Arkansas
Godfather

Arkansas Godfather

The Story of Owney Madden and How He Hijacked Middle America

Graham Nown

BUTLER
CENTER
BOOKS

Copyright 2013 by Sylvana Nown
(Former title: *The English Godfather*, UK copyright 1987 by Graham Nown)
All rights reserved. Published by Butler Center Books, part of the Butler
Center for Arkansas Studies, a division of the Central Arkansas Library
System. No part of this book may be reproduced in any form, except for brief
passages quoted within reviews, without the express written consent of Butler
Center Books.

The Butler Center for Arkansas Studies
Central Arkansas Library System
100 Rock Street
BUTLER   Little Rock, Arkansas 72201
CENTER
BOOKS   www.bultercenter.org

First Printing: April 2013

ISBN 978-1-935106-51-7
e-ISBN 978-1-935106-57-9

Project director: Rod Lorenzen
Proofreader: Ali Welky
Book design: H. K. Stewart

All photographs appear courtesy of Sylvana Nown unless otherwise noted.

Library of Congress Cataloging-in-Publication Data
Nown, Graham.
  [English godfather]
  Arkansas godfather : the story of Owney Madden and how he hijacked Middle America /
Graham Nown.
    pages cm
  Originally published under title: The English godfather. London : Ward Lock, 1987.
  Includes bibliographical references and index.
  ISBN 978-1-935106-51-7 (pbk. : alk. paper)
  1. Madden, Owney, 1891-1980. 2. Criminals–New York (State)–New York–Biography. 3. Criminals–
Arkansas–Hot Springs–Biography. I. Butler Center for Arkansas Studies, issuing body. II. Title.

  HV6248.M245N68 2013
  364.1092–dc23
  [B]
                            2013001989
Printed in the United States of America
This book is printed on archival-quality paper that meets requirements of the
American National Standard for Information Sciences, Permanence of Paper, Printed
Library Materials, ANSI Z39.48-1984.

The publishing division of the Butler Center for Arkansas Studies
was made possible by the generosity of Dora Johnson Ragsdale and
John G. Ragsdale Jr.

Contents

Introduction

Our fascination with gangsters and the sinister lives they pursue never seems to end. For the better part of one hundred years now, gangsters have been glamorized in film and fiction despite the terrible crimes they commit and the violence they perpetuate. In the American psyche, they seem to function like shadow selves by defying convention and living just outside the law. Vicariously, we live through them, maybe feeling a bit of envy for those who can make a living on their own terms, legal or not. Successful mobsters enforce the idea that criminality exists not as the exception but as the rule and that people can break the law without ever getting caught. Sometimes, the criminal life is totally entwined in government and society, so much so that one might wonder about what is law and what isn't.

The world of organized crime is oddly compelling, and we want to know what gangsters do and how they live. This is how it was for Graham Nown, an enterprising British journalist and eloquent broadcaster. He was a smart, engaging man who was liked by all, and his journey into the underworld of organized crime started innocently enough. Fueled by a reporter's insatiable curiosity, he spent four years tracking down the truth about a former countryman who later became one of America's most notorious criminals. Where many others had failed to get the goods on Owney Madden, Graham Nown succeeded, and, above all, this is his story.

Nown's book about Madden, *The English Godfather*, first appeared in Great Britain in 1987. It was never distributed in the United States, and the public here learned of it only by word of mouth. A few libraries acquired it, but those interested in owning a copy had to pay an exorbitant sum for it through rare-book dealers. With the publication of this new, indexed edition, an extraordinary piece of American history is now preserved, thanks to Sylvana Nown, Graham Nown's widow, who allowed us to reprint her late husband's book. An author herself, she also collated all of Nown's research on Madden, who was born in Leeds in the north of England. Madden's family, originally from Ireland, later lived for a few years in Wigan, a town in Greater Manchester, England, before immigrating to the Hell's Kitchen area of New York City.

By 1980, Nown was a journalist based in Wigan and was acquiring a finely tuned antenna for the unusual and quirky. His interest in gangsters was piqued by the memories of an old man in Wigan who once had dinner in Hot Springs, Arkansas, with Madden. He recalled that Madden spoke of nothing but his boyhood days in England. Later, Nown was bemused to find that, in researching Madden, he actually had discovered a love story involving a notorious underworld figure from New York who moved to a small resort town in the middle of the country and married the daughter of the postmaster. Nown showed up in Hot Springs in the mid-1980s, determined to track down and interview Madden's widow, Agnes, who still lived just outside the downtown area in the same house she had shared with her gangster husband, dead since 1965. Day after day, Nown knocked on the front door of the Madden home on West Grand Avenue, only to be turned away every time by the bodyguard, Roger Rucker. Mrs. Madden, who had never discussed her infamous husband with any outsider, finally relented after talking with Nown on the phone.

"Roger Rucker told Graham that she would never have consented to meet him if she hadn't heard him speak," recalls Sylvana Nown. "He said that Graham's voice on the phone had brought tears to her eyes because he sounded just like her Owney. She had never heard anyone else with a northern English accent." Because of her involvement in her late husband's business deals, Agnes herself was practically a real part of the mob. Now, would their vaunted code of silence finally be broken? And what would Nown find when he walked into the home of a mobster whose career in organized crime had spanned five decades?

In the America of the Depression-era 1930s, crime often seems to fill the main news headlines. It is irresistible for reporters and sells lots of papers. The criminals are usually taking matters into their own hands and thwarting a government that has been pushed to the verge of collapse. A cast of well-known thugs—Bonnie and Clyde Barrow, Al Capone, and Pretty Boy Floyd among them—dominates the news, and criminals often become folk heroes of sorts in the popular imagination. In New York City, Owney Madden is the undisputed champion of crime—the Duke of the West Side. He is the prototypical gangster, the first to wear expensive suits and insulate himself from the physical violence of the gang life by using intermediaries.

Big-time gangsters like Madden suddenly found themselves with large piles of cash, mainly from bootlegging during Prohibition, but are denied entry into New York's "high society." One remedy for this was to buy a nightclub and supply the booze so the society people would come to them. And come they did. Madden bought a nightclub in the African American community of Harlem from former heavyweight boxing champion Jack Johnson and renamed it the Cotton Club. There, Madden sold his own beer—"Madden's Number One"—manufactured in an illegal brewery protected by "New York's finest." Even though the club was in a black neighborhood, it was off-limits to black patrons. This was a "whites only" club, and the only exceptions were the staff and the performers, including such greats as Cab Calloway, Louis Armstrong, Duke Ellington, and Billie Holiday.

"Madden was the unlikeliest gangster," Nown liked to recall, "a reclusive oddball who clung to his British passport, spoke in soft, rounded Yorkshire vowels with a hint of his Irish parentage, wore a flat cap as his trade-mark and bred pigeons."

Prohibition and illegal booze made him one of the biggest gangsters in America. Madden, also nicknamed "the Killer," had already served time in prison for the murder of rival gang leader "Little Patsy" Doyle, and, in the early '30s, the law began to close in on him once again. He finally concocted an amazing secret deal—worth one million dollars according to Nown—with state prosecutors that allowed him to escape further prosecution and have himself "banished" forever to the quieter environs of Hot Springs, a resort town nestled in the hills of central Arkansas. It is the town where, decades later, Madden's shadow would finally fall across Nown's path.

Hot Springs and Madden were a natural, if unlikely, fit for each other. Oaklawn Park, a national thoroughbred racetrack, was one of the few places in America where gambling was legal. But there was always plenty of illegal gambling going on away from the track, along with a host of other vices. Madden simply took over a lot of it, bankrolled by New York mobsters Meyer Lansky and Frank Costello. Big-time gangsters had been retreating to Hot Springs—they called it "Bubbles"—for years. Madden continued to make Hot Springs a safe haven for his gangster pals in Chicago, New York, and New Orleans. There were no mob hits in Hot Springs. That kind of thing was simply bad for business, and what Owney Madden and the vice lords wanted in Hot Springs was business as usual. More mysterious is the fact that, after he relocated to Hot Springs in the '30s, Madden was never convicted of a crime in spite of his criminal activities and incredible scrutiny by the U.S. government.

From the time of his arrival in Hot Springs, Madden was followed every day for the rest of his life by an agent from the Federal Bureau of Investigation. On one occasion, he actually gave the agent a tour of the illegal "racing wires" he controlled. These were telephone lines that came into Hot Springs and brought news from race tracks all over the country into casinos, which used the information to chalk up the tote boards of their "horse books." Madden also told the agent how he first got into crime as a boy in Hell's Kitchen. He watched as a neighborhood kid snipped the handles of Madden's mother's shopping bag with a pair of scissors and ran away with the groceries. "When I saw what that kid had got away with," Madden said, "I decided I was a fool not to try it myself."

As a "Top National Hoodlum," Madden was long a person of special interest to J. Edgar Hoover, director of the FBI, and also appeared as a witness at Senate hearings on organized crime in 1950 run by Sen. Estes Kefauver of Tennessee and Sen. John L. McClellan of Arkansas. In 1963, Attorney General Bobby Kennedy began another taskforce to investigate the mob, although Madden's subsequent testimony revealed nothing about his life of crime. Kennedy's chairman for the congressional hearings was McClellan. (Madden and his wife had been campaign contributors, and, interestingly enough, illegal gambling in Hot Springs had flourished for years right in McClellan's own backyard.) Madden resented this new intrusion by Kennedy. After all, he and Kennedy's father, Joseph P. Kennedy, had been partners in bootlegging operations during the Prohibition era, and Madden's pals in the Chicago mob, by some accounts, helped swing Illinois and the 1960 presidential race to Kennedy's brother, John F. Kennedy.

In spite of their good intentions, Bobby Kennedy and the FBI were only embarrassed when visits to Hot Springs by the national press found that Hot Springs was a wide-open town where illegal gambling thrived. Kennedy actually had solid evidence about Madden's gambling operations, but the federal government bungled its attempts to prosecute him. Despite years of effort, the FBI was never even able to obtain a decent photo of Madden for its files.

During his years in Hot Springs, Madden looked more like a benevolent retiree. A modern-day Robin Hood, he stuffed cash in his pockets and doled it out to needy folks during his daily rounds in Hot Springs, not to mention what he and his "syndicate" pals might have set aside in a black bag that, according to some accounts, was sent routinely to the governor's office in Little Rock until 1965. He owned the local politicians, too (they got their money in little envelopes). Madden had bank-

rolled the careers of film stars such as George Raft, a boyhood pal, and
Mae West, a favorite girlfriend. Raft even copied Madden's mannerisms
for his gangster movies when Hollywood first began to engender public
interest in real-life, cold-blooded killers. They were glamorized and mawk-
ish, these godfathers of cinema. But Madden learned the hard way to
avoid the spotlight. John Gotti, a New York godfather from the 1990s,
seemed to bask in it. And decades earlier, Chicago's Al Capone had carefully groomed his public image by employing his own publicist. Madden,
however, actually paid famous columnists like Walter Winchell to keep
his name *out* of the news. Madden knew from experience that publicity
easily could be his downfall.

Although Madden's friends were movie stars and big-time mobsters,
he managed to live a quiet life near downtown Hot Springs and died just
as quietly in 1965. By then, he was known mainly as a benefactor of the
city because he gave money to schools and churches. But his long career
as a criminal had thrived because he paid off the local police and county
and state officials while decent people often looked the other way. When
Madden's wife, Agnes, died twenty-five years later, one of the items in
the estate—her jewelry collection—was alone worth $2 million.

This is Graham Nown's story about how one man achieved his own
version of the American Dream, even though he paid a price to do it.
Madden was hounded by the law and hampered by old gunshot wounds.
He was angst-ridden and he constantly chain-smoked, but he was still
"the Duke." Whenever Washington DC urged Arkansas officials to shut
down illegal gambling in Hot Springs, the officials claimed that it was a
local matter and it would be unconstitutional for them to interfere.
During Madden's rule, Hot Springs was one of the wealthiest, most politically corrupt illegal gambling towns in America long before Las Vegas
started up. Unsurprisingly, future president Bill Clinton would choose
to bill himself as "the man from Hope" (Hope, Arkansas) although his
formative years were spent in nearby Hot Springs and he was a graduate
of Hot Springs High School.

It is difficult to understand American history without first understanding the prominent role of organized crime. The history of Owen Vincent Madden is our history, too, regardless of whether we want to claim a part in it. A few years after *The English Godfather* was published, Graham Nown offered up this postscript to his indefatigable search for the truth about the Duke of the West Side:

"Owney Madden's story is about an era when capitalism and organized crime were in their infancy. The Duke was a catalyst who ensured that each of the two great forces of modern American history moved forward side by side. Above all, he was a survivor at a time when few in his chosen line of business died of natural causes."

Rod Lorenzen
Butler Center for Arkansas Studies
Little Rock, Arkansas
February 2013

1.

Duke of the West Side

first heard of Owney Madden on a cold winter night in England. Jimmy Murphy had come to stay. We basked on each side of a roaring fire with the wind moaning down the chimney like a muted siren. When Murphy talked of the 1920s and 1930s, he gazed deep into the fire, his eyes lighting up with memories of Hollywood and Manhattan.

He had worked as a butler for the famous comedy team of Laurel and Hardy and later ran the household of film star Joan Crawford. Rich, turbulent years were etched into his face. Murphy was a roly-poly old man in a black shirt and white tie. Sitting there with his hands clasped, he might have been at the table next to author Damon Runyon in Lindy's, the trendy New York restaurant. Like Stan Laurel, Murphy came from Lancashire and the years had failed to rub away the corners from that wry, working-class humor.

Perhaps it was being back on home ground again, with the gale shrieking over the sand dunes from the Irish Sea—or perhaps because we were so near to where Owney Madden grew up—that he started to talk about the war. Murphy had been caught in the draft and posted to Arkansas. After Hollywood, it was rather like watching paint dry. He and Stan had a tearful farewell at the Greyhound bus station and promised to keep in touch. Months later, with a weekend pass burning a hole in his pocket, Murphy called California and asked Stan if he knew a good place to unwind. Stan thought for a minute and said: "Call you back."

When the phone rang, he told Murphy to be at the Arlington Hotel in Hot Springs, Arkansas, at a certain time. "And make sure you dress up," he warned. Murphy, who was an orderly for a five-star general, borrowed his uniform and a jeep and disappeared into the great Mid-South.

"I was waiting in the hotel," he recalled, "when I heard a quiet voice say, 'Now then, lad.' It was so English it made me turn. A guy wearing a cap stuck out his hand and said: 'Owney Madden.' He bought me dinner and told the manager he would pick up the tab for the weekend. They said he was the biggest gangster in New York, but he only wanted to talk about his old hometown in England. I never forgot him."

Four years later, after assembling enough FBI files, district attorneys' reports, and police records to fill a large suitcase, I reached the conclusion that I still knew nothing about Owney Madden. The answer, perhaps, was to follow the same route he had taken more than eighty years before and begin at the end.

Twenty years earlier, in 1965, the shy, quietly spoken, enormously polite Madden died in Hot Springs, the mountain spa in the buckle of the Bible belt to which he had been exiled for the past thirty years. Two hundred policemen, lawyers, members of the underworld, and solid citizens of the small Arkansas town assembled in the calm following a tornado which had left a trail of destruction along the nearby Mississippi River. They had gathered to pay their last respects to one of the most influential, yet perhaps least known, figures in America. Throughout his seventy-two years, the man who had wielded enormous power in the stratosphere of organized crime was, in fact, America's unlikeliest gangster. He was a man of many secrets who, unlike Dutch Schultz and Al Capone, never courted the cameras or basked in notoriety. He was a nervous, thoughtful man who avoided publicity and anonymously gave away millions to the poor and needy. Owney never granted an interview, rarely had his picture taken, and even paid columnist Walter Winchell to keep his name out of the news.

In the 1920s and 1930s, Owney Madden could cause ripples of excitement simply by strolling the sidewalks of Manhattan. He owned the famous Cotton Club, which lightened the Depression with exquisite jazz and helped Duke Ellington on his way to the top. In the dry years of Prohibition, he provided the sweet life of the Stork Club, the Silver Slipper, and a chain of others he ran in partnership with Texas Guinan, a nightclub queen whose favorite line was, "Hello, Sucker." He was the gangster on whom Hollywood based its greatest gangsters. George Raft, his best friend and later a movie star, rode shotgun on his beer trucks while waiting for a break in show business. When Owney was in prison at Sing Sing, George visited him regularly, hungry for stories about life inside. Later, in Hollywood, Raft modeled himself on his old pal in his classic gangster roles.

Owney, with a frail appearance which belied an iron toughness, was born in Leeds, schooled in Wigan, and raised in Liverpool. His young adulthood was spent in New York where, in the volatile melting pot of Hell's Kitchen, poverty forced him to turn to crime. Raft, who lived a few blocks away, escaped to earn his living in the movies, while Owney rose from leading the Gophers, New York's most feared street gang, to become one of America's godfathers of organized crime. In a tough world of musclemen with sinister bulges under their coats, Madden was surprisingly different. He was always stylishly dressed with an understated manner and an economy of words. He was slim, intelligent, good-looking—more like a movie star behind the wheel of the bulletproof Duesenberg given to him by former dictator Fulgencio Batista of Cuba—yet often too shy to meet people in case they were embarrassed by his reputation.

What genuinely distanced him from the thugs and murderers around him was a lifelong struggle to adhere to his own values in a world where "legitimate" success was all but impossible. Police, politicians, and judges thrived on bribery and Owney used them to his advantage while trying to retain his individual moral code. If the history of America can be viewed as the history of lawlessness, then Owney Madden's progress through corruption in high places was the backstage story of twentieth-century America.

Madden's story has never been told simply because, throughout his life, he intended it to remain that way. It lies in the yellowing pages of court records, buried in FBI files and forgotten transcripts of Senate hearings. There were chapters so secret that they could never be officially recorded, like the million-dollar deal which resulted in his exile to Arkansas at the height of his career and the officials who turned from persecuting him to offering protection. His story endures most strongly in the memory of those who retain a genuine pride in having known him. A close circle guarded him loyally, viewing outsiders with caution and suspicion. For almost half a century, a succession of writers, newsmen, movie producers, and radio reporters knocked at the door of his pretty, white clapboard house in Hot Springs, only to return empty-handed. There was no reason to believe that I could succeed where others more plausible had failed. Along the way, however, I knew there might be some missing pieces.

Sex goddess and movie star Mae West was among those who protected his memory. Their relationship ran so deep that she never discussed it until shortly before her death. When Mae spoke of Owney, her friends were left with no doubt that it was "her hottest affair." Madden helped her out of vaudeville and onto Broadway, just as he once loaned Raft the money to get to California. His two closest friends repaid him by risking their reputations to hide him during a Hollywood police hunt. When he was finally arrested, Mae played her finest role by slipping into a favorite dress and seducing the district attorney to secure his release.

Owney Madden was never as he appeared to be. On the surface, his life seemed one of endless dazzle and wild caprice, running close to the abandoned madness of the Jazz Age. In reality, the most famous figure on Broadway was a gentle, introspective man who loved nothing better than living quietly at home tending to his pigeons. He seldom drank and never gambled but smoked heavily and would start at the slightest unexpected sound. Even to his friends he was intensely private, often complex, and full of contradictions. In rising from poor immigrant to multi-millionaire, he was the embodiment of the American Dream, yet remained proudly British, carrying his passport for half a century until, threatened with deportation, he finally took U.S. citizenship. Try as I could, as I traced his footsteps on a 10,000-mile journey from his English birthplace, I found no one who did not recall him with fondness and affection. Though perhaps one or two of the dead, they say, might have voiced a different opinion.

When Owney was exiled by the authorities, Hot Springs was a wild gambling town that paid little heed to Arkansas laws. He gave the spa some of the sparkle of Manhattan, and movie stars, mobsters, gamblers, fighters, and politicians poured in to drink their fill at the wealthiest watering hole in America. Power and money stretched dreams like fiddle strings and everyone danced to the tune. While gambling was illegal in most of America, Hot Springs and the state of Arkansas managed to overlook these details. The Rock Island and Missouri Pacific railroad lines disgorged them at the depot in the thousands from all over the country. Visitors from the west arrived with their elegant alligator luggage, golf bags, and two-tone Florsheim shoes. They were there for the dice and roulette games and healing thermal waters.

By the 1980s, however, the railroad tracks are overgrown with weeds, the ironwork rusted and leading to nowhere. Gambling was wiped out by the outcome of one election, and the old Duke of the West Side died in the town's St. Joseph's hospital. An era passed with him, and part of Hot Springs slipped into alcoholism and unemployment.

The day I arrived, Hot Springs had been edgy, waiting for the rain. Yellow-brown dust and fallen leaves drifted along the bleached shoulder of Highway 70. The earth was cracked and calloused, and farmers scanned the sky. Hot Springs needed not only rain, but anything which stood for some growth and hope. It was the beginning of the tornado season, when vicious twisters could tear down from the Ozark and Ouachita Mountains, cutting through the pinewoods like a scythe through wheat. On days like these, there was always tension in the air. It was a foreboding which had hung around the boarded-up shops, silent restaurants, and peeling frame houses since the town had buried Owney Madden way back in 1965.

The rain finally came in a wild, uncompromising assault, sweeping across the narrow valley in tall sheets as it chased the tail of a tornado rampaging upstate. It fell solidly for forty-eight hours, crashing from the flat roofs of roadside motels, hammering on billboards, and pouring in rivers down the parking lots of gas stations and diners.

Then, early in the morning, it stopped as suddenly as it had begun, leaving a musty smell of old potatoes on the cool breeze from East Mountain. In the clear air, I had my first view of the city, encircled by tree-covered hills—tinted by the fall into green, brown, yellow, and mauve, like a patchwork quilt stitched by Baptist ladies. The only real clues to the private life of the English Godfather lay a mile south in the elegant fifteen-room wooden house which had been his home for thirty years.

In Hot Springs, Madden had married Agnes Demby, the postmaster's daughter, a long-legged, spirited girl, full of independence. Agnes turned away the unwanted callers during Owney's life and, now eighty-five, had refused to see anyone since his death. It was both a marriage, they said, and a business arrangement. Nowadays, she seldom went out and then only chauffeured by her well-built bodyguard for a slice of home-made coconut cake at his mother's. The only piece ever written about her was by her cousin, a Memphis journalist, years after Owney's death. That was after long months of persuasion and only because she was family.

This was the house where George Raft stayed to swap yarns about the old days. Outside, the cars used to crawl bumper to bumper along West Grand, hoping to catch a glimpse of him. It was the house where Frank Costello, prime minister of the underworld, relaxed and formulated his plans over Agnes's home-made pasta. Champion boxers Gene

Tunney and Rocky Marciano dropped by to pick up Owney for a game of golf. Duke Ellington, the famous band leader, and Red Buttons, a Hollywood comedian, used to pay their respects, along with politicians, the police chief who lived next door, and Owney's shrewd attorney from around the corner on Woodbine, Senator Q. Byrum Hurst Sr.

Somewhere in there was the unlisted phone which often rang all day with calls from Chicago and New York, as well as the local sheriff's office. Few of Hot Springs's well-known visitors realized it, but they were in town only with Owney's permission. Underworld figures outside his circle of friends and business associates were likely to be met at the city limits by a sheriff's roadblock and drawn guns.

In its heyday, the rambling house, presided over by strolling cats, Sissie the fox terrier, and a yellow-headed parrot named Prince, literally gleamed. Its wooden floors were highly polished and vases were crammed with flowers from the immaculate garden tended by Agnes and Willie, the handyman. No one could pass without glancing in. Even the dog was a celebrity, with her own printed pass to visit movie theaters. The New York papers ran an obituary when Sissie was laid to rest beneath a tree on the lawn.

The house of secrets lay overgrown now and, from the outside, looked abandoned. The undergrowth was almost impenetrable, the roof covered in fallen leaves and the paintwork faded. A white picket gate, twined with wisteria, opened onto a path shaded by a beautiful old walnut tree. Beneath its branches, thyme, fennel, mint, and lemon balm had grown into each other to form a thick, sweet-smelling carpet.

An air of faded grandeur hung about the place as I approached the black-and-white front door. It was mid-morning but most of the window blinds were drawn. A chandelier burned brightly in a downstairs room. The house number plaque, 506, lay on the front step where it had rotted from the wall.

Mrs. Madden, it seemed, was looked after by an implacable young man named Roger Rucker. Other men were often seen in the house, helping with his protective duties. He never left, day or night, and carried out his work as bodyguard and housekeeper with daunting efficiency.

I knocked on the door and waited for a reply. A sash window shot up a few feet away. Behind a thin curtain, I could make out the figure of a muscled man of about thirty wearing a white athletic vest.

"Roger Rucker?" I asked.

He did not answer for a moment. Then the voice behind the screen said, "Yes?"

I introduced myself and told him I would like to talk to him.

"Go ahead," he said, making no attempt to move.

"Could I come in for a moment?"

"Sorry. You can't."

"Well, could you come to the door? It's a little difficult talking through the screen."

"I can hear you."

Two other men were moving around in the room behind him.

"I'd appreciate it," I said. "If you wouldn't mind."

The window slid down but minutes passed and nothing happened. I stood at the door, wondering what to do next. To pass the time I knocked again. A few seconds later, I heard the door unlock. Roger Rucker stepped outside, pulling the door shut behind him so that it was impossible to glimpse the interior.

He wore a pair of beige tracksuit bottoms and stood with arms folded across his chest and his legs planted apart like a gym instructor. He was not unfriendly but seemed as amenable as a block of concrete.

"Is Mrs. Madden home?"

"She's home," he said, looking over my head.

"Could you tell her I'm here?"

"Mrs. Madden don't want visitors today."

I began to tell him that I was not a casual caller and that I had been researching Owney's story for almost four years when he interrupted.

"Mr. Madden," he said. "I always called him Mr. Madden."

I knew all about Mr. Madden's life, I told him. It was just a matter of putting one or two things into perspective. Roger Rucker smiled and leaned on the door post. "It won't work," he said. I was beginning to feel like a door-to-door salesman.

* * *

In Greenwood Cemetery, where they laid him to rest, Owney's black marble slab rose impressively on a grassy knoll above the adjoining graves. There was a slight drizzle drifting between the oaks and magnolias scattered across the landscaped lawns. Pine needles, swept by the wind into round, brown patches, mottled the gravel walk. Even in these somber surroundings, beyond the rattle of trucks passing the iron cemetery gates, there was a smile on the face of the exile. Beneath the name, they had carved his date of birth—December 25th, 1891. According to his birth certificate in Leeds Register Office, it was December 18th. The misleading information he had fed to the police, the FBI, and the immigration authorities all his life had followed him in death. When she authorized his tombstone, and had her own name carved on it in readiness, Agnes decided to let it remain.

I stumbled back into town over rocks and through water-filled potholes which made up the sidewalks of Hot Springs, to the forest of gas stations and motel signs marking the main intersection.

Mrs. Madden's white wooden fortress was around the corner on West Grand. With a couple of pictures of the house I would not feel too bad about returning home empty-handed. I had just raised the camera to my eye, managing to keep discreetly out of view of the windows, when there was a piercing whistle behind me. Roger Rucker was standing on the median of the highway watching me.

He wore a loose jacket over his vest and tracksuit pants and a pair of blue, flip-up designer sunglasses.

"Hope the pictures turn out alright," he said, obviously displeased.

I apologized and said I hoped he didn't get the wrong impression. He ambled over and leaned on the trunk of his tan Buick.

"You're sneaky," he said, flipping up the lenses of his shades with a forefinger. "'Course, if you want to be like that, well, it's your business." He looked thoughtful. "Where are you staying?"

After a moment's hesitation, I told him. "I was walking back from the cemetery," I said, as casually as possible. "I wanted to pay my respects."

He drew a semi-circle in the dirt with the toe of his running shoe and said: "You found the grave, then?"

I nodded and asked if he knew that the birth date listed on Owney's tombstone was wrong.

"Sure, we know that." He grinned so wide that I could see a gold filling in his bottom molar.

We fell silent. It was an awkward situation but I was reluctant to leave.

"Everything you need is in there," Roger said finally, nodding toward the house beyond the white picket gate. He paused. "Papers, newspaper articles, photographs." His manner made it clear that nothing short of the entire Arkansas National Guard would be able to get inside. "I even found the medals Mr. Madden won for his pigeons back in New York, when I was cleaning out the other day."

"It's a pity you can't leave the house to talk, Roger. We could have had dinner—maybe a few beers."

"I can't think why," he replied, levering himself off his car. He turned to go, then clicked his fingers. "Hey, I forgot to tell you. I told Mrs. Madden you were by."

"Thanks." I picked up my briefcase. "What did she say?"

He took off his designer sunglasses. "Mrs. Madden is a very, very, very private person," Roger said with slow emphasis. "You get me? Private. She said she wasn't seeing anyone today. She's tired."

He turned and disappeared toward the house where the lights were burning brightly in a front room behind the thin curtain.

As I trudged off to call a cab, I remembered Hank Messick, the great and fearless Miami crime reporter. He had opened the white picket gate here two years before Owney's death on the off-chance of getting an interview.

"Mrs. Madden, stout and motherly, answered the bell," Messick wrote. "Owney was 'awfully busy.' She was busy, too—the floors were being sanded. Could I come back next week perhaps?

"The cab driver smiled as I returned through the white picket fence. An ex-deputy, he knew Mr. Madden well. He could set up an interview easily.

"I accompanied him into the two-car garage and examined the two cars parked there while he entered the house through a rear door. In less than a minute he came out. I noticed his face was white and I followed as he ran down the driveway to his cab. The car moved away before I could close the door. We were two blocks away before he slowed.

"'What happened?' I asked.

"The cabbie mopped his face with a colored handkerchief, sighed deeply and remarked, 'He don't want to see no writer.'

"I waited. The cabbie took a deep breath.

"'Mr. Madden said if I ever brought anybody to his house again he hadn't sent for first, he'd cut my heart out.'

"'Did he mean it?'

"The cabbie turned his blue eyes upon me. 'Hell, yes, he meant it. They don't call him "Killer" for nothing, you know.'"

A few paces up the road, Roger Rucker called me back.

"You see this garden?" he asked, leaning on the side of his Buick. "People drop by all the time looking for work, asking if they can clip the grass, maybe tidy it up a little. You know something? Mrs. Madden *always* says no."

He folded his arms and looked at his shoes. "But one guy, he just kept coming back. He pushed and pushed. He wasn't pushy though, if you get my meaning. In the end I guess she must have said to herself: 'This man is sincere.' So, Mrs. Madden gave him some work. Not much. Just enough to get him by."

I felt rather tired. At that moment, an ice-cold beer seemed most appealing. "I haven't really come to do the garden, Roger," I said, patiently.

He laughed and turned toward the house. "I *know* what you want," he called. Halfway up the path he turned and jabbed a finger at me. "You remember what I told you."

As I walked back into town, one piece of our conversation came back to me. I had been curious to discover whether Mrs. Madden had seen Francis Coppola's movie, *Cotton Club.* Bob Hoskins, I recalled, played a very unconvincing Owney Madden—brash, aggressive, and prone to throwing tantrums. Roger had looked very serious when I mentioned it.

"It came 'round on TV," he said hesitantly. "I pulled the chair up for Mrs. Madden—she's eighty-five now, you know—and I switched on the program. She watched it without saying a word. Sat there for all of ten minutes, I guess. Then, she just slowly got up out of her chair and turned the thing off. She's never mentioned it since."

Around the corner was the law office of Owney's friend and attorney, Q. Byrum Hurst Sr. It was a tiny, red-tiled building on Woodbine across the street from the Garland County Library. He offered to talk to me on a Saturday morning when his son, Q. Byrum Hurst Jr. was away in Memphis on legal business and the building was empty. Hurst arrived in a smart, gleaming limousine which bounced on air cushions over the curb to its parking spot. The former state senator and county judge looked like a distinguished Southern gentleman, with his tanned complexion and grey hair swept over his ears.

He had seen the Duke almost every day and knew him better than most people in Hot Springs. At first, he thought deeply after each question, gazing in introspection for up to two minutes before he spoke. His words came slowly, like the autumn leaves zig-zagging gracefully to the ground on the tree-lined street outside. Hurst, who had encountered numerous media men inquisitive about Owney, was trying to figure me out. He spoke frankly about Owney's past and business activities. It was only when he tried to recapture the nature of the man that he drifted pensively into half-forgotten memories.

"He was a dear, sweet little guy," he said. "So shy about everything he did. He always took precautions—not for his safety or his life—but so that he wouldn't hurt people or offend them. He wouldn't push himself on anyone—all his life he tried to be secluded. Owney loved children. He looked after our babies and was crazy about our daughter, little Byretta. I remember he bought her those holsters that gangsters wore, with a gun on each side. She would walk around with it on and it would just tickle him to death 'That's my gangster, right there,' he would say.

"He was so good to people. He would do things that Agnes absolutely could not understand. Owney was a cash man—he always carried. They had a safe up at the house and every morning he would fill his pockets. He knew what he needed to give away. A five here, a ten there. He'd help children out with shoes, saw them through school. Sometimes he'd stop their mothers out on the street to check if they needed anything. It cost him a hundred dollars a day to live. He was private. If he wanted to give my wife a diamond, or something, he would go and buy it quietly and that would be the end of it. He was always doing something for somebody. Agnes was not like that. She was a businesswoman.

"Frank Costello came down here a lot. He would stay at the Arlington and bring maybe fifty or sixty people with him by train. Then he wouldn't want any of them near him. He and Owney were devoted to each other. They would sit quietly and discuss things, maybe play a little golf. But there was so much heat on them from the federal authorities, especially Costello. Every time he moved there was someone after him.

"Those visitors cost Owney a fortune because he picked up the tabs whenever they came. Agnes was always mentioning it to him. Some of them were high livers. Lord have mercy! You can't imagine it. But he would just pick up the tab. If they insisted, he'd say: 'Now don't hurt me like that,' and send them on their way.

"He missed New York. Yes, he did. Nearly every day somebody was trying to get him on the telephone. It kept refreshing all those memories. A lot of people respected his advice and his experience and they'd call him. They would fly down from Chicago or New York, talk to him, and go back that night. It was not unusual."

Hurst spoke with more than a touch of sadness about times past. Agnes, he explained, was a very different person from Owney—even in politics she was a Republican and he a Democrat—but they both liked to spend time at home. Despite the life he had led running New York's liveliest nightclubs, he preferred to retire early. While he slept, Agnes would often sew into the early hours or sit reading in bed surrounded by magazines.

"Owney was sick at home before he died," Hurst reflected. "Friends came from all over the United States to see him. I had to go to California and I was worried about him. He told me he didn't want a minister or anything at the funeral. He just wanted me to say a few words about him. That night, after the funeral, we all went back to the house and it was full. Agnes was very gracious and tried to talk to them all. She did her part. She had already lived through it maybe a hundred times."

I explained to Hurst the problem I'd had in trying to see Agnes and asked if he could help pave the way with an introduction. He thought about it for a long time and said: "When you go up to the house, tell them you have talked to me."

"You have the phone number," I suggested. "It isn't listed. Perhaps you can call and talk to the people up there to make things easier."

He stared deep into his coffee cup in silence for several minutes, then raised his eyes. They looked tired, as though he had returned from a long journey, but his face gave nothing away.

"No," he said. "I'd rather not."

My attempts to see Mrs. Madden increased as the days went by. She alone held the missing pieces of Owney's life, particularly as to how the Duke of the West Side came to fall in love with a postmaster's daughter to form one of the most formidable partnerships in the South. Roger Rucker continued to keep the door firmly closed behind him as we talked for hours in the damp and mellow garden speckled with the bronze and gold of fallen leaves. Occasionally, he stepped from his post to offer a conducted tour of the shrubbery, where the gravestones of Owney's pets lay half-buried in the undergrowth. High on the side of the house hung the pigeon loft he had built with Willie the handyman. Two dogs patrolled a rear orchard behind wire fencing, and there were invariably other people moving around inside the house. In a conservatory screened by trees, an empty wheelchair stood facing the garden. Owney had been confined to it by his doctor in his final days.

I came to realize that these excursions and conversations were not polite stonewalling but the opening moves in a complicated process of vetting my intentions. One day, after perhaps sixteen visits—I had begun to lose count of the number of times I had stood on the front step—Roger announced that Mrs. Madden had expressed an interest in the books I had written. When I remarked by chance that I had some in my hotel room, he opened the door to his Buick and, to my surprise, said: "Let's go."

Next day, the first thing I noticed was that Roger Rucker's Buick was missing from its usual parking place. It was unlike him to go out and leave Agnes alone, I mused, unless some of the other people were looking after her. The only other possibility was that Roger had driven away somewhere, taking Mrs. Madden with him. I knocked on the door but there was no reply. After tapping, rapping, and finally hammering for five minutes, I sat down on the front step to write a note. The Manx cat emerged from behind a rambling wisteria to keep me company. I was screwing the top back on my pen when the door behind me opened wide to reveal Roger with a warm smile of welcome.

"Well, how are you?" he beamed. "Come on inside, make yourself at home."

It was as though a new director had been brought in and the whole script rewritten. I stepped through into a comfortable drawing room with a pink-and-beige chintz sofa and a pale blue rug spread over the polished floorboards. The mantelshelf and antique tables overflowed with photographs of Owney and Agnes. On the south side of the room all the shades were drawn and the lights blazed in the morning half-light.

"Through here," Roger invited, leading the way into a dining room with a long, lace-covered table and Chippendale chairs. The floral beige-and-blue wallpaper belonged to a grander era. Above the table hung a huge, ornate chandelier made of crystal and amethyst. Roger caught me admiring it.

"Agnes has a cutlery set in amethyst to match the chandelier," he remarked, beckoning me to sit down.

Three chairs had been pulled out at the end of the oblong table where the most powerful figures in American crime once had sat down to dinner. Roger motioned for me to sit facing him across an expanse of neat piles of photographs, letters, press clippings, and memorabilia that covered a third of the table. The seat at the end remained empty.

"Agnes will be here shortly," he said, making himself comfortable.

I was engrossed in the forgotten flotsam of the Duke's life when a floorboard creaked, betraying the presence of Mrs. Madden in the doorway. She was small and frail and wrapped in a pale dressing gown. Her grey hair was pinned into a neat bun, framing a strong face which lit up when she smiled. Roger took her arm and steered her fragile steps toward the chair.

"I'm not too good today," she said, easing herself into the seat and examining me closely. Her face was lined like the Mississippi Delta but the eyes belonged to a woman half her age. "I believe," she said, "that you are interested in Owen."

I told her that I was interested in both her and Owney and especially how two such unlikely people came to meet. Mrs. Madden gave a girlish half-smile and shook her head.

"Oh, all that was a long time ago," she murmured with a touch of wistfulness.

"You must miss him."

She folded one hand slowly on top of the other. "I loved him," she said simply, in a thin southern voice as smooth as juniper.

Mrs. Madden's eyes never left me as she hesitantly told her story. As she relived the memories, her face was sometimes illuminated and, at other times, cast with private shadows. A man in dark wrap-around sunglasses entered the doorway behind her and leaned in silence on the jamb, taking in the scene. No one turned to acknowledge his presence. As we sat beneath the cool, eggshell blue ceiling with the branches of the old walnut tree brushing the window outside, I wondered what she was hiding. The answer, I concluded, was devoid of any mystery or intrigue. The treasure chest Agnes was so anxious to protect contained neither wealth nor dangerous secrets but simply memories. She had wished them to remain undisturbed as she lived out her remaining years.

Why she had decided to share them with me was a question I made no attempt to fathom but, after an hour had passed, I had a better understanding. Agnes looked tired and asked Roger to fetch her morning glass of ice water. When he had gone, we talked about her failing health. I gave her hand a friendly squeeze and told her to look after herself. She took hold of my hand in both of hers and her eyes began to moisten inexplicably. Agnes kept my hand imprisoned and looked as though she was about to tell me something, then changed her mind.

"You're okay," she said, releasing me. "I like you."

It was only later that I recalled my conversation with Q. Byrum Hurst. I had asked him how Owney spoke and if he could describe his voice and accent. Was it, for instance, typically American or something quite different?

"Lord," he laughed, "It was like yours, of course. Real soft. You talk just the way he did."

Somehow a tone, an inflection had brought memories flooding back over the years. Owney never returned to England for fear that he would not be readmitted to America. His manner and voice, the cloth cap which became his trademark, and his lifelong love of pigeons belonged, it seemed, many miles from the endless bedlam of New York or a remote mountain town in Arkansas.

2.

Huddled Masses

Owen Vincent Madden was born on December 18, 1891, in a tiny, terraced house on Somerset Street, Leeds. It has long since been pulled down and replaced by the Home Office building, which *Yorkshire Life* magazine once wryly suggested should be named Madden House.

His parents, Francis and Mary, were Irish. They were driven by the dark aftermath of the potato famine to search for work in the English mills and factories which were turning villages into towns. There was plenty of work for Francis in the industrial north and, like many of his countrymen, his dreams were dulled by long hours and little pay. As a boy, Owney watched him walk wearily home from the Leeds "sweat shop" where he worked, developing an early distaste for manual labor.

Pressing and cutting wool and manhandling heavy rolls onto horse-drawn carts was exhausting labor. In the evening, they gathered around the smoking kitchen fire at Somerset Street. With Francis coaxing heat from the coal fire, Mary darning clothes, and the children playing on the rag rug, there were times when it was almost like the old country again.

A restless search for prosperity took them over the black Pennines to Wigan—a town thick with yellow smoke and the ring of hollow coughs. Each morning, carts clattered on the cobbles and machines whined into life as the mills and mines opened for business. Rows of terraced cottages climbed up the surrounding hills as though trying to escape from the grime.

Owney never forgot the bleakness of his boyhood and occasionally referred to it even in his declining years. The public school he attended was strict and the teachers unsmiling. A polished cane hovered over them, ready to swoop, as they sat in rows chanting edifying maxims such as "a healthy mind in a healthy body" and "discipline is the backbone of the British empire." When the bell rang at the end of the day, he ran home to perform his favorite task—tending his father's pigeons. He fed them grain, cleaned out the tiny loft, and released them. As they took flight, banking in tight formation above the chimneys against a backdrop of mist-covered moors, there was no greater expression of freedom.

It was a passion which was to remain with him for the rest of his life. His prize birds later earned him a drawer full of medals as they sailed with the same graceful poetry above the rooftops of New York. He built pigeon lofts on top of the Cotton Club and most of the buildings he owned. In exile in Hot Springs, he built a white loft on his garage roof. It became home to a flock which once belonged to Senator Huey Long of Louisiana. Homing pigeons were unheard of in Arkansas at the time. A generation after his death, they flew wild over Central Avenue, descending in huge flocks to peck for food around the deserted stores. A cloth cap and the pigeons became Owney's trademarks, rather than the more formal trilby and gun.

The *Washington Post* once wrote of the Duke of the West Side: "Owney Madden is a connoisseur of fine pigeons of every description. Feeding, mating, and studying them are his relaxations, and he has flocks scattered in various roosts about New Jersey, Brooklyn, and Long Island. Lonely folk so often turn to pigeons somehow."

One day, as though drawn ever westward toward Ireland, Owney's father, Francis, announced that they were moving on, this time twenty-five miles away to Liverpool. The city overflowed with Irish, Welsh, and faces from every corner of the world, attracted by its booming cosmopolitan port and bustling optimism. Liverpool, like New York, was a melting pot. People were friendly and shouldered poverty with a cocky resilience. They were always ready with a self-deprecating joke and a quick reply and would not have felt out of place in the Borscht Belt or the Lower East Side.

Sparse documentation of Owney's early life in England refers to a brief spell as a child entertainer in the music halls. The British Music Hall Society has no record of this but halls teemed with acts which often rose and sank without a trace. Accounts suggest that Francis and Mary found a brief kind of escape in rehearsing Owney in an unpolished song-and-dance routine to help boost the family income. It was the time when future movie stars Stan Laurel and Charlie Chaplin were treading the boards of provincial halls, performing a clog dance and knockabout comedy act with Fred Karno's company. Owney's friendship with Stan was possibly based on memories of those early days. There is no doubt that the shimmering spell of show business had an easygoing appeal which always made him feel at home. Francis, at this time, was working in a fish mill, pulverizing dockside catches into powdered concentrate. Owney found the theater a welcome antidote to the grim world of industrial work, which he had come to instinctively resent. In his teens, he was to boast to a police sergeant that he had never worked a day in his life.

The satisfaction in creating a show—the eternal quest for perfection—always transcended mere investment in the rackets he ran later in New York. At the Cotton Club, which he bought as an outlet for his Prohibition beer, Owney brought in celebrated interior designer Josef Urban to create the right atmosphere. Even his illicit beer—Madden's Number One—was hailed as the best in New York ("creamy," one connoisseur described it). Dutch Schultz, a rival gangster, was dispensing little more than colored water at the time. He used to scoff at Owney's efforts to improve his brew. The same interest and enthusiasm was evident when Owney bankrolled Mae West's Broadway shows.

Owney's Liverpool boyhood was also galvanized by the drama and fleeting riches of the boxing ring. He was too young to take up the gloves himself but spent hours watching an uncle fight for cash purses in halls and boxing booths. Owney hung around the dressing rooms, as he is said to have done in the music halls, discovering a world far removed from the drudgery outside. He retained a love for fighters and show people, not for the reasons that some gangsters found them attractive, but because he found them to be "real people." While Schultz flirted with the Ziegfeld Follies and Capone was pictured with showgirls on his arm, Owney would be deep in conversation with them until the early hours. Show people were open and genuine in an age of high corruption. Like them, he followed a precarious calling and they seemed to understand each other.

Many English fighters like Jackie "Kid" Berg, the British Lightweight Champion, were his close friends. Some, in the North of England, kept in touch by sending him clippings from the sports pages of the *Yorkshire Post*, which he kept in a cigar box. With all the worldclass fighters he owned, he was content to take a back seat and watch their progress. Boxing, like crime, was a tough way to reach the top and it was not difficult to see parallels between the professional ring and the streets of the West Side.

Dick O'Brien, the *Washington Times-Herald* sports columnist, deeply missed Owney's unique appreciation of the fight game. In 1950, he wrote:

"A fight manager I knew once went to Madden and said: 'Owen, I've got a good fighter and I need about $5,000 to promote the guy. He can win the championship of the world. Loan me the money and I'll cut you in.'

"'You're on,' Madden told him, 'but I don't want your fighter. Just tell the boys I loaned you the money. That's good enough for me. Pay me when the guy gets to the top.'

"That's how Madden started lending money to managers for the promotion of their fighters. He was sort of proud to be associated in a strictly unofficial capacity.

"But he didn't come out in the open and flaunt himself to the public. He remained in the background while others ran the boxing business in New York.

"How different today. Gamblers are no longer the shy boys they used to be. They started with boxing and racing. Now they're moving up. To them it's just as legitimate to walk up to a twenty-one-year-old college boy and offer him a bribe as it is for them to call on the phone and lay off a $10 bet on a horse.

"I think if one of Madden's men was caught attempting to bribe an amateur or a college boy, there would have been an 'investigation' inside the mob itself."

Liverpool was Owney's kind of town. From the waterfront, life ranged from rich and classy to poor and brassy in a single sweep of the eye. The city, however, harbored no sentiment for those who chose to leave its rough embrace. Dockside boarding houses, jammed shoulder to shoulder along the five-mile waterfront, preyed mercilessly on poor emigrants. The long wait for a passage to America was fraught with uncertainty, and timetables were notoriously unreliable. Glib promises of comfortable berths proved no more than confidence tricks. Ships often sailed days late, depleting passengers' precious savings. Queues on the quayside hummed with every kind of low-life opportunist, from tricksters selling dud currency to urchin pickpockets darting nimbly among the crowds.

In 1902, at the age of eleven, Owney stood with his mother, brother Marty, and sister Mary on the same wharf where his father had disembarked from an Irish packet years earlier in search of the promised land. Francis, always the optimist, had laid plans for a new life in America but, after saving the fare, died before they could book their passage. Mary summoned the courage to take the children on alone and live the dream for him. If she failed to find work, there was always the hope that Aunt Lizzie living in Manhattan might take them in.

Owney assumed the role of family protector, guarding their bundles and shaping up his fists on gangs of street kids buzzing like flies around a honey pot. His last view of Liverpool was a thicket of masts and rigging and sandstone waterfront buildings burnished by the setting sun. As a bobbing tender filled its decks to make another run out to the gaunt outline of S.S. *Teutonic* waiting at anchor, the queue edged along the landing stage. The scene is recalled in faded photographs in Liverpool Museum. Rickety legs and emaciated faces—a river of cloth caps and bonnets moving inexorably toward the unknown. Women clutched tightly wrapped babies, while men comforted sobbing relatives. Children shielded their eyes against the low sun to catch a glimpse of the ship building up steam for the long voyage ahead.

If leaving Liverpool was painful, there was nothing to prepare passengers—cold, hungry, and invariably ill—for their arrival in New York thirty-eight days later.

Those lucky not to have been beaten up and have their belongings stolen in Liverpool's dockland were destined to encounter exactly the same problems on the waterfront of New York. The year the Maddens embarked, 195,000 other emigrants from England endured the same suffering and pitfalls. Owney, shouldering his mother's bundle down the gangplank, soon learned that the first rule of the promised land was to survive or die. In his perilous future profession, he was to attain legendary respect as one of the few who outlived them all.

The family settled on 10th Avenue, where Hell's Kitchen yawned like a mouthful of rotten teeth to the north and south of 34th Street. It was considered to be the most notorious area in all of New York. Mary, a righteous, respectable Irishwoman, felt beleaguered in trying to bring up her children with any semblance of values. Owney—softly spoken and reserved—clung more to his English upbringing than his elder brother, Martin. Marty, as kids on the block called him, soon became indistinguishable from a native New Yorker. Owney, in contrast, never completely lost his native roots.

Each day, at the age of twelve, he walked down the stone steps of their building, Number 352, to St. Michael's Parochial School, a few blocks down on West 33rd Street. In the distance, the newly built trian-gular tower of the Flatiron Building soared twenty-two miraculous stories above Madison Square—the highest of the tall blocks New Yorkers had dubbed "skyscrapers." But that was on the days he made it to school. Like many of his classmates, Owney often didn't bother with school. There was too much to do on the crowded streets. He preferred to hang around livery stables and gyms, run messages for local villains, and re-ceive his education on the sidewalk.

Lessons in life came thick and fast in the scramble for survival which characterized life on the Lower West Side. For almost two years, the Maddens were the only neighborhood children who had not turned to crime. Mary prayed that it would last, but in her heart probably knew that the chances were slight. She told the boys that she wanted them to fulfill the hopes of their father. Francis believed that in the New World everyone had an equal chance of success. It was, he thought, a place where honest work would be rewarded. What he underestimated was the extent of corruption in New York's poorer quarters. Everything, down to the price of food, was ruled by the power of the rackets, even at a time when organized crime was still in its infancy. Police and politi-cians, far from being the upholders of law and justice, were often as ruth-less as the gangs. In Hell's Kitchen, the only sure way to the American Dream was to get a break in the movies, show business, or "the mob."

Mary, who had managed to find work scrubbing floors, must have missed her husband's strength and optimism. Despite giving the children as much as she could, there was no doubt that they were pale, thin and plainly starving. She naturally began to look to Owney—fast maturing and showing signs of manhood—with a mixture of hope and anxiety.

"On your father's grave, Owney," she warned her potential bread-winner, "I'll have no dishonest money in this house."

Soon afterward, he was walking home with his mother, helping to carry the family groceries. Before he had a chance to turn at the sound of scuttering footsteps, a boy about his own age snipped the handles of his mother's shopping bag and made off with the contents into the crowd. All the way home, Mary raged with indignation. Owney, toting the remaining bag, trotted quietly at her side, turning the incident over in his mind. He often told friends the story to illustrate the first time he became aware of crime as a paying proposition and recalled thinking: "Hell, I could do that—and better, too."

It was one of a handful of turning points in his life which appeared to dramatically affect his character and attitude. At the age of barely fourteen, desperate to ease the family's hopeless situation, he planned his first crime. In Hell's Kitchen, it had proved impossible to blow against the wind and, before long, Marty was following in his footsteps.

Years later, in middle life, Owney was lounging on the sidewalk outside his Hot Springs gambling joint, the Southern Club, when FBI special agent Clay White strolled by. The Duke of the West Side and the man who was to tail him until the day he died, exchanged greetings and fell into conversation.

"Owney never talked about much except general things," White said. "But I remember that day because he suddenly said, 'Do you know about the beginning, Clay? How I got involved? My mother, brother, and I didn't have a thing in the house to eat in New York City. Didn't know where the next dollar was going to come from. Mother was worried about how she was going to provide for us—about what we were going to do.

"'I decided that I was going to get some money somewhere and I went out on the street.' Owney even told me the street, but I don't recall where it was," White said, slowly revolving a yellow pencil during an interview in Hot Springs. "He got himself a club and told me that he waited in a darkened doorway until a certain individual came along. The man was alone. Owney told me: 'As he passed the doorway, I hit him with that club and knocked him out. He had $500 on him. I took what he had, but only the money, nothing else. I knew I couldn't take it home and give it to Mother, because she would want to know where it all came from. I couldn't do that—she'd be after me. I gave a little bit at a time to my aunt and she loaned it to my mother. That was the first crime I ever committed.'"

White, who served as sheriff of Garland County, Arkansas, after his FBI days, laid his pencil down on the desk. "I thought that was kind of interesting. He never did get into too much with me about his early days."

The story indicates the first sign of a certain Madden style which became more sophisticated as he grew older. Our sympathies, of course, must lie with the man with the sore head and empty wallet, but behind the crudeness of the crime lay a distinctive moral finesse. Owney, unobtrusive to the point of shyness, always made a point of taking the unexpected course. Friends, attorneys, hard-bitten newsmen, and underworld figures alike have remarked on the quiet, self-effacing way he handled himself. He had none of the swagger of the mobsters who hogged the headlines, they said. The toughness came from within—a rock strata compressed in the Lancashire coalfields, Liverpool's dockland, and the mean streets of Hell's Kitchen. Owney achieved what he wanted, not by the wild ravings of contemporaries like Capone, Schultz, or Legs Diamond, but by taking a man aside and talking quietly and directly to him until there was no misunderstanding. "He could nail someone with a look when he wanted to," one New York reporter recalled.

"There was never a day that I did not notice him give something to someone," said Hot Springs attorney Q. Byrum Hurst. "But never in an obvious way. That wasn't his style. You might never know he had done it. He was calm, sweet, unassuming, grateful. So quiet that you would never, ever dream that this little man had done some of the things he was reputed to have done."

At the tender age of fourteen, Owney was on the verge of a wild rampage of murder, ballot-rigging, and robbery which would take him right to the top of the most violent, unpredictable street gang in New York—the Gophers. They called him "the Killer," a nickname he hated all his life. There is a creased and aging photograph that shows him posing in a back alley with his soldiers. In the foreground are the inevitable pigeons.

Owney, in the center, looks every inch the wild thug, ready to knock down anything or anybody that stood in his way. In ten years, he built up a fearsome reputation that was equal, some say, to Capone's in Chicago. It was not, however, until maturity that he really earned respect. He abruptly abandoned the gun and heavy blackjack in his twenties but found it hard to divest the hard, ruthless image he had acquired along the way. As his youth receded, however, Owney became an intelligent commander and subtle philanthropist. The change was so fundamental that many found it difficult to equate the man they met with the legend.

Whitney Bolton, a former newspaper columnist in New York, fondly remembered the iron fist in the hand-tailored kid glove. At the time of Owney's death, Bolton published a revealing story, knowing that the old Duke would have lapsed into self-conscious silence had it been published when he was alive.

"The best you can do when a colorful man dies, a man you have known, is to recite the relations he had with other people," Bolton wrote in his widely syndicated column. "Owen Madden, once a gangster, reputedly a killer, a hard man with a hard business going for him, was at all times, to me, a quiet-voiced, enormously polite man who on at least one occasion went out of his way to be helpful to a kid newspaperman in his twenties who didn't know too much about anything but was willing to learn. The kid was me 40 years ago.

"A high-placed lady of New York society telephoned me to say that friends of hers had a supper check padded the previous Saturday night, and asked if I could do anything about it. Could I, for example, find out what outlaws owned the club so she could complain to the police with some accuracy? I said I thought she didn't need me, since the police probably would know the ownership anyway. We argued that around for a while, and I finally yielded. I said I'd try to find out.

"I mentioned this situation to a columnist friend, who nodded casually, and we let it drop. An hour later, my telephone rang and a soft, still British voice said: 'This is Owen Madden. I have been told you have a problem. Would you like to tell me about it in my office? It's in the Longacre Building and I'm here now.'

"Fifteen minutes later, having been ushered through a waiting room in which sat four or five dour-looking bravos, I was in Owney's office, a simple, even severe room devoid of any garish decor of any kind. His desk top was clear.

"'I understand the problem only generally,' he said in that quiet way he had. 'Would you give it to me in detail?'

"I did. He smiled once, a fleeting, small smile, and when I finished, he said: 'Actually, I already have taken some steps to correct this unfortunate thing. The waiter who mis-added the check is bringing over in person the $21.90 due your friend's friends. I am happy to have been told of the matter. If you will wait, I'll give you the money and you can pass it on, with our regrets.'

"A slim, dark, and fearfully anxious little man came in after about five minutes, starting at the door with, 'Owney, you got me wrong. I didn't do it purposely. We was rushed, see, and I added too fast.'

"'My name is Mr. Madden,' said Owney, never raising his voice. 'You won't be adding at all for a while. I am having you replaced. Give this gentleman the money and I shan't detain you.'

"After he left, I stood up. Owney asked me to sit down. I sat.

"If your friend still wants to know the ownership, it is easy. All New York nightclubs are incorporated. Therefore, the names of all officers and principal stockholders are on file in Albany in the Corporation Office. There is no secret as to identities. If she persists, I'd be happy to save her the trip and show her this book, in the drawer here. It lists them all for every club. You may copy from it if you wish.'

"Soon after that I was assigned by the newspaper to cover gangster developments and nothing else. One night, just before the first edition went to press, the receptionist said, 'A Mr. Madden is here to see you.' I asked that he be shown in and he was. He sat on the edge of the desk and said, more quietly than usual: 'I heard about your assignment. I thought it might be helpful to you if you were seen talking to me. Your editor might be impressed. We'll talk about nothing very important and in a few minutes I'll go on my way.'

"I found a $10 raise in my pay the next week, after Owney Madden's city room call on me had ceased to be an excitement to the staff.

"And I'll tell you this—Owney Madden always talked that way, good English, spoken at a quiet level.

"About all the murders, I wouldn't know. I never asked him."

3.

Fire in the Streets

New York City, 1912

It was the Gophers' night out. They drifted out of pool halls and dingy apartments in the gas-lit streets off 10th Avenue to meet up outside the nickelodeon. Some wore caps and roll-neck jerseys, others battered derbies and collarless shirts. Nearly all of them sported heavy side-laced boots, which had become a fashion with the gang. The toughest boys on the West Side were relaxed on their home turf, and the cinema was still novel enough to be something of an occasion. They caught every new movie that came their way, from cops and robbers to romance in the Klondike. This one was something new—*Les Miserables* the billboard announced, but no one was quite sure how to pronounce it.

The only non-member of the gang was young George Raft, a kid from up the block who had left home and scratched out a living by picking fruit upstate, with a short spell in between as a professional boxer. He was a friend of Owney's and, as far as the boys were concerned, this made him all right. Georgie liked the Gophers. Sometimes he hung around with them when he was not at Lindy's Restaurant making a coffee and cheesecake last for hours and watching the famous entertainers who dropped in. In the back of his mind, he had bigger plans for the future than the Gophers, who spent their time raiding freight cars in the sprawling train yards at New York Central.

Georgie could handle himself well at boxing but quit the fight game when an Irish giant beat the daylights out of him. He valued his dark good looks and resumed his career chasing girls instead. Georgie's latest job was as a seven-cents-a-dance ballroom instructor, and the girls were queuing for lessons with outstretched arms. He was light on his feet and liked to show off his fancy footwork in local clubs and dancehalls.

At twenty-one, Owney was five years older than Georgie and had a fond regard for his two-fisted style. Occasionally, he would stuff a handful of bills in the kid's pocket because he knew he was sleeping rough. Georgie would always count the money carefully and make a point of repaying him. After the movie, there was a good chance the young dancer would hide in the lavatory until the crowds had gone so he could sleep across the seats in the warm theater.

Georgie, like many youngsters in Hell's Kitchen, tried to model himself on the tough, restrained, and slightly gracious style of the leader of the Gophers. In many ways, they were both different from the Irish roughnecks under Owney's command. When *Les Miserables* flickered silently onto the screen, Georgie, with a sense of shame, tried to hide the fact that he was deeply moved by it.

Later, toward the end of his career as a movie actor, Raft recalled the night for his biographer, Lewis Yablonsky, who wrote: "Jean Valjean, the hero of Victor Hugo's classic, reached his greatest dilemma in the film when he had to decide whether or not he could save the life of a young boy pinned under the wheels of a carriage. Saving the boy meant revealing his identity (by exhibiting his strength) to the police and returning to prison. Of course, he chose to lift the carriage. George could not contain his emotions and began to sob. His tough pals roared with laughter at George's sentimentality and the experience taught him to conceal his emotions and maintain an impenetrable exterior."

George's transparent honesty endeared him to Owney. The antics of other earnest, hero-worshipping youngsters amused him, but he treated them with stern authority. One street urchin, Jack Diamond, an orphan who hung around the Gophers running errands, begged Owney to let him join them on their moonlight raids on shops, warehouses, and freight cars. Owney turned him down and, to prove himself, Jack took to stealing parcels from the back of passing delivery vans. He could run through the streets clutching his loot faster than anyone in the neighborhood had ever seen.

"He had not arrived in his crime apprenticeship at a point where he was on a social or business parity with his idolized chieftain," wrote Fred D. Pasley in the *New York Daily Illustrated News*. "Owney just tolerated him—good-naturedly, certainly—but still just tolerated him.

"'Legs,' Owney would say, as father to son, 'you're only a kid. You're only a punk. All you can do so far is to chase express and delivery wagons along Death Avenue, snatch a likely-looking package, and then beat it.'

"'Yeh, but you say yourself, I do pretty well,' Legs would protest.

"'Sure,' Owney would admit, 'you ain't so bad. You're faster on your feet than any of the other kids. The coppers can't catch you—you run so fast—that's why we call you Legs. Say, you ought to be proud of that—a kid like you and already with a swell nickname.'

"Proud? Legs Diamond would tell the world. Only fourteen years old—still in knee pants—and the speediest fellow in the Junior Gophers' Wagon Package Snatchers Association. Owney himself had said so."

Diamond rose to run the Hotsy Totsy Club on Broadway and, after miraculously escaping several attempts on his life, made the error of thinking he was "unkillable." Legs Diamond's greed and recklessness finally upset the delicate balance of underworld life. He was regarded as a nuisance and, in 1931, a contract was finally taken out on him. Two gunmen burst into his safe-house in Albany when he was sleeping. One held him down by the ears while the other pumped three bullets into his head. Such killings were not unusual, and Owney's straight dealing and quiet diplomacy were undoubtedly one reason why he survived to be an old man.

One journalist, looking back on his career in the mid-1930s, concluded: "His word, except among madmen and low competitors with designs upon his life or his money, was always, in the days of his glory, regarded as absolutely good. This man, whose long-ago record caused him to be referred to occasionally as a sneak-thief and worse, actually had a great many admirable qualities. It would have been impossible for even the most strict moralist to have passed an afternoon listening to Owney without feeling that, according to his own lights, he was an honest man."

After a night at the movies, Madden loved to saunter down 41st Street, the heartland of Irish tribal anarchy. He was a familiar figure, walking with his chest out like one of his prize pigeons, or a duke making the rounds of his estate. His manner once prompted an old sergeant at the West 37th Street police station—the "Hell's Kitchen precinct"—to call him "a banty little rooster from hell." As he strolled along, he would take everything in. He watched faces in the crowd, noting which shops had changed hands. He absorbed every detail with the alert, restless eye of a born survivor. An urge to know everything that was happening preoccupied him. At home, he would read every column inch of the newspapers, marking up items which caught his eye and putting them to one side for reference. Even on his deathbed, his attorney's secretary sat for hours reading every page of the New York dailies to him while he nodded knowingly at one story or another.

The Hell's Kitchen precinct was one of the city's most violent police postings. Locals called the place "the slaughterhouse" because of the shouts and disturbances which emanated long into the night as officers worked out on uncooperative young bloods to keep their hand in. One of the most formidable characters ever stationed at the fortress-like precinct house was Officer Patrick H. Diamond, known throughout the West Side as "the Iron Claw." He was a man so tough that he regarded police-issue revolvers with contempt and was never known to draw a firearm while making an arrest.

"He was reported to wear out a couple of night-sticks a week," Hell's Kitchen historian Richard O'Connor related. When his weapon broke in his hands, he would haul out a cargo hook—hence his sobriquet—and "continue the argument," as a reporter for the *New York Sun* put it. When Diamond finally retired, five hundred gangsters and policemen joined forces to treat him to dinner at the Old Homestead, a restaurant at 23rd and 8th Avenue. They raised their glasses in salute and genuinely mourned the passing of an era.

Hell's Kitchen officers—many of them from Ireland themselves—had to wage a running war to make their presence felt against the brawling warlords from vast families of Gallaghers, Brennans, Malarkeys, and Mulraneys. Protection rackets flourished openly, houses were ransacked in broad daylight, and anyone with a hint of cash in his pocket ran a serious risk of being blackjacked to the ground.

"When he was in a mellow mood (he rarely ever drank much, but he could unwind), he liked to talk of the old days when he and his wild hellions ravaged the West Side from 42nd to 14th Streets," Stanley Walker wrote of Madden in *The Night Club Era* in the 1930s: "In retrospect, these lads would appear not as bruisers, loft thieves, pickpockets or whatnot, but as good-hearted lads full of the spirit of fun and horseplay. 'Wildest bunch of roosters you ever saw,' is how he remembered them."

Burglary was one of Owney's early specialties but, despite many arrests, he was never brought to justice. The New York District Attorney files reveal a typical case in 1910, when a patrolling policeman spotted him boarding a 10th Avenue trolley car at 3 a.m. in the company of three other men. Owney and another Gopher, Eddie Jordan, were each carrying heavy bags, which aroused the suspicions of a Patrolman Collins. He leapt onto the moving car after them and drew his revolver. Jordan threw the bag at him and all four escaped in the confusion. Owney and Eddie were later arrested and charged with stealing $34 worth of scrap metal, three watches, and 160 foreign coins from a junk shop on West 33rd Street. Both pleaded "not guilty" when they appeared before city magistrate Paul Krotel and were acquitted. How they managed to achieve this remarkable feat will unfortunately never be known, as the court records have since been destroyed.

The West Side gangs feared no one and displayed a strutting confidence in the power of the knife and club. One of the Gopher leaders, Lung Curran, was one of the wildest figures on the street. He believed that anything that caught his fancy was his for the taking. High among the legends about him, which ran like brush fires through the sawdust saloons, was one set on a cold winter's day as Curran strolled along with his girlfriend on a street west of 8th Avenue. The girl shivered in the freezing wind that gusted up the riverside canyons. Curran decided to do something about it. He ambled over to a patrolling policeman and, without exchanging a word, clubbed him to the sidewalk and tore off his blue serge tunic.

Curran's girl bundled it up and took it home. After a few hours at the kitchen table with scissors and thread, she had cut it down, nipped the waist and altered it to fit her. Even among the mixture of styles parading in Hell's Kitchen, it was an instant hit. She wore it with a swagger and, hanging onto Curran's arm, imbued him with new authority. Soon, no law officer could feel safe. Gangs waylaid them at every street corner to beat them up and take home uniforms as trophies for their girlfriends. It was around this time, when patrolmen were forced to walk in pairs, that the authorities decided that the blatant rampage of the Irish warlords could not be allowed to continue.

The Gophers—in Hell's Kitchen they pronounced it as "Goofers"— earned their name because they tended to congregate in cellars and basements like their subterranean namesakes. Owney was proudly English. With Irish parents, however, his credentials were good enough for the Gophers. It may have been a slightly eccentric pedigree but, in the gang's rigid code, it was infinitely preferable to being Jewish or Italian. The boy was small and wiry, with a raw nerve and self-reliance which quickly won their admiration. He made his early reputation with a curiously Victorian weapon—a length of lead pipe wrapped in newspaper. It was an English novelty in Hell's Kitchen and remembered for generations.

The factor which set him apart, perhaps more than any other, was that from the age of fifteen he was one of the very few hoodlums anywhere on the West Side to carry a gun and use it with deadly efficiency. Owney, with his well-oiled .38 Smith and Wesson, was regarded from the East River to the Hudson as "the finest shot in New York." It was not until World War I, when many hoodlums were conscripted and trained in weaponry, that firearms became fashionable on the streets of Hell's Kitchen.

The Gophers defended their territory with clubs, knives, brass knuckles, and blackjacks against hit-and-run raids by rivals. The Gas Housers, the Five Pointers, the 14th Street Gang and, above all, the Hudson Dusters, were their sworn enemies. In times of emergency, the Gophers could muster up to 500 street fighters to put the opposition to flight. Skirmishes were bloody and ferocious, occasionally resulting in death, as they defended rich pickings provided by the freight cars waiting in depots along 11th Avenue. Some nights, the cars—loaded with commodities—strung out almost the entire length of Manhattan, from Battery to Riverside Drive at 72nd Street, protected by battle-weary railroad guards.

Gophers regarded work with disdain. They were lazy and lived well, cooling their heels until the dancehalls and movies opened, or darkness gave cover for their raids. During one of Owney's many spells in Hell's Kitchen Precinct House (he was said to have been arrested more than 140 times and convicted only twice), a sergeant asked him about his movements. A curious reporter hanging around the desk had put the officer up to it. Owney, amused by his growing notoriety, obliged them by borrowing a police pad and writing:

"Thursday: Went to a dance in the afternoon. Went to a dance at night and then to a cabaret. Took some girls home. Went to a restaurant and stayed there until seven o'clock Friday morning.

"Friday: Spent the day with Freda Horner. Looked at some fancy pigeons. Met some friends in a saloon early in the evening and stayed with them until five o'clock in the morning.

"Saturday: Slept all day. Went to a dance in the Bronx late in the afternoon, and to a dance on Park Avenue at night.

"Sunday: Slept until three o'clock. Went to a dance in the afternoon and to another in the same place at night. After that I went to a cabaret and stayed there almost all night."

There was, of course, no mention of any crime. Freda Horner, a blonde with bobbed hair who hung around with the gang, was one of several steady girlfriends. She was what came to be known in the early 1920s as a "moll." Molls were a breed of steel-hard girls, often with gang mottoes, such as "death before dishonor," tattooed on their forearms. They carried their boyfriends' guns in their clutch bags in case of a police shakedown and were known for putting up a formidable fight when arrested. Freda, like many of them, was attracted to Owney's growing reputation. He was also more of an attentive ladies' man than his rough-and-ready Gopher associates. They liked his generosity and were aware that, beneath the polite exterior, he could command authority with just a look.

Stanley Walker recalled him in the 1930s—less of the wild rover in those days, but still possessing a magnetic charm: "Ladies who heard of him were thrilled at meeting him—to some, he appeared cute. His forehead was not high, and it receded a little. The nose was a fierce beak. He had that first requisite of leadership, 'a bone in the face.'

"His mouth and chin dropped away almost straight to the neck. No offense meant, but, when viewed from the front, there was something fishlike about the way the mouth drooped at the corners. His face was sometimes pallid, and sometimes flushed.

"His body bore the scars of many bullets, and the condition of his lungs always made him fear that he would die of tuberculosis. His hair was black and sleek. His eyes were blue, a very bright and piercing blue. Sometimes they were friendly enough, and in repose they were even sad, but usually they were hard, and shining, and they saw everything."

Owney would take Freda, or any of the other girls he picked up around the crowded dancehalls, back to his apartment. Freda had several sexual partners and, like her best friend, Margaret Everdeane, contracted a mild form of syphilis. Freda's medical records at Bellevue Hospital noted that it was "not infectious and that no person is in danger of con-tracting the said disease." Margaret, who came from a well-to-do back-ground, was less fortunate and had to be admitted to the hospital for prolonged treatment.

Freda saw less of Owney when he married another of his girlfriends, Dorothy "Loretta" Rogers, in 1911. For a while, they lived at his apart-ment near 41st Street and 8th Avenue, where Dorothy gave birth to a baby girl, Margaret. The marriage, by all accounts, lasted barely two years. Owney's turbulent street life was unsuited to domesticity, and Dorothy moved in with her mother on West 42nd Street. She remained on the fringe of the Hell's Kitchen scene and was later reported to have drifted into bootlegging. For almost twenty years, they remained man and wife, at least on paper. Owney, chastened by the experience, never considered remarrying until he met Agnes Demby many years later in Hot Springs. By then, Madden had lost touch with Dorothy and had to have her traced in order for them to obtain a "quickie" divorce in Reno, Nevada. She disappeared again, cushioned by a $75,000 cash settlement, a yacht, and a house in Yonkers to ease the discomfort of old memories. Margaret grew up in New York barely knowing her father.

Freda Horner reappeared on the scene when Dorothy moved back with her mother. It was a rekindling which Owney was to regret for the rest of his life. Freda had thrown over a wild gunman named Patsy Doyle to move back with the Duke and, for a while, it was apparently like old times. Later, when Doyle was fatally cut down by two gunmen after being lured into a saloon, she pointed the finger squarely at her lover. Owney clearly had an ability to arouse the strongest emotions in the opposite sex.

Gang troubles in the early months of their marriage undoubtedly contributed to the breakup with Dorothy. At the time, he was a fast-rising, able lieutenant and the gang, facing its darkest hour, desperately needed his services. The New York Central Railroad Company was not amused by the Gophers and their nightly forays and decided that their days of unchallenged power were numbered. Thousands of dollars worth of freight had been looted and a number of company patrolmen seriously injured. If the police were unable, or unwilling, to handle them, New York Central decided, then the time had come to take its own preventative measures. Under conditions of great secrecy, the railroad company assembled a huge squad of handpicked security men, all chosen for their willingness to take on the Gophers. Some were keen to settle old scores while others were simply hungry for a rumble to relieve the monotony of the freight yards.

A few weeks earlier, the New York police had launched a concerted show of strength against the West Side mobs by staging coordinated assaults on their respective neighborhoods. The battle left the Gophers winded, but far from defeated. When the police withdrew, a semblance of peace returned, but the gang was unprepared for subsequent raids by the railroad company.

Among the casualties of the long battle with New York's police were Gopher leaders Marty Brennan and Newburgh Gallagher, who had been captured and hauled away to Sing Sing prison. Other passengers in the fleet of trucks which carted away bleeding prisoners included Willie Jones, boss of the Gas Housers, Itsky Joe Hickman of the Five Pointers, and Al Rooney, who ran the fearsome 14th Street gang.

The railroad swoop was planned at a time when the walking wounded felt demoralized by the loss of their leaders. The special force divided into groups and fanned through Hell's Kitchen, smashing down the doors of Gopher hangouts and beating them senseless with nightsticks. A bloody battle raged over several hours, with residents fleeing the streets. When some gang members followed Owney's example and pulled out firearms, they were stunned to be met by a hail of accurate gunfire. The railroad police, anticipating tough opposition, had trained especially for the occasion.

Over the next few weeks, wave upon wave of fresh attacks broke the Gopher resistance. One patrolman, watching from a street corner, was so impressed that he said the Gophers had been "clubbed from hell to breakfast."

"Many thugs were wounded and several sent to prison," gangland historian Herbert Asbury was to recall a decade later. "There was scarcely a Gopher who did not receive a sound thumping. Within a few months, the new force devastated Hell's Kitchen with clubs and blackjacks and, thereafter, the Gophers avoided railroad property as they would a plague. To this day, a New York Central watchman is regarded as the natural enemy of a Hell's Kitchen hoodlum."

Owney was seen in the thick of the fighting but somehow managed to avoid arrest. As Richard O'Connor remarked, "He had the cherubic smile and general appearance of an altar boy, so he might well have been overlooked." The Gophers, broken and decimated, convened a conference and decided to split into two main gangs—one commanded by a roughneck known as Buck O'Brien, the other by Owney.

He had now been in America just nine years and was on the threshold of achieving impressive gangland power. In the process, he had run up a long arrest record for assault, burglary, carrying burglar's tools, and petty larceny, without once being jailed. Rival gangs, circling like vultures for the pickings offered by Owney's new territory, considered the Gophers a spent force. The young Englishman knew that his leadership was about to be tested. To give himself breathing space and time to consolidate his weary troops, he entered into a peaceful agreement with Tanner Smith, leader of the Marginals, who controlled the streets to the south of his domain. The Hudson Dusters, the Gophers' oldest enemies, showed interest in a similar arrangement. "Unlike the old Gophers, Madden's gang refused any peace treaty with the Dusters and often battled in the streets with them," O'Connor noted.

It was a period when gangs were evolving all over New York, waging territorial wars which occasionally turned to gun battles on the streets. East Side and West Side, neighborhood racketeers and petty criminals emerged from the age of innocence before Prohibition to run organizations more profitable and influential than legitimate corporations. A major figure in organized crime, Meyer Lansky, later boasted to his colleagues that "we're bigger than U.S. Steel." The single factor which provided the means to help major figures such as Owney to awesome power was the misguided intention of moralists who wanted to see America alcohol-free. The organizational flair and business talent of these master gangsters stemmed from apprenticeships in the crude street rackets of their youth. Hell's Kitchen, like similar slum areas across the city, became a proving ground in which only the strongest managed to survive.

As a warning to the Dusters, and in an effort to raise his standing among his own men, Owney shot a young Italian, Luigi Mollinucci, on the corner of 11th Avenue and 30th Street. He stepped out onto the sidewalk and calmly squeezed the trigger in full view of passersby. It was a cold-blooded slaying, and detectives were convinced they at last had a case against him. As the weeks passed by, proceedings had to be dropped when several key witnesses packed their bags and vanished from the neighborhood. Owney, arrested on suspicion of homicide, was freed.

His leadership of the Gophers instilled a fear in the Dusters which was never quite forgotten. Many years later, when Owney was investing heavily in boxers, he called in to see Joe Jacobs, an old promoter who shared an office in New York's Putnam Building with his partner, William McCarney. Bill Corum, the *Chicago Herald-American* columnist, heard the story in 1946 and ran it under the headline: "When a Duster Tasted Dust." McCarney told him:

"One day, a slight, soft-spoken man came in and asked for Joe. I told him that Jacobs wasn't around but that he might be in later.

"'Mind if I wait?' he asked.

"Not at all," I told him.

"There were a lot of fight pictures on the wall, if you recall, and pretty soon the visitor got up and started walking 'round looking at them. I could see the pictures interested him and, of course, with me a story went with every one of 'em. I started telling him about the various fights and some of the angles and situations that had come up in my, if I may say so, varied experience.

"I guess I must have gassed him for almost an hour when he interrupted me and said, 'I'm afraid I'm taking up too much of your time, Mr. McCarney.'

"I told him he wasn't and that I had nothing to do. So, I cut up some more old fights, with him only asking a question now and then to keep me going.

"Finally, when he got up to leave, he said, 'I've enjoyed this. I'm sort of out of action these days. Would it be alright if I drop in again sometime when you're not busy.'

"So, a couple of weeks later he comes again and it happens that, again, I'm the only one in the office.

"'This is the second time,' he said, 'that I have sat around here talking fights with you without introducing myself. I'm Owney Madden.'

"Well, if he had said he was King Tut I couldn't have been more astonished. My mouth opened up so wide I almost swallowed my cigarette. I'd read a lot about Owney Madden in the papers and the picture I had formed of him wasn't anything like this almost shy fellow that just seemed to want to fan about boxing."

In his article, Corum went on to describe how Owney told the elderly promoter that, if he could ever be of any service to him, not to hesitate to ask. A short time later, Owney took a suite of offices in the Putnam building. A few floors below, McCarney—known in boxing circles as "the Professor"—was paid an unexpected visit by an unsavory mobster named Linky Mitchell. Corum's article continued:

"Mitchell walked in and demanded, 'Where's the Monkey?'

"'We don't have any monkeys here,' the Professor told him. 'Who is it you wish to see?'

"'I want to see that monkey Jacobs. I've just taken over ten percent of his fighters and I'd better see him quick if he knows what's good for him.'

"'That's funny. I'm his partner and he didn't tell me.'

"'He don't have to tell you, I'm telling you,' sneered Mitchell, and he patted himself lightly under his armpit. That was where McCarney phoned Madden. Three minutes later, Owney was at the door.

"'Get out of here,' ordered Owney Madden.

"'Yes sir, yes sir,' Mitchell mumbled and started sidling toward the door.

"Madden still filled most of the doorway, and the man made himself so thin he scratched his back against the jamb as he eased out and went away from there.

"'He won't bother you again,' Owney promised the Prof as the Link sneaked off down the hall. Nor did he.

"Linky Mitchell was a supposedly tough member and trigger-happy hood of a West Side New York gang that had once been called the Dusters."

The slaying of Luigi Mollinucci took place in September of 1911 just three months after Owney's marriage. Devoting his energies to diversifying the Gophers' interests meant spending less time at home, and there are indications he and Dorothy were beginning to lead separate lives. Six months later, Owney was having an affair with someone else—some say Freda Hopper—and taking advantage of the separation. His relationships were rarely casual and, in return, he expected a certain loyalty with his lovers. Throughout his life, until his second marriage, Owney's girls were treated royally by the underworld and given a wide berth by those who knew how protective he could be toward them.

George Raft and Owney ran into each other regularly and had slightly different views on women. Georgie, with slick hair and polished shoes, had become a small-time dance celebrity around town. He had a fast way of talking and an amusing line of flattery which won hearts wherever there happened to be a dance contest. The handsome young man with the flashing feet and Valentino looks had no interest in pursuing steady relationships. The tango, waltz, and jazz dancing provided an endless supply of willing partners. By night, he was a dancehall sensation. A friend recalled a typical Raft routine to biographer Lewis Yablonsky:

"The hall was dark. Suddenly, there's a spotlight on George. He had a jaunty look. Jet black hair, wearing a black suit with flare trousers. Over one eye is a sharp derby. He got a tremendous ovation even before he began the dance because he looked so perfect."

In the afternoons, he worked tea dances for two dollars plus tips. Often, the female clientele were interested in paying for private sessions of a more intimate nature.

Owney would listen to tales of his conquests and laugh until it seemed he would never stop. Throughout their lives, they were to meet up and yarn away the hours together. George's escapades always amused him, and the young gigolo enjoyed relaxing with his childhood hero. On Gopher ground he knew he was safe, but Raft encountered girl trouble in other gang areas where they were as keen as Owney to protect their women.

His dancehall companion of the time told Yablonsky about a memorable trip to Yonkers with ten friends:

"George was just unbelievable with women. This one attached herself to George—a beautiful girl. Then three tough guys came up to me. One said: 'Your friend's dancing with my girl.' Next, he pulled a knife and said: 'I'm going to get him. Not now. In a little while.' Then they walked away. I told George and he said, '—— him.' He was just carried away dancing with this girl. Finally, the last thing I remember is the whole crowd of us running down the street trying to catch the streetcar for New York City. The guy with the knife and his gang were after us. We just barely made it onto the rear of the streetcar. It scared the hell out of us and I felt certain that George, and all of us, had just escaped with our lives."

Owney was occasionally known to warn off the opposition in a similar fashion. According to Jay Robert Nash, author of *Bootleggers and Badmen*, "Madden was girl happy. Any girl he knew was his girl. Any man who made a pass at his girl was beaten senseless."

In February of 1912, when he was leading the Gophers and ruled a vast tract of New York, only a fool, or someone far removed from the world of crime, would have made advances to a girl he was known to show affection for. The reckless—or naive—man in question was a clerk named William Henshaw. By all accounts, Owney had warned him off with his usual quiet understatement though one version says they argued. Henshaw, either through stubbornness or misunderstanding, did not take the advice of the Duke of the West Side.

Owney watched him drop the girl off at her home in uptown Manhattan after a date and waited until Henshaw boarded a trolley car. As the trolley passed the corner of 16th Street and 9th Avenue, he swung aboard, leveled his Smith and Wesson coolly at the clerk and shot him in front of a dozen passengers. Before alighting, Owney paused on the rear step and tolled the trolley car's brass bell in a sinister death knell. A moment later, he vanished into the night, leaving the passengers in turmoil. Those who rushed to help Henshaw detected faint signs of life, and he was quickly taken to a New York hospital. Before he died, he managed to tell detectives the identity of his killer.

After the shooting, the Duke went underground, lying low in various Gopher apartments until he was sighted ten days later as he emerged from the doorway of a Hell's Kitchen tenement. Three detectives who had been watching the neighborhood gave pursuit when he disappeared back into the building. Owney made for the fire escape, and a long, desperate chase ensued over the rooftops of 10th Avenue. This was familiar territory to Owney, who kept his pigeon lofts here, but he still couldn't shake the cops. He was finally cornered when reinforcements were brought in to surround the area and arrested. The police, for the second time, were convinced they had a watertight homicide charge against him and he was on his way to the electric chair. However, by the time Owney appeared in court two days later, relaxed and untroubled, they discovered that key witnesses from the trolley car had decided to leave town, and the case was dismissed.

Oddly, despite the killings, Madden never quite achieved a murderous reputation among those who knew him. "Old playmates of his say he wasn't so homicidal as the authorities made him out to be," Richard O'Connor concluded.

From 1911 to 1914, Owney built the Gophers into the most powerful criminal organization on the West Side. After the railroad raid, his first priority was to establish an unassailable headquarters and to spread the gang's interests beyond merely robbing freight cars. A building was found soon after the Henshaw killing. The grand plan took a little longer and included forging links with influential Democrats. This eventually led to Owney's close, lifelong association with men of political power.

Owney's two close escapes from prison encouraged him to keep a low profile and devote more time to diversifying the Gophers' activities. Three experienced killers—Eddie Egan, Bill Tammany, and Chick Hyland—carried out his orders, overseeing rackets which terrorized new areas of the community and provided Owney with a personal income of $200 a day. The Madden family, in a way that none of them ever could have anticipated, were at last living the dream they believed America would provide for them. Mary Madden had a vague idea of her son's affairs but tended to turn a blind eye. As far as she was concerned, Owney was loving, loyal, and looked after the family as his father Francis always hoped he would.

Owney joined forces with his new ally, Tanner Smith of the Marginals, to invest in a secure new headquarters. After touring the neighborhood, they settled on a suite of rooms two floors above a blacksmith's shop and turned it into a bar and bistro called the Winona Club. Owney kept a small apartment there and the inevitable pigeon loft on the roof.

Looking after his collection of prize birds was becoming so time-consuming that he paid one of the Gophers $75 a week to feed them and clean out the loft. "Owney liked pigeons almost as well as blondes," one journalist recalled. "In his spare time, he would putter about the nests or do a bit of flying with them. All the hoodlums in Hell's Kitchen knew Owney's pigeons and they were immune from bullets. You could kill a

Hudson Duster, but lay off Owney's pigeons. Owney didn't even have the heart to eat squab under glass."

Owney's well-protected pigeons were, however, not beyond causing trouble themselves. "He spent much money on them," one observer noted, "Nun's Caps, Hollanders, Budapest Tiplitzes, and other breeds. These birds used to fly round New York, enticing birds from other coops to come home with them, and many fights ensued."

Perhaps only one other man wielded as much power as Owney did on the West Side. His name was Jimmy Hines, a chisel-featured blacksmith turned city alderman. The two met as their respective careers were blossoming. Owney instinctively saw, like generations of later gangsters in all great cities in America, that a powerful, tightly run political machine that controlled the police and judiciary could be of enormous advantage. In New York, it happened to be the Democrats, and their fastest-rising star was Jimmy Hines. Party politics in such matters were secondary to personalities and power.

Hines, at times ambitious to the point of desperation, was a vastly different character than Owney but their backgrounds and outlook were largely similar. "Hines was a man who commanded loyalty from others by giving loyalty," wrote Craig Thompson and Allen Raymond in *Gang Rule in New York*. He never deserted a pal and he never, if he could help it, refused to grant a favor. He believed, as those who worked for him and supported him believed, that in his lifetime he did "a lot of good." According to Thompson and Raymond:

"Whether it went for good things or bad, the undeniable fact is that, of the enormous financial return that came into his hands through crime, relatively little of it stayed with him. Certainly a large percentage of this blood-stained money was scattered by him in service of the poor. He gave it lavishly to men and women who said they needed food, or coal, or rent, or hundreds of other things that required money they did not have. That was the system to which he adhered, in which he was raised, and he served it without apology or much deviation. That he left his people to be preyed upon by those who operated the rackets was a fact he never looked in the eye."

Electioneering in the roughneck days before the First World War was a bloody, street-corner business. Hines had vowed to wrestle the influential office of district leader from a tough Irish plasterer named Jimmy Ahearn, who was equally determined to hang onto it. The bitter campaign began in 1907 with Hines suffering two narrow defeats before a third, all-or-nothing attempt in 1912. The two candidates, accompanied by hired toughs, would stand on the backs of open wagons and harangue each other from opposite sides of the street. Ahearn was the more accomplished orator and made capital of his rival's lumbering way with words. Hines hated to lose anything and had a quick temper which was easily aroused. On one occasion, in the 1907 round, Ahearn shouted a jibe from his platform, leaving Hines speechless at his own inability to come up with an appropriate reply. He stormed across the street and landed Ahearn a right hook which knocked him from the wagon.

Listening intently to these heated exchanges from a street corner was a small, bright young law student called Joe Shalleck. He had already formed a college Democratic club at Columbia University to back the reelection of New York's Democratic mayor Bill Gaynor and had been studying Hines's campaign from the sidelines with interest. As Jimmy climbed down from the back of his wagon, Joe shook his hand and said:

"Mr. Hines, I listened to you. You have some very good ideas. But you are unquestionably the lousiest speaker I ever heard."

For a second, Jimmy looked as if he might floor him, then asked: "What's your name?"

Joe explained who he was and about the support he had given Bill Gaynor. He appeared confident and was highly articulate.

"All right," said Hines, finally. "From now on, you're going to be my speechmaker."

Joe's skill, which later made him one of the most successful criminal lawyers in New York, began to have a marked effect on Hines's popularity.

When Shalleck graduated from law school, one of his most celebrated clients was the other silent partner in Hines's team, Owney Madden.

In his first two attempts for district leadership, Hines had the advantage of a powerful speech writer, but his Gopher muscle yet lacked the benefit of Owney's leadership. They were unruly and unpredictable and failed to appreciate the importance of organization and time in the run-up to the polls. The flow of voters had to be carefully monitored at each polling station and a constant record kept of Democrats' fortunes. If the pendulum began to swing the wrong way, steps had to be taken immediately to rectify it, either by keeping the wrong voters out, persuading them to change their minds, or bringing more of the right voters in. In emergencies, votes were cast on behalf of the dead or someone who had not turned up to register. If the hapless voter did not materialize, they would hotly accuse him of trying to vote twice, usually with the admonition: "What do you think this is, Bud, a personality contest? Get the hell outta here!"

On the credit side, the Gophers were good with their fists and, in the stormy first round of the contest with Ahearn, little else mattered. Each street-corner campaigner carefully picked his own protection squad. Ahearn's hired muscle was led by a stone-faced pugilist named Spike Sullivan whose hatred for the Gophers made a bloodbath inevitable. Several Gophers were beaten up in the scuffle which followed. Hines knocked Ahearn from the wagon, and immediate retaliation was considered essential.

"Degnan's saloon was on the same corner, and Spike Sullivan, apparently unaware of what had gone before, made the mistake of entering the bar room alone," gangland historians Thompson and Raymond recorded. "The Hines gang went in after him. In the carnage that followed, chairs, tables, beer mugs, and many another quick weapon flew wildly. The battle surged into the bar. The place was wrecked and so was Sullivan, who did not get out of the hospital in time to do any voting. Had he been able to get around, Hines would probably have lost by more than he did—Ahearn kept his control by forty-seven votes that year."

Hines lost the next election by twenty-seven votes, the narrow margin making him even more determined to succeed in 1912. By this time, Owney, as boss of the Gophers, had honed them into an efficient and highly effective election force. To cover his overheads, Hines mortgaged his blacksmith shop and borrowed the rest, raising $4,000 for what proved to be a profitable investment. With shrewd presence of mind and an awareness of the wealth political power could bring, he had already closed his bank account, leaving no evidence of the vast income which was to come his way in the years ahead.

Hines, with Owney's tactical advice, planned his 1912 campaign following the basic rule of West Side political warfare: "The more an opponent's hoodlum resources were crippled in advance of an election day, the less opportunity he then would have of winning at the polls."

With Shalleck's eloquent speech-writing and Owney's battle skills, Hines swept to victory by a margin of 1,500 votes. The memorable and exhausting campaign forged a relationship which operated to their mutual benefit throughout the 1920s and 1930s. When the celebrations were over, Joe acted as Jimmy's political manager while building up his law practice. Hines moved into the freight business and, with a fleet of trucks, obtained lucrative city contracts. Owney returned to expanding his rackets empire, knowing that he could now call on Hines's friendship at any time.

4.

Enemies

In the same year, another election—a hard-fought campaign for president of the United States—was to keep Owney Madden busy. William Howard (Big Bill) Taft was running for reelection, but a rival Republican faction known as the Progressives or Bull Moosers had funded a popular hero, ex-president Theodore Roosevelt. Democrat Woodrow Wilson, Governor of New Jersey, finally won the presidency with a united party behind him. Owney's services were heavily in demand at the polls but, despite his efforts, it became apparent soon after the voting opened that New Yorkers were less than enthusiastic about the Presbyterian, rather opinionated Wilson. "Persuading" West Side Democrats to the polls proved an unexpectedly demanding and, at times, impossible business.

When the hour arrived for the ballot boxes to be secured, Owney was not the happiest of men. To add to his troubles, Dorothy deeply resented seeing so little of him and demanded that he should abandon the last vital hours of voting and take her out instead. One way or another, all New York would be celebrating and she was anxious to be part of it.

When Owney told her it was out of the question, Dorothy angrily announced that she was going to an election party at the Arbor Dance Hall "with who the hell I like." It was calculated to make her neglectful husband furious, particularly since the Arbor lay well outside the Gophers' territory and was known to be a favorite haunt of the Hudson Dusters.

Owney hung around until the West Side count was under way, sinking deeper into gloom at the Democrats' local performance. He returned to the Winona Club where he had a drink and went to his apartment to change. The room, simply furnished with a bed and little furniture, contained nothing unusual to the casual visitor except perhaps for a punching bag suspended in the corner. Those who called regularly, such as the errand boy Legs Diamond, knew that the apartment housed a formidable arsenal. The punching bag, Diamond recalled, was used by Owney to work out with brass knuckles. In the closet, below an assortment of caps and hats, a concealed shelf opened up to reveal rows of neatly-stacked revolvers, scatter guns, ready-primed bombs, and burglary tools. Within easy reach on the mantelshelf above a cast-iron fireplace sat two expensive vases stuffed full of bullets and shotgun shells, respectively.

Owney eventually headed uptown to the Arbor Dance Hall. It had been a popular meeting place since the days when it was known as the Eldorado. Under new management, it had been refurbished and renamed and was reportedly doing better business than ever. On November 6th, 1912, there was an election party atmosphere all across town. To beat the licensing regulations, many night spots formed impromptu clubs or associations to qualify for an after-hours extension on serving drinks. The Arbor, on the corner of 52nd Street and 7th Avenue, had been awarded a late license on the grounds that the Dave Hyson Association was holding a commemorative dance. Hyson, in fact, was a waiter at the dance hall. Such late-night liquor dances were known as "rackets," a term which was rapidly gaining wider connotations.

Dorothy was already there when Owney arrived. "She said she would turkey-trot, bunny-hug, or grizzly-bear with anyone she pleased," one observer noted, "and she did just that."

Owney's entrance caused a ripple of consternation. He was rarely seen alone outside the safety of Gopher territory and was clearly not in the best of humor. Several couples were seen to stop dancing.

"Go on and have your fun," he waved to them, adding with a wry smile. "I won't bump anybody off here tonight."

Then, according to Herbert Asbury, he beckoned to Dave Hyson and graciously shook the trembling waiter's hand:

"Let them dance, Dave," Madden said. "I don't want to spoil the party."

He made his way up to the balcony that overlooked the dance floor and watched Dorothy—or, Loretta, as she was widely known—enjoying herself. "She was in her best clothes," the *New York Morning Sun* reported the next day, "and she danced everything that came along. She saw Owney and he saw her but they did not speak. She made a few side remarks and he grinned. She did not like the grin."

After he selected a balcony table, various small-time hoodlums called briefly to pay their respects and pass along comments about various girls on the dance floor below. Shortly before 2 a.m. they had drifted away, and an attractive girl walked over and sat down beside him. As she held his attention and prattled charmingly in obvious hero worship, Owney failed to notice that the occupants of all the adjoining tables had been quietly replaced by eleven members of the Hudson Dusters.

When they were all seated, the girl discreetly rose and made her way downstairs, leaving Owney alone to watch the dancers. He turned around in his seat to see who else was on the balcony and found himself surrounded on three sides by a frigid crescent of all too familiar faces. "He knew that they intended to kill him," Asbury noted, "and would shoot before he could even so much as make a movement toward his pocket." It was obvious he had little chance, but the "banty little rooster" rose to his feet with great courage and swept them all a glance.

"Come on, you guys," he taunted. "You couldn't shoot anybody. Who did you ever bump off?"

The tension was electric and, for a second, none of the Dusters spoke. Then one of them cursed Owney and suddenly all eleven drew their guns and fired at almost point-blank range at him. As the Duke of the West

Side crumpled to the floor beneath his table, they pocketed their weapons and unhurriedly made their way downstairs and out into the night. No one in the crowded dance hall made any attempt to intervene.

"A rush of bouncers and waiters found Owney lying doubled up on the floor," reported the *New York Morning Sun*, which managed to get the story on the streets in two hours. "There were men and women within five feet of him but no one was looking at him.

"'Who done it, Owney?'" asked a waiter, as a matter of form.

"'I done it myself,' came the answer.

"Loretta rushed back up the stairs with the strident outburst, "'Who done it, Owney?'

"'How do I know?' was the answer she got.'"

Minutes later, a flying wedge of police officers from West 47th Street Precinct forced a path through the packed dance floor onto the balcony. Patrolman Mitchell took one look at Owney's abdominal wounds and raced back to call for an ambulance. Two detectives, Fitzsimmons and Fitzpatrick, knelt beside him asking questions but the victim stuck by the tough code of the streets and refused to answer.

"Nothing doing," Owney told them, rapidly losing blood. "It's nobody's business but mine."

By the time the ambulance arrived, his condition had worsened and there was little sign of life. At one stage on the journey to Flower Hospital, the doctor accompanying him gave him only minutes to live and ordered the driver to detour to the morgue. Owney rallied a little and they made straight for the hospital. By the time they were wheeling him to the operating theater, he managed to exchange a few words with the surgeon. They were characteristically brief:

"Get busy with the knife, Doc," the Duke told him. "I can feel it got me bad."

The medical team removed six bullets from him and found five others too deeply embedded to be removed. The surgeon felt he had done all he could and stitched up the wounds, leaving the other bullets inside him.

Newspapers at first jumped to the conclusion that the gunmen were friends of William Henshaw, the trolley-car murder victim, but it soon became clear that the Dusters were involved.

Reporters began digging around for background information in their own distinctive style. "Owney 'got his' because he could not stand a bluff his wife put up, some of his friends say," ran one account. "Loretta told the police, among the few things she did tell, that she and Owney had been scrapping for about two weeks. He passed her downtown one day and gave her the 'frozen lamp,' as she explained, whereupon she gave him a call right there. Then she got sore and beat it out of the flat. Election night she sent him word that she was going to a dance at the Eldorado, as the Arbor was once called. The police believed that Mrs. Madden's message was to the effect that she was going to the dance and was going to dance with whomsoever she pleased, the Hudson Dusters and the Buck O'Briens by preference. Owney's prestige could not permit this."

After the operation, Owney regained consciousness and made remarkable progress. Indeed, his constitution appeared to astound the medical staff which, at one stage, had given him up for dead. Within days, he was sitting up and receiving visitors. Muted conversations took place between the Duke and his trusted lieutenants at the bedside. Within a week, six of the eleven Dusters who had made the attempt on his life were murdered. Hell's Kitchen now knew unmistakably that Owney was still in command despite his long convalescence.

One man, however, was reluctant to acknowledge the news. Patsy Doyle, a psychotic killer known for his crazed behavior in the early Gopher days, had reappeared from nowhere in the old haunts.

Doyle, a husky guy with a gold tooth, hung around the fringes of the gang, spreading rumors that Owney's injuries had left him permanently crippled. Madden was finished, Doyle told them, and it soon became clear that he was bidding for leadership. There were even rumors, perhaps not beyond the bounds of possibility, that he had been involved in the Arbor incident. Doyle's trouble-making was not unconnected with his girlfriend, Owney's old flame, Freda Horner. Upset by the Arbor shooting, she had walked out on Doyle, telling him that she had to be with Owney to help speed up his recovery. "Doyle's ego was bent all out of shape when she announced that she preferred Madden," one account ran. During weeks of giving out incorrect information, Doyle had even succeeded in gathering around him a small group of disconnected and impressionable gang members from the lower ranks.

Reports on his activities filtered back to the hospital and within days of Owney's discharge Doyle was discovered unconscious, almost dead, in an alley. A length of lead pipe rolled in newspaper was found nearby. Three weeks and a day after the Arbor shooting, Owney was back on the streets and everyone was aware of his presence.

To men of greater wisdom, that would probably have been the end of it. Doyle, however, became consumed with jealous fury and retaliated by blackjacking several of Owney's closest friends. There was no doubt, in gangland terms, that he was becoming a nuisance. When Tony Romanello, one of the Duke's most faithful deputies, taunted Doyle about Freda Horner, he lost control. A short time later, Romanello was found clubbed, stabbed, and shot.

It is interesting to note that, by this time, Owney had broken with the recognized tradition and opened up the Gophers to non-Irish members. Romanello, like several of his associates, was Italian. Madden never displayed much regard for national or racial differences though there were a handful of Irish families in New York and Chicago who received protection from him all his life. Later, he became one of the few non-Italians with whom the Mafia shared its innermost secrets, to the point of seeking his advice on sensitive questions of appointments and succession. Frank Costello and Jewish mobster Meyer Lansky were to become his closest working partners. Even when he was in exile in Arkansas, in the heartland of racial segregation, Madden spent many leisure hours in socializing with African Americans.

"The Doyle-Madden feud sputtered away for months and the whole West Side waited for the blow-off," Richard O'Connor wrote. "Most of the betting was on Madden. But he refused to be hurried; like most gangsters, he had a vast fund of patience when it came to paying off an old score."

Owney was once again back at his Winona Club headquarters which, at the time, was causing what might be called "environmental problems" in Hell's Kitchen. Local residents grumbled about all the singing, shouting, and loud music emanating like a St. Patrick's Day Parade from the second-floor windows. The Gophers were an unruly bunch and, to the annoyance of blacksmith Dennis Keating on the ground floor, appeared unaware that people slept at night. Keating was also angry because he had no idea that a bar was operating in his building.

Local patrolmen were reluctant to intervene. Many knew from experience that the Gophers were prepared to repel all unwelcome visitors with a hail of bottles and chairs. There was also growing anxiety among officers about the strong friendship Owney had forged at Tammany Hall, the New York Democratic Party headquarters on 14th Street. Jimmy Hines and friends, as the precinct knew, had authority to approve the transfer of officers to any part of the city they wished.

Keating reportedly was a huge fellow and felt capable of handling the disturbance by himself. One day, he stormed up the stairs to complain about the noise.

Fred D. Pasley once floridly described a typical Winona scene: "A skinny, hatchet-faced runt was thumping away at a battered upright piano, which stood in a rear corner of a room thirty feet wide and sixty feet long. The instrument was sadly out of tune, but the melody issuing from it was unmistakable. The maestro was rendering 'In the Good Old Summer Time.'

"Occasionally, he paused to sip from an eight-ounce glass of beer reposing on the square of mahogany at the right end of the keys. The glass was half empty, but the collar of frothy foam lingered on, leaving bands of white about the glass as the contents diminished.

"A cigarette dropped from the left corner of the man's mouth. It was of white rice-paper, enclosing a quantum of Duke's Mixture. The maestro rolled his own.

"Now the jangling tune ceased whilst he enjoyed another draught of lager. Its effect was magical. The ballad of tender hearts and loving hands gave way to a rollicking rag, to be followed by a scintillate foxtrot.

"The shuffling rhythm of dozens of dancing feet shifted in two-four time on the rough oak floor, and the young fellows tossed their willing girls about with a new abandon. Voices rose above the twanging din of the piano to mingle in the thick haze of tobacco smoke that floated about the room. The voices came from men standing at the bar running the length of the room—wicked-looking, cold-eyed men....They were discussing the business of safe-blowing, burglary, hold-ups. They paid no attention to the dancers."

Perhaps the blacksmith encountered a similar scene when, according to an eyewitness, he threw open the door and ordered: "Keep it down, or I'll throw the lot of you out of my house."

Owney, who was having a drink at a table with Tanner Smith, is reported to have said quietly: "You'll throw *me* out of your house? Mister, did you ever hear of Owney Madden?"

Keating appeared suddenly unsure of himself.

"Well, mister," said the Englishman without a trace of bravado, "I am Owney Madden."

The blacksmith left the room without a word and was afraid to report the incident. Among the Gophers' rackets, he was presumably aware, was the practice of bombing shops when the owners refused to pay protection money. They had also diversified into beating up strikers on picket lines at the request of employers—a "service" started some years earlier by an unpolished thug known as Dopey Benny Fein and developed by the Hell's Kitchen gang into a lucrative source of income.

A few days later, however, as the Gophers' seemingly endless party continued, someone else complained and Patrolman Sindt was dispatched to investigate the disturbance. It took him only a short time to send for some reinforcements.

The Gophers, suspecting he might be back, posted watches on the street to give themselves time to prepare for a showdown. About an hour later, one of the gang, watching from the Winona window, picked up hand signals from a lookout on the corner of the block. Within minutes, the familiar figure of Sergeant O'Connell, a rock-hard officer of the old school, swung boldly into view leading a detachment of officers.

Owney had ordered all the furniture in the club to be piled high against the door and was prepared to dig in for a siege. There was probably enough drink and food to last for days. The squad clattered up the narrow staircase and tried unsuccessfully to shoulder the door. Sergeant O'Connell moved forward and banged on it with his nightstick. In a voice which had the reputation of sending Hell's Kitchen residents scurrying for cover, he ordered the Gophers to open the door or have it broken down.

As he leaned toward the door to listen for a reply, there was a loud revolver report. The bullet tore a hole in the door, grazed the side of the sergeant's skull, and spun him around. If one of his men had not had the presence of mind to grab him, he probably would have rolled right down the stairs.

Then, the distinctive voice of Owney Madden called from the other side of the door: "That's just a taste. We shoot the gizzard out of any cop who tries to come in here."

The squad hastily retreated from the scene and regrouped around the corner. O'Connell issued instructions to two experienced officers to circle the building and try to find a way in from the rear fire escape. To give them time, he marched his men across the road in full view of the second-floor window of the club and began calling up to the Gophers.

Owney and Tanner threw open one of the windows and began shouting abuse at him. The Gophers, obviously enjoying every minute, opened adjoining windows and leaned out to jeer.

O'Connell, who was something of a character, played for time by shouting back at them. The exchange was enough to lure all the Gophers to the street side of the club, leaving a back window onto the fire escape unguarded. The first the gang knew of this pincer movement was when one of them was clubbed to the floor with a nightstick. The two officers laid into the rest of the gang, relying on speed and surprise. O'Connell, taking his cue from the ensuing commotion, led his men up the stairs and smashed the door from its hinges. In fifteen minutes, the last of the Gophers lay trussed and bleeding, ready to be taken to the precinct house. Even as they lined up one by one to be booked, the wheels of the political machine were already turning.

The next morning, as the Gophers shuffled handcuffed into court, Owney was cleaned up and immaculate. The judge, after brusquely disposing of the other gang members, listened to a short, mitigating statement from his lawyer. It was the moving story of a misunderstood minor whose father had died at an early age. The judge listened understandingly and addressed Owney like a father lecturing a son who had taken the family car without permission. He was a smart young man, the judge said, with a promising future. Unfortunately, along the way, he had fallen into bad company. With a rap of his gavel, the Duke was dismissed with a $500 bond to keep the peace for six months. As one commentator put it: "Hines owed him and Owney called in the debt."

The long arm of politics did not stop there. Owney's stature and value to the Tammany machine had to be underlined to deter further displays of enthusiasm from the Hell's Kitchen precinct. Tanner Smith, who was dealt with by the judge in a similar fashion, left the court building and went straight to City Hall where an appointment had been made for him with the mayor. During a long, private discussion, Tanner opened his shirt to show Bill Gaynor the injuries he had sustained while sitting in a quiet card game with friends. He then returned to the Winona Club.

Hell's Kitchen held few secrets and it did not take long for word to filter back to the jubilant Gophers that the entire police squad involved in the siege had been disciplined for using excessive force. Sometime later, as a direct result of the incident, Mayor Gaynor issued Order No. 7. The ruling "prohibited a patrolman from using his club unless he was prepared to prove that it was in defense of his life" and left nothing to the discretion of an inspector or captain if a citizen, honest or otherwise, complained that he had been clubbed.

Two years later this order was rescinded by another mayor, John Purroy, but the gangs had welcomed the cover of Order No. 7 to build up their empires. Old grievances, however, died hard. Within days after the order was reversed, Tanner Smith was under arrest for carrying a revolver. Early in 1915, he began a year's sentence. On his release, he found that the police once more had the upper hand. Tanner decided it was time to retire and set up a waterfront business employing stevedores. Even though he now had a respectable job, the old life exerted a steady pull on him. Cargo handling seemed no way to earn a living and in 1919 he opened the Marginal Club above an 8th Avenue saloon, seeking to recreate the atmosphere he had so dearly missed. Apparently, he recreated it too well! Just a few months after opening night, Tanner was shot in the back as he sat at his favorite table. The estate he left was worth $100,000.

The Winona case proved Jimmy Hines to be a man of his word, and he rapidly gained a reputation for fixing court cases for friends and constituents. As the years passed, the stream of supplicants at his home grew longer. Hines would put each morning aside to deal with them. After he was shaved in bed by his personal barber, the door would open promptly at 8:30 a.m. A long queue often reached through the house into the bedroom where Jimmy received his callers in a silk dressing gown. At his side by the bed were a note pad and pen, a fat roll of dollar bills, and two telephones with unlisted numbers. On occasion, more than fifty favor-seekers might be found waiting on the stairs to see him.

No one, it seemed, was outside his sphere of influence. One retired New York City judge recalled a case tried by a panel of three judges. The presiding judge, who was sitting between the other two, was Jimmy's man. The two flanking him were not, but there was a glimmer of hope. Following an old personal disagreement, they were widely known not to be on speaking terms with one another. A two-to-one majority was required to secure the defendant's release. For a while, things looked bleak as both secondary judges were renowned for their punitive approach to criminal work.

After hearing the submissions, the presiding judge turned to the colleague on his left and asked in a low voice:

"Guilty or not guilty?"

"Guilty," he murmured.

Then, turning to the other judge, he whispered the same question.

"Guilty," his colleague said quietly.

At this point, a clear way out of the dilemma became apparent.

"The verdict of the court," the presiding judge intoned, "is not guilty."

And neither of his colleagues considered any reason to question it.

The police and district attorney's office, hoping to see Owney safely behind bars after the Winona incident, were cheated of the pleasure once again. For his part, the Duke had too many other problems to think of celebrating. His gunshot wounds were almost constantly giving him trouble, and he had already made several hospital visits to have them treated. Friends noticed that his usual, easy-going expression was now often furrowed by a frown. Little Patsy Doyle was still stirring up trouble around the neighborhood and going to the unthinkable—by gang standards—extreme of reporting Owney's activities to the police. Officers noted his tips gratefully but still felt reluctant to move against Madden again until they felt absolutely sure of their evidence. Word began to spread among the Gophers and local residents that Doyle was a stool-pigeon or informer and should be avoided. The handful of gang members he had wooed away from Owney began to drift back in two's and three's. Still, he increased his insane determination to avenge himself for losing Freda.

Suddenly, on October 23, 1914, Owney was arrested and charged with burglary. Many had little doubt that Doyle was somehow behind it.

The case papers, still on file with the New York District Attorney's records of 1914, state that he was accused of pigeon rustling—an unlikely offense when one considers that the dedicated pigeon fanciers of Hell's Kitchen knew their own birds and everyone else's almost blindfolded.

His alleged accomplice was Emil Klatt, a twenty-four-year-old German longshoreman who obligingly jumped bail before the case came to court. Owney, who gave his occupation on the charge sheet as a driver, pleaded not guilty and requested the magistrate to note that he demanded a full inquiry into the circumstances leading to his arrest.

A poultry dealer named Joe Schweitzer had locked his two-story shop on Hewitt Avenue and gone home for the evening. At nine the next morning he found the lock broken and two hundred pigeons, valued at $1,000, missing. Suspecting that he knew who was responsible, Schweitzer went to Klatt's apartment on West 30th Street and found seventy-five pigeons kept in a loft on the roof. Twenty-three of them were part of the stolen birds.

Detective Joe Daly immediately called on Owney, the most celebrated pigeon fancier in the neighborhood. Klatt had merely said that he had acquired the birds from an unknown man on 8th Avenue but Daly appeared convinced that only Madden could have been responsible. The visit seemed to come as little surprise to the Duke. "Defendant Madden stated that he knew he could be arrested for the burglary," the court files note. "He also stated that he would try to recover the stolen pigeons for the deponent. He knew where seventeen of the stolen pigeons were at the said time." There is every probability that, with customary honesty, Owney was telling the truth. He answered to a bail of $1,000, convinced the magistrate of his innocence, and was acquitted. Klatt was last heard of working under the assumed name of Ellendt.

There was a growing feeling that something had to be done about Doyle. A month later, on November 28th, a Saturday night when the first snow of winter began to lightly cover New York, steps were taken to silence him permanently. Doyle had been arrested for the vicious assault on Tony Romanello, but "Tee," as he was known among the Gophers, refused to help detectives or to press charges. Little Patsy was released, smiling, from custody but remained unaware that his days were now limited. The violent events which followed were thought to be in revenge for his attack on the Italian.

The last hours of Patsy Doyle are still clouded by half-truth and subterfuge but the most likely account is that, late one evening, he received a phone call from Margaret Everdeane, Freda Horner's close friend. Freda, she told Doyle, wanted to make up to him for walking out and reviving her affair with Owney.

"The poor kid's all busted up over the way she treated you, Patsy," Margaret said. "She wants to see you, Patsy. I'll have her with me and Willie and you can talk to her."

Willie "the Sailor" Mott, Margaret's boyfriend, was a gunner on the battleship *Florida* and was so smitten with her that, at sea, he used to write endearing letters beginning, "Dear Wifey."

Margaret and Willie the Sailor waited for Doyle in the back of a saloon, Nash's Café, on the corner of 41st Street and 8th Avenue. Patsy is said to have had a phone call tipping him off that, if he went there, he was to be killed. His obsession with Freda, however, and the chance of winning her back swept all considerations of safety from his mind. He slipped a gun into his overcoat pocket and set out full of anticipation to meet his former lover.

When he walked through the double doors of the saloon, a site that later became the New York City bus terminal, the place was empty except for the bartender cleaning glasses and, at a far table, Margaret and Willie. Doyle evidently did not pause to consider that, for a Saturday night, business was unusually quiet.

"Where's Freda?" he asked.

"She's gone out a minute," Margaret told him. "She'll be right back. Sit down, Patsy."

As he was about to pull out a chair, the bartender called over: "Hey, Patsy. There's someone here wants to have words with you."

"Who?" asked Doyle, starting to turn toward the bar.

"Me," said a voice close behind him as Doyle came face to face with two armed men. One of them jabbed a revolver in his chest and fired. An explosion of shots followed. Patsy tottered backward and collapsed to the floor. Gasping for breath, he levered himself to his feet and tried to pull the gun from his overcoat pocket. The butt emerged but he lacked the strength to remove it completely. Bleeding from the chest, he staggered the length of the bar and out through the swinging doors into the snow-covered street. Patrolman Henry Star from the 22nd Precinct heard the shots and found his body lying nearby on a tenement doorstep. The officer counted six bullet holes in his clothing.

Johnny "Hoppo" McArdle and Art Bieler, the Gophers' top hitmen, were arrested for the shooting. Two days later, Owney was picked up by detectives and also charged with murder. It took the district attorney almost six months to prepare a case against him and bring it to trial. While Owney waited in the Tombs, New York's oldest and dampest prison, McArdle was sentenced to thirteen years and Bieler to eighteen.

The prison, situated between Mulberry and Lafayette where Foley Square now stands, was originally built on a swamp. Its official name was the Hall of Justice but the name Tombs somehow stuck. The original design had been sketched from an Egyptian mausoleum by John L. Stevens, a traveler from Hoboken, New Jersey. Conditions in the prison were notoriously bad, but Owney, through the intervention of Jimmy Hines, was given a comfortable cell and had his meals delivered from a nearby restaurant. "He was given a double cell all to himself and a room service that would have been the envy of any Fifth Avenue hotel," Richard O'Connor recalled.

Dick Butler, a Hell's Kitchen desperado, was also in the Tombs at the same time, on trial for arranging the escape of millionaire Harry K. Thaw from Matteawan Asylum where he had been incarcerated for murder. On the night before Butler was acquitted, Owney invited the anxious longshoreman to have supper in his cell. The meal was followed by a whisky nightcap. Breakfast the following morning was comprised of orange juice, boiled eggs, toast, and coffee. "Owney sure was boss of the place," Butler told friends later.

When Madden came up for trial in May, the week-long hearing was far from comfortable. He knew he could depend on the testimony of Bieler and McArdle, who were called as witnesses. Freda, Margaret, and Willie the Sailor, however, completely changed their stories and accused him of complicity. Walter Deuel of the district attorney's office made it clear from his opening speech that the authorities were out for blood. The story of Doyle's attempt to take over the Gophers provided the main thrust of the case.

At the earlier Bieler-McArdle trial, Freda and Margaret had gone to great lengths to protect Owney, swearing under oath that he knew nothing of the slaying. Now, strangely, they changed their stories and seemed bent on convicting him.

"I used to go around with Patsy Doyle until three days before he was shot," Freda told the jury, apparently forgetting her long affair with Owney. "At that time, I met Madden at a racket in Tammany Hall. I was with Madden for two nights after that. On the night that Doyle was killed, I was in a 10th Avenue lunchroom with the Madden crowd. I told them Doyle had said that they were a bunch of bums. Arthur Bieler got me to get Doyle on the telephone. I did so and Bieler talked with him."

Freda followed this up with the damaging claim that Owney was standing outside the saloon at the time of the killing, watching it all happen.

Then, Margaret Everdeane gave her version of the incident. Madden, she said, had persuaded her to meet Doyle in the saloon. "I told him, 'No, I don't want to make any trouble,'" she testified, but eventually she went anyway. Margaret added that she and Willie the Sailor walked out of the saloon before the shots started, leaving Doyle, who was on the phone with Freda. As they were leaving, they passed Bieler and McArdle, who were entering.

Margaret told the court that, back at the lunchroom, she had been crying and Owney asked her what was the matter:

"'You not only did a lot of shooting—you killed him,' I told him.

"'What are you going to do?' he asked me.

"'Anything you want me to,' I answered.

"'Stop crying, then,' he said. 'If you don't, people will get wise.'"

Margaret later went to a dance with the Gophers at the Moose Inn, a Democrat Club where Owney was on the committee. There, they ran into a character named Arthur Stein, whom everyone knew as "the King." Margaret continued:

"Madden told him: 'We dropped a guy at 41st Street. Take these girls and keep them under cover.'

"We went to King's apartment in West 30th Street. Madden asked me if I saw him on the corner when Patsy was killed. I told him I didn't, and he said: 'Do you remember bumping into someone when you left? That was me.'"

The next day, according to Margaret, Bieler walked into the King's apartment and said: "We got Patsy all right—we got him right through the heart."

Both Hoppo McArdle and Art Bieler were brought from Sing Sing prison where they were serving their sentences to testify on Owney's behalf. Their stories varied little from the original evidence they had given at their own trial. Bieler, jauntily sporting a lapel button which said, "Sing Sing," tried to clear both Madden and McArdle. He said he had killed Doyle in self-defense when two shots were fired at him. He explained away the two different types of bullets found in Doyle's body by saying that he carried two revolvers. As for Madden, he claimed, they were not even on speaking terms at the time because of an argument over some pigeons.

Freda Horner, he said, had told him that Doyle had been abusing her so he had asked McArdle to take him to the saloon and point Doyle out. McArdle had identified him and then left before the shooting.

The jury further had to grapple with problems presented by Owney's alibis. Witnesses testified that he was nowhere near the saloon on the night of the shooting and was at the hospital having his stomach wounds treated. Later, he went to a barber shop two doors from the lunchroom where he got his hair cut and stayed for an hour and twenty minutes.

Someone, somewhere was clearly being less than honest and Madden's lawyer, Charles Colligan, suspected the hand of the district attorney's office. There was nothing he could prove, but he sensed that something may have happened at Waverly House, a welfare home for girls, where Freda and Margaret had been staying for the duration of the trial. A frequent visitor there had been Walter Deuel, the assistant district attorney. Several other visits, seemingly unnecessary, had also been made by a probation office investigator named Mrs. Marion Goldman. Colligan was also unhappy about Freda, Margaret, and Willie the Sailor being taken out on a pleasure trip to North Beach by Detective Patrick Flood of Homicide.

The atmosphere of the Court of General Sessions was becoming increasingly tense. "Friends of Madden were standing in the corridors of the building," the *New York Times* reported. "They were barred from the courtroom by a squad of reserves from the Elizabeth Street Station. During the day, for the first time since he took office, District Attorney Perkins went about the courts accompanied by a uniformed policeman."

Owney took the stand and handled his three-hour cross-examination calmly. He did, however, appear to become increasingly exasperated as the assistant district attorney tried to trip him up with questions based on Freda Horner's and Margaret Everdeane's testimony. The prosecutor, perhaps sensing his discomfort, began to refer at length to the evidence provided by the women. Owney rose from his chair to complain, but two court officers pushed him down again. Having taken more than he felt he could stand, he lost his temper and shouted at the judge: "For what I'm getting here, I might as well plead guilty. I'm not getting a fair chance. Give me a show. I'm innocent. You might as well take me out and kill me, and have it over with. I won't testify anymore."

Owney was led away in handcuffs to cool down in the Tombs for the rest of the morning. By the time he returned after lunch, the jury had retired. After seven hours of deliberation, the jury returned with a verdict of guilty on the lesser charge of first-degree manslaughter rather than murder. Owney looked relieved and asked the judge if he would pass sentence immediately.

Word of Owney's courtroom outburst had spread throughout Hell's Kitchen and the Gophers, along with local residents, had turned out in force to follow the rest of the proceedings. "The fear that gangsters could gather in the courtroom in large numbers led Deputy Police Commissioner Lord to put on duty a heavy guard of detectives, which he headed himself," the New York Times reported. "In addition, there were a dozen uniformed men in the corridors."

Judge Charles Nott asked if the defendant had anything to say before sentence was passed. Colligan immediately got to his feet and asked for a retrial. "Motion denied," Judge Nott said firmly.

Colligan felt unable to let it go. "I had not expected to say a word, your Honor," he replied, "but I think I ought to say this. The peculiar thing about this case is that there was no evidence against Madden, absolutely no evidence, until after the trial of McArdle.

"It is a most significant thing that the sailor testified as he did. He never said anything at all, so far as we can find out, with reference to Madden being on the corner at the time Doyle was killed. There isn't the slightest doubt in my mind that the man was coached by someone, and I say that with due deliberation. There is not the slightest doubt in my mind that someone else coached the girl Freda and also the girl Maggie.

"There is not any doubt that Madden knew that Doyle was killed. But there is the gravest doubt, from all the investigation that I have been able to make, from every standpoint, that he instigated it.

"What I say, of course, is not evidence. I know how the community feels as to alleged gangsters. I know the influence that the newspapers have on juries. I know what the atmosphere of a case of this kind is—lived through it for days during this trial. But I say now that I believe, just as surely as I am standing here, that Madden did not know that Bieler was going to kill Doyle.

"Nevertheless, the jury has found him guilty, and I ask you to be as generous as possible under the circumstances. I feel that, no matter what he has done in the past, what his record has been, or what his life has been—I feel that he knew of that murder only after it had been committed. I am making a very strong statement to you, sir, absolutely from the bottom of my heart that this man is innocent. That is all I can say."

It was an extraordinarily impassioned outburst but despite Colligan's apparent sincerity Judge Nott was unmoved. He had a reputation for toughness and was well aware of Owney's influence on the West Side.

"It seems to me," the judge said, "from the relation that this defendant got to this other young man that did the shooting—the close relations these men bore, associating together every day—and the fact that undoubtedly there had been some ill feeling on their part toward the deceased, that it was well nigh impossible that this defendant should have been ignorant in advance of what was to happen.

"This section of the city has been more or less terrorized by these sort of acts. I hope in pronouncing sentence it will be a warning to other men of like character in that vicinity to desist from this course of action. It will be a warning to them that, if they come before the courts charged with homicide and are found guilty, they will be punished.

"The sentence of the court is that he be committed in the State prison for not less than ten, not more than twenty, years."

No sooner had Owney been led downstairs and the crowds drifted home than a defense fund was launched from door to door in Hell's Kitchen to pay for an appeal. Some gave freely and those who did not finally dug in their pockets when the Gophers shook the tin a little harder.

A few months later, hopes were raised when Freda Horner, Margaret Everdeane, and Willie the Sailor had a change of heart about the part they had played in Owney's trial. The girls swore statements that both Walter Deuel and Marion Goldman had pressured them into changing their original story. Over a series of visits to Waverly House, they were said to have written out a "script" on yellow notepaper and coached the girls on their respective lines. Freda, Margaret, and Willie also made statements alleging that, on the trip out to North Beach, Detective Patrick Flood had told them what to say in court and how to make it all sound plausible.

Deuel, Goldman, and Flood naturally all swore depositions denying any conspiracy. Deuel admitted that he had made numerous visits to Waverly House. "Because of the unwillingness of the witnesses, it was necessary to have many conversations with them to urge them to tell the truth," he declared. "At no time did I coerce or threaten them."

Colligan, encouraged by new evidence, renewed his appeal for a fresh trial. Almost five months to the day after sentencing Owney, Judge Nott turned down the application. "How this remarkable change occurred in the feelings of the two women toward the defendant is not apparent," the judge concluded. "It is evident that, in view of their character, their admitted perjury, and all the surrounding circumstances, that their accusations against Mrs. Goldman and Mr. Deuel are entitled to no weight. I am convinced from a careful study of their testimony—together with my observations of them while on the stand—that it is their testimony on this motion that is a willful and deliberate perjury, and not their testimony given upon the trial."

The war against the Gophers was all but over. New York City police records show that by the following month sixteen leading members of the gang had been rounded up and convicted of various offenses. It was the end of an era, and a new age was about to dawn in which both criminals and politicians would prosper side by side. Never again would the wild flame of youth burn quite so fiercely across the West Side. Owney put the old days behind him and resigned himself to life up the Hudson River in Sing Sing prison.

He always maintained his innocence of the Patsy Doyle killing and, even years later, could not pass Nash's Café on 41st and 8th Avenue without becoming emotional. He took his sentence philosophically and considered that it wiped the slate clean. "I believe in the law of compensation," he would say. "All those times I was arrested in all those years, the cops often had me right but I lied my way out of it. They never had enough evidence. Then they got me for something I didn't do and wouldn't believe me when I told the truth. But that's all right. I'm not sore at anybody. I've paid my debt. That's all wiped out now."

The maturing of Owney Madden was about to begin.

"He decided to serve his term without further battling," recalled Stanley Walker, who knew Owney in the 1930s. "The day he made the decision was the day on which began his greatness."

5.

The Big Thirst

Owney had barely completed a year of his sentence before the Winona was deserted and the remaining Gophers scattered to the winds. Sing Sing was designed to be a shock to the system—a bleak, remote institution made of grey stone from which chances of any escape were very slim. Each day, a bus full of new prisoners swung through the iron gates for registration. On the first floor of the administration building, they were lined up against the wall before the chief clerk. One by one, the prisoners were asked to step forward while he completed a long form of personal particulars—name, date of birth, religion, occupation, home background, education, and the standard question, "What made you do this?" Experienced prisoners knew the right answer to avoid further questions. "Bad associations," they replied, one after another, and newcomers waiting in line quickly followed their example.

After emptying out their pockets, they were led to the Bertillon Department for photographs and fingerprinting. The Bertillon system, all but abandoned by the time Owney entered Sing Sing, was a detailed method of measuring criminals from elbow to wrist, and knee to ankle, for identification purposes. Police departments and prisons used it widely—fingerprinting was in its infancy—until two prisoners in the same penitentiary were found to have identical Bertillon measurements and its popularity began to wane.

Across the yard at the State Shop, they were handed boots and blue prison-issue clothes before being led to the showers and then the barber shop. Many prisons completely shaved inmates' heads but Sing Sing, under its humanitarian warden, Lewis Lawes, insisted only on a light trim around the sides. For the next two weeks, Owney and the rest of the new intake were kept in virtual isolation due to the first instruction in penitentiary discipline. Lesson One was on privileges:

"Recreation in the yard after working hours is a privilege.

The visiting room without screens is a privilege.

Motion pictures, baseball and football games, and all others forms of amusement are privileges.

Purchasing supplies from the commissary is a privilege.

Receiving packages of food and clothing from relatives and friends is a privilege.

Writing and receiving letters is a privilege.

Receiving newspapers and magazines is a privilege.

Wearing any articles of apparel not supplied by the state is a privilege.

Smoking in the yard and cells is a privilege.

The warden may confer these privileges, or he can revoke any or all of them, whenever he thinks it necessary to maintain the discipline or the general welfare of his administration."

Owney, after two weeks in the reception block, was registered as a "C" Class prisoner. In Sing Sing penal jargon, this was known as the "restricted prolonged tractable group"—roughly translated this meant long-term prisoners who were generally considered well behaved. Warden Lawes was curious about the leader of the Gophers, a young man who was only in his mid-twenties but who was treated as a celebrity among the 2,500 inmates. Owney was put to work cleaning the yard and tending the gardens and behaved like a model prisoner. In common with all other Sing Sing inmates, he was allowed to write one letter a week—the "Sunday" letter—at the expense of the state. The Duke found little need to avail himself of the privilege. On visiting days, his mother, sister, and brother called regularly, interspersed with visits from familiar faces at Tammany Hall. As his sentence and the years wore on, only a handful of close, dedicated friends and relatives took the trouble to make the tedious rail trip up the bank of the Hudson.

Among the faithful was George Raft, who would sit in the cavernous visiting hall with a gift of Lucky Strike cigarettes and talk incessantly. His visits always lifted Owney's spirits and provided a line of communication with the outside world, where so many changes were taking place. George would always talk about the movies, which excited him, and how stars like Valentino, Fairbanks, and Barrymore were earning their fortunes. He was always alert and observant, absorbing the atmosphere and detail of "the Big House" and asking to have characters pointed out to him. In later years, he put his memories to use in the classic convict drama *Each Dawn I Die* when he played a role created almost exclusively from his visits to Owney in Sing Sing.

During his friend's imprisonment, George was performing in the clubs and illicit gambling dens which were sprouting wildly across New York. He was on familiar terms with most of the gangsters who ran them. It was a glittering, underground world in which fortunes were made or lost and the risk of arrest was never far away. The big games were run by Arnold Rothstein, a shadowy figure who was later to become the secret banker of the biggest criminal organization in the country. "The cast of gangsters who enjoyed Rothstein's crap games included men who were to become legendary heroes of American crime," Raft's biographer, Lewis Yablonsky, recalled: "Al Capone, then known as Al Brown, was a regular; Huge Waxey Gordon, another notorious hood from the Lower East Side; Lucky Luciano; and Larry Fay, a local rum runner. Large sums changed hands rapidly. One night, Lou Clayton, Jimmy Durante's partner and a serious gambler, pawned his wife's diamond ring and managed to win a hundred thousand from Rothstein. Happy and excited with his big score, Lou came to George's dressing room in the club where he was working and threw him a fifty-dollar bill. A few days later, he lost every cent at the same time. Broke again, he came to George to borrow a few hundred to stake his 'getting even.'

"Many nights, a big crap game was warned in advance from police headquarters to fold because the cops were on their way to raid the place. Big shots would vanish through a rear exit and lesser lights were left behind to be arrested and give the raid some authenticity. Once, George was trapped in a raid and, along with the others, taken to the police station. Raft did not use his own name, was neither fingerprinted nor booked, and the charges were dismissed."

Owney listened to such tales with unconcealed delight and a growing awareness that the old order had been replaced by organized rackets with vast sums of money at stake. After George's visits, the wild rover's mind must have teemed with schemes and restless plans. In Sing Sing, he could do little but patiently dream. The only solution to the intense frustration of being excluded from the action was to serve his sentence in a textbook fashion and hope for an early release. The decision required much self-discipline and a certain strength of character. Sing Sing was rife with rackets, warring factions, and constant rows triggered by the tension of close confinement. Owney's exemplary behavior attracted the attention of Warden Lawes, and a friendly relationship developed between them.

Some mornings, when new prisoners were lined up for processing, Lawes would take Owney up to the Bertillon Department and ask his opinion of certain individuals. The pair would stand out of earshot at one end of the hall and Lawes would ask:

"How 'bout that man, Owney? What do you think of him?"

"Oh, he's okay. He's smart," Owney would smile, as he recognized a familiar face.

"And how 'bout that guy there?" Lawes asked, pointing out another man.

When the conversation had gone on in this light-hearted vein for some time, Lawes said: "You know, I've been thinking, Owney. If all these guys are so smart, as you say, then how come they're all in Sing Sing?"

The comment clearly hit home and, little by little over the years, Lawes gave the exiled Duke of the West Side plenty to think about. Because of the discomfort still caused by his bullet wounds, Owney did not take part in prison sports activities. From time to time, he watched the energetic baseball and football games from the sidelines, but often preferred just to ruminate alone. His disability provided many opportunities to mull over his present situation. The claustrophobic experience of prison life urged him in later years to pass on fatherly advice to the errant men who regularly crossed his path. Many trigger-happy young hoods reminded him of his own renegade past with the Gophers. He would take them to one side to warn them in his quiet, man-to-man way: "Don't go wrong. Whatever happens, don't get into trouble. Always be able to say you have a respectable job."

"It is not unusual for a man to form friendships in prison," said one commentator. "But Madden did more than that. It is quite probable that he did more to set ex-convicts on their feet, though he may have done it in curious ways, than all the other social agencies put together. In the years when he was a big shot, as authentic a big shot as the underworld ever saw, he was responsible for the employment of many men who otherwise might have gone back to banditry."

The long years in Sing Sing were responsible for a curious renaissance. He was always a thoughtful man and, with so much time on his hands, reflected at great length on the pattern his life had taken. Prison became a watershed. When he was finally free, he left behind the violence of his youth and became, in many ways, wiser and more sophisticated in his methods.

"Sometimes," said Stanley Walker, "he would hear of a young man, a counterpart of one of the 'roosters' of the old Gopher days, who was showing signs of cutting up—robbing people, carrying a gun, talking too much and too loudly. He would either send word to the young man to behave himself or he would call the problem child before him and deliver a fierce, fatherly lecture on the blessings which come to the man who keeps out of trouble."

In 1920, the cornerstone was laid for Sing Sing's new prison building. Built almost entirely by convict labor, it was to transform the 47-acre penitentiary into America's biggest prison. Owney had little part in the building work in its early stages because he contracted pneumonia and his old wounds also were affecting his health so badly that he had to be transferred to the hospital wing. At the same time the prison was slowly turning into a huge construction site, Dr. Charles Sweet, the prison surgeon, told him that he would have to undergo major surgery. The bullets Owney still carried inside him had, at this stage, given him only minor problems. The wounds left by the bullets which had been removed at Flower Hospital, however, had now become severely ulcerated.

Dr. Sweet was a brilliant surgeon, highly experienced in treating a bizarre range of afflictions encountered in the course of criminal life. Hundreds of criminals were discharged from Sing Sing immensely grateful for his skills. Among them was a gangster whose nose had been shot away in a gunfight. Sweet painstakingly rebuilt it using plastic surgery. "As a precautionary measure, our Bertillon Department was directed to take a set of new photographs for our records," the warden noted. "The old ones were, of course, utterly useless."

Another prisoner, registering on arrival, could only sign his name with an "X." The registration clerk noticed that his right arm was stiff, and he was sent to Dr. Sweet, who concluded that the arm had been broken in a fight years ago and improperly set. The surgeon corrected this and the arm was restored to full use. One of his greatest successes was with a hunchbacked prisoner whose deformity was found to be caused by a large cyst. Sweet removed it and the patient later became the star player of the Sing Sing baseball team.

Owney, who had become disillusioned after several years of unproductive hospital treatment, recovered from the operation and came to trust Dr. Sweet implicitly. Even when he was discharged from prison, he still preferred the surgeon to attend to his recurring stomach problem. Once, he even drove all the way to Sing Sing for an operation in the hospital wing rather than place himself in the hands of an expensive New York consultant. Owney's friends, incidentally, maintained that he was shot on four separate occasions throughout his career. Most of these instances are unrecorded though it is known that Sweet always treated his wounds.

Owney spent a week convalescing after this particular operation. Ray Arcel, his fight trainer, took some boxers to Sing Sing to sit around Owney's bed and tell stories about the fight game to cheer him up. "He was sick real bad at the time," Arcel recalled. "When he was feeling better, he asked me to stage a boxing tournament for the prisoners. Owney introduced me to the warden, Lewis Lawes, and we talked over details. I took a whole load of fighters up there and put on a show. I suppose it was Owney's way of saying 'thank you.'"

Back home, inactivity after the operation left him with a backache. Arcel, who would drop by regularly to give him a massage, recalled: "He was a very quiet guy. Never talked about himself, and I think he loved to be at home better than going around all the clubs and speakeasies he owned."

British Lightweight Champion Jackie Berg, an East-ender who accompanied Ray to Owney's apartment, remembered him well: "He was small, thin, and softly-spoken, but very, very tough. You could take a glance at him and perhaps imagine he went each day to an office or a bank."

On February 1, 1923, Owney finally stepped from the prison gates a free man after earning his release for good behavior. He had served only seven-and-a-half years of his sentence and was released with the sword of parole hanging over him. Even the slightest violation, he was aware, could result in him returning to serve the rest of his sentence. This sobering realization, together with the wisdom of Warden Lawes and years of self-examination, served to dramatically change his attitude toward crime.

For many years to come, the experience of prison "caused him to insist always upon outward order and decency in the conduct of the rackets of New York," an acquaintance said. "He was suspicious of the swaggering tough boys from Chicago, Philadelphia, and Boston. He saw no reason for killing anyone. There was plenty of money for everybody. His hatred for Jack 'Legs' Diamond, the human sieve, may be traced to his realization that Diamond was a shallow thinker, too quick on the trigger, with a lust for blood and torture when there was no need for anything except a smile and an occasional firm command on the telephone."

Of all the New York underbosses, possibly only Owney and his future partner, Frank Costello, achieved power without always looking down the barrel of a gun. The *Police Gazette* was to call Madden, "the most feared mobland boss in the United States, and possibly the most powerful," a position he gained largely through the force of his personality. As Joe Bonanno, the Sicilian Don of Dons, reflected in old age: "I have learned that true power comes only from self-control." Unlike many leading hoods, however, Owney was a sensitive man, and the precarious lifestyle took a toll on his nerves. The more his wealth and influence expanded, the more monastic and stressful his private life became.

In Hot Springs, where he spent his later years, he would physically start at an unexpected noise. "Everything disturbed him, you know," said his friend and attorney Q. Byrum Hurst of Hot Springs. "If a squirrel got into his attic at night, he would leap out of bed. The least little thing would make him jump. When we had people around at the house, Owney might call and we would introduce him. They'd say, 'the Owney Madden?' and he would step back looking nervous. That kind of thing made him feel bad."

The "best shot in New York" rarely carried his Smith and Wesson after his release from Sing Sing, a time when bloody gangland battles were being fought on city streets. His nervousness was hardly improved by quickly becoming one of the likeliest targets in town. In Arkansas, he kept weapons at home to protect his property, like most other citizens, but never carried them with him. Perhaps, as the result of a lifetime of glancing over his shoulder, he appeared constantly alert and never was completely able to relax unless with close friends. A former shop worker in the Sears Roebuck department store in Hot Springs remembered

Owney coming in one Christmas to purchase $100 worth of toys to send anonymously to a local children's home: "He walked to the rear of the store and stood with his back to the wall, pointing out articles for the staff to bring to him."

In the 1920s, few of those who knew him were foolish enough to conclude that his nervousness was a sign of weakness. "Madden could be firm," a *Herald* reporter noted. "For all his nervousness, for all his fear of being framed or killed or betrayed, he would not back down in the face of minor racketeers who thought they could cow him." Despite his mild manner and soft-voiced English politeness, he was still "the Killer," and no one was ever completely prepared to take the risk of thinking otherwise. Only a handful of friends knew how much he had mellowed, and there was little doubt that his enduring reputation from Gopher days ensured his survival into old age.

His first weeks of freedom in 1923 were a time of personal turmoil. Sing Sing had been tranquil in comparison to the mayhem caused by the Prohibition era. Owney had kept abreast of gossip from George Raft's visits and by reading the newspapers. At the time of his release from prison, America had been dry for three years and vast changes were taking place among the ragtag army of hoods supplying booze to thirsty New Yorkers.

Prohibition had been imposed by the Volstead Act on January 16th, 1920, a day when a *New York Times* headline noted: "John Barleycorn Died Peacefully at the Toll of 12." The *Times* was, of course, not quite right. John Barleycorn was alive and well, and the 122,000,000 Americans who drank more than 2,000,000,000 gallons of alcoholic beverages a year showed little inclination to take the pledge of sobriety.

Despite changes in the law, drinking was never universally regarded as a crime. On the contrary, there was a strong feeling that raising a glass of bootleg booze was a determined stand for the U.S. Constitution. Bishop James Cannon Jr. of Virginia denounced New York as "Satan's seat" when it was revealed that the city's 15,000 pre-Prohibition bars had been replaced by 32,000 "speakeasies"—the slang term for secret places where people could buy alcoholic beverages. The high sentiment behind Prohibition was a misplaced urge to curb drunkenness and increase productivity. Its effect was to create a national obsession with alcohol and to send production in the bootleg industry soaring.

Supplies of alcohol had been chaotic and unreliable during Owney's stay in Sing Sing. Small-time crooks all over the country scrambled to make a fast buck during the first two years of Prohibition. One of the main sources of supply was alcohol that was still being produced legally in the form of medicinal whisky and sacramental wine for churches. Vast stocks of booze that were "frozen" on the hour of midnight when the Volstead Act came into force could also, with the right authority, be released for medicinal purposes. Warehouses required a federal withdrawal permit to release them, and there was soon a brisk trade in permits stolen from government offices and hastily printed counterfeits. Warehouse workers were happy to hand over supplies, providing they were handed an authorized permit which placed them above suspicion.

Demand was so great that the system led to what was known as the Curb Exchange, something akin to the Stock Exchange, only busier and probably more lucrative. Bootleggers met at appointed times, by day and night, at the curbs of a great circle of streets along Kenmare, Broome, Grand, and Elizabeth. Some had permits for warehouses holding brands which their particular customers did not want, so exchanges took place to enable orders to be filled. Right in the center of this teeming clearing house was New York City police headquarters. As arguments over permits or territorial rights erupted into gunfights, officers would rush to the windows to watch the outcome. "Fledgling detectives did not have far to walk to practice the investigation of murders," one observer noted.

The weakness of the system was that it flourished on little more than luck and improvisation. In these early days of Prohibition, influential crime figures had stood on the sidelines, watching developments with interest. As Owney began to explore the streets of New York again, they were just beginning to move in and put haphazard distribution on an organized level. Small operators were quickly forced out of business, and bootlegging rapidly rose from a cottage industry to a corporate enterprise.

Owney had arrived back in New York, clutching a bundle of personal belongings. He went to stay with his mother on 10th Avenue where he looked up old friends and caught up with the news. Like all newly released Sing Sing inmates, he looked tanned and healthy. Sunbathing was a prison tradition in the final weeks of confinement to dispel any impression that one was pale due to prison confinement. Owney was now thirty-two and something of a living legend to those who recalled the old Gophers. He had little money and wielded no power, but in the eyes of the underworld and political bosses, he still had a certain respect and standing. Events had overtaken him during the long prison years, but what he found suited his new outlook—a world in which money could be made through crime that nobody considered crime. It was a business which was almost legitimate and could utilize his talent and experience to get a good monetary return. Grey areas like this had begun to appeal to him. Owney found the drugs and vice rackets distasteful and, characteristically, on the repeal of Prohibition, moved into gambling, the victim of the second-most unpopular law ever passed in the United States.

Prohibition had been proceeding like a comic opera between 1920 and 1923. Home brew sales soared and people were drinking with a desperation born of the belief that every glass might be their last. "When they opened a bottle, they didn't drink it, they killed it," one journalist observed. Determined to cover any possible loopholes in the law, Washington's Prohibition Bureau ruled that hip flasks were illegal and anyone caught with one technically could have his trousers confiscated as a "vehicle of transportation." Disregard for the law became so widespread that Henry Ford, the automobile magnate, threatened to fire any of his automobile workers who concealed drink in their homes. "So far as our organization is concerned," Ford warned, "the law is going to be enforced to the letter." Family members who once drank only in moderation suddenly began fermenting potatoes, yeast, and sugar in their bathtubs. As the bubbling concoctions rose to the brim, bodily hygiene gave way to an insatiable desire for booze. In the first year of Prohibition, 32,000 illicit stills were raided. Within five years, the number of seizures had risen to a total of 172,000.

Some shops, hoping to sidestep the law, ran a brisk business in "wine bricks" at two dollars each. A reporter for the *Cincinnati Enquirer* paid one establishment a visit to find dozens of customers elbowing each other and shouting out orders for "a block of Burgundy" or "a dozen blocks of Rhine wine." The lady behind the counter handed them out as fast as she could, while impassively reciting instructions which placed her on the right side of the law.

"You dissolve the brick in a gallon of water. Do not put the liquid into a cupboard for twenty-one days because it will turn into wine. Do not put the patent red rubber siphon hose into a glass of water because it helps to make the liquor tasty and potable. Do not shake the bottle once a day because that makes the liquor work."

Confidence tricksters were soon selling useless counterfeits made from compressed sawdust or seaweed. Others hastily prepared brews that resulted in outbreaks of gastric trouble and even fatalities. Clearly, something had to be done to regulate the hysteria and, in the highest American tradition of public service, the entrepreneurial New York gangsters finally stepped in to help out. Within a year of Owney's release from prison, booze supplies were being established on an organized basis. Thirsty New Yorkers could visit a speakeasy no different from their old corner bar or simply pick up the telephone and have supplies delivered. The way in which this efficient distribution system was developed, however, was not without heartache.

Some wag once remarked that all the organized crime in America can be directly traced to two sources—the Anti-Saloon League and Henry Ford. One provided the market and the other the means of transportation. Once the system was operating successfully, it became only a matter of investing the profits in other rackets. Larry Fay, a New York taxi proprietor, was one of the first to discover the high profits to be made from smuggling booze. In the spring of 1920, he was a self-employed driver with his own cab, earning $25 a week. When someone flagged him down in Manhattan and tried to book a fare over the border to Montreal, Fay thought twice about doing the long journey. He reluctantly agreed to go and discovered, to his good fortune, that whisky could be bought in Canada for only ten dollars a case. To cover his expenses, he bought two cases, concealed them in the car trunk and drove back to New York, where he sold them for $100 each. Encouraged by his profit, he began to make regular trips north, buying and reselling on his return. Soon, he'd made enough to afford a fleet of several cabs and a truck.

Fay was a cautious man who varied his routes, times, and border crossings and was content not to buy too much at one time. If he was arrested, the loss would then only be small. The system worked well for almost a year until his truck was stopped in Lawrence, Massachusetts, carrying a full shipment of scotch from Trois Rivieres in Canada. He escaped lightly with no more than a fine, but the incident was enough to deter him from moving on to a large-scale bootlegging operation. Instead, Fay used his accumulated profits to build up his cab company to one of the biggest in New York and then invested the rest in night clubs.

New York teemed with hundreds of independent cab operators and sizeable fleets, all jockeying for business around the speakeasies and busy railroad stations. One of Fay's early enterprises had been to ferry out-of-towners to "clip joints"—disreputable speakeasies—where they were quickly relieved of their money. His cabs were the most eye-catching in town. They glittered with polished alloy trims, small customized windows for privacy, strings of tiny lights shining across the roofs and down the sides, and were topped with chromium-plated musical horns which played popular tunes. In Fay's words, they had "class." His drivers were the roughest in New York, picked for an ability to beat off the opposition and backed by a team of bruisers who made sure no one dared encroach on his territory. Larry Fay was "Mr. Cabs" and felt proud that he expressed his personality through his company.

It was around this time that Owney started working for Fay. His main function was to defend two crucial stands from marauding rival operators. The Grand Central and Pennsylvania stations were the most lucrative taxi stands in the whole of New York and constantly under attack by cruising flotillas from other cab companies. Owney dispatched his muscle with the precision of a general defending a besieged city. Thugs were quickly sent wherever there was trouble or to stands that required heavy protection at peak periods.

The Duke proved to be highly efficient and was well paid for his efforts, but the job was to last only a few months. Before the year had ended, Fay sold out to a big fleet operator for a large sum, plus a $10,000-a-year seat on the board. Fay's problem was that he had a desperate, fundamental urge to become a star. His gleaming cabs were an expression of his yearning for glamour but, however he looked at them, they still did not satisfy him.

He believed that his destiny lay in night clubs. As outlets for the tidal wave of booze pouring into New York, they promised a quick return. Fay lavished the same blitz on their décor as he had on his fleet of taxis. He embarked on a grand tour of Europe, returning with twelve trunks of expensive suits and shirts and a wealth of ideas from Paris and London. Everything he gleaned from the trip went into his first venture—an overpoweringly decorated club called the El Fey ("after my name, Larry Fay, get it?" he often said).

Owney, who valued loyalty, later backed Fay's night club ventures because he had helped him in his time of need. Fay, however, had played a greater role in the Duke's affairs than he might at first have realized. He persuaded Owney and a formidable member of the old Hudson Dusters to get together and bury their grievances. Times had changed and Larry felt that they ought to get to know each other. For all his brashness, he detected a common thread in Owney and George Jean "Big

Frenchy" DeMange, a former top enforcer for the Dusters. The recon-
ciliation must have raised a smile among New York's underworld.
Physically, little Owney and Big Frenchy were not unlike the popular
comedy team of Laurel and Hardy, though with vastly different tempera-
ments. Fay, convinced that some unknown potential lay buried, was
happy that they made the peace and forgot their differences. He proved
to be a man of perception—Owney and Frenchy ended up becoming in-
separable working partners and had one of the most enduring business
relationships in the history of New York crime.

DeMange liked what he saw in Owney—a tough Englishman, but
with inbred politeness and a gentlemanly way of handling himself. He
also had a sharp brain, which DeMange lacked, and a solid reputation.
DeMange amused the Duke—he was big, well over six feet, with the lumbering mannerisms of a heavyweight boxer. Frenchy was clumsy and had
no way with words. With a poker deck in his ham hands, however, he
could clean out the best players in New York. Above all, he had a big
heart and appeared trustworthy and straight—attributes which always carried great weight with Owney.

They were the perfect partnership and created a huge empire in a stag-
geringly short period. Their dealings, both with each other and the rest of
the city's gangland, were treated with affection and respect, particularly by
the increasingly powerful Italian and Jewish mobs. It would have surprised
no one during a Madden-DeMange disagreement if thin, nervous Owney
had snatched off his cap and battered his slow, gigantic partner over the
head with it. To those in the know, they were a fearful combination, with
immense leverage and power in the burgeoning booze rackets.

Owney's initiation into the easy money provided by Prohibition
came when, with friends, he broke into a warehouse and loaded up a
truck with barrels of bonded whisky. Back in their hiding place, he re-
sisted the temptation to sell it outright to established booze runners for
a quick killing. After inquiring around the neighborhood, he found a
supply of suitable containers and bottled the whisky, complete with

printed labels. His team loaded them into a car and cruised around Manhattan, selling them to speakeasies. "The profits were so spectacular," the Police Gazette reported, "that Madden decided to devote all his energies to bootlegging."

Ready-bottled scotch was to prove less time-consuming, and Owney soon earmarked the target of his first big raid—the fortress-like Liberty Storage Warehouse, which dominated a block on West 64th Street. Late one winter night, the telephone rang in the office and the puzzled watchman, seventy-one-year-old James Stafford, stumped up the steps to answer it. It was highly unusual for anyone to ring during the long hours of darkness and Stafford wondered who on earth it could be.

To his surprise, it was one of the warehouse directors.

"This is Mr. Woods," said the caller brusquely. "I left a package at the office earlier this evening. My secretary is calling over for it. Please let him in when he rings."

The caller had a cultured, business-like voice, and the old man, convinced that it was indeed Mr. Woods, replaced the receiver and went to look for the package. The caller had described the package in detail, so there could be no mistaking the authenticity of his request. James Stafford searched the office for the package but could not find it.

When the front bell rang, he opened the door to face a well-dressed man who introduced himself as Mr. Wood's personal assistant.

"Have you got the package?" he asked.

"I can't find it anywhere," Stafford apologized. "You'd better come and look for yourself."

The watchman opened the main door and led the way to the office, where the "secretary" suddenly pinioned his arms from behind. Three other men materialized from nowhere and bound and gagged the old man. Between them, they carried him upstairs to the second floor and lowered him onto a mat so he would be more comfortable. In the next room, he could hear the scraping of cases across the floor and, after a while, the sound of a truck starting up and driving away. The watchman had been tied loosely enough so that he could free himself, and he raised the alarm. The missing stock amounted to two hundred cases of rye whisky, valued at $16,000.

Four detectives were immediately assigned to the case and began making house-to-house inquiries along the block. Residents reported that the truck, which had been closely followed by a Cadillac sedan, had broken down not far from the Liberty Warehouse. Another truck had appeared a short time later and towed it away. The detectives, guessing that the first truck had probably been abandoned, made a street-by-street search of the area early the next morning. On West 44th Street, they found it—emptied of its contents—and decided to keep watch on it. About two hours later, a Cadillac sedan drew up and three men got out and tried to get the engine started. When the detectives surrounded them with drawn guns, the trio surrendered without a struggle.

Back at the precinct, they identified themselves as Harry Jacobs, a known hood; George DeMange, who had an arrest record for homicide, safe-cracking, and burglary but no convictions; and Owney Madden. All three were charged with assault and robbery and bailed out at $10,000 each. Strangely, a few days later, detectives informed the district attorney that they did not have enough evidence to bring a case, and the incident never came to court.

Owney was hard at work, day and night, building a bootleg empire with an energy and determination which had not been displayed since his Gopher days. Curiously, none of the people who remembered him, regardless of which side of the law they might have been on, considered him to have had what might be called a criminal mentality. They recalled him essentially as a tough character, a businessman, and someone generous to those worse off than himself. Questioned further, a picture emerges of a man who acquired a shady past because of the milieu in which he was raised and operated, rather than because of any terrible deeds he might have perpetrated. His leadership and financial acumen were beyond question. The truth is that, while he was perhaps a victim of a corrupt system, Owney made no secret about enjoying gangland life. No doubt he would have been highly successful in legitimate commerce, but would have felt stifled without the zest and thrill of living dangerously. He was, too, a great judge of people and loved the rough, larger-than-life characters who dominated the underworld. They lived on a perpetual knife-edge, with little regard for the risk of death or imprisonment, and Owney felt a kinship with them. The renegade life had an intensity and dimension which he considered lacking in the law-abiding world.

After his stay in Sing Sing, violence was absent from most of the crimes he committed. If he went out of town, however, he still carried a gun for protection. A month after the Liberty raid, early in January 1924, a posse of state troopers flagged down a truck on the outskirts of Bedford Village, Westchester County, for a routine check. Using their flashlights, they saw six men crammed into the cab. On inspection, the truck was found to be loaded with $25,000 worth of pre–World War I whisky, which was said to have been stolen from the secluded estate of Charles Mayer in Stockbridge, Massachusetts. What Mr. Mayer was planning to do with such a large quantity of illegal alcohol was never established.

Back at the Westchester police station, the leader of the six gave his name as James Malloy, but a fingerprint check revealed him to be Owney Madden. The gang members were released on a bail of $15,000 each. Additionally, Owney was charged with being in possession of a firearm. Once again, mysteriously, the police failed to put a case together and the six men were never brought to court.

Police officers were not only notoriously lenient in bootlegging cases, but extensively corrupt. An indication of their general willingness to accept bribes emerged in a Prohibition investigation of the Philadelphia police department where one inspector, on a $3,000 salary, had managed to bank a total of $193,553. A captain on a salary of $2,500 had likewise managed to put away $102,829. Philadelphia, incidentally, was considered one of the quieter bootlegging corners of the United States.

"On a frightening scale, policemen in almost every precinct in every city were corrupted because bootleg money, unlike dollars from the prostitution and narcotics rackets, was 'clean' graft," New York journalist Henry Lee recalled. "Besides, politicians from the mayor down would not tolerate unauthorized raids. In New York City, a captain suffered years of exile in an outlying precinct because of his unwanted but honest views on enforcement. And, the poor commissioner who held office there during the first five years of Prohibition confessed to an interviewer: 'Prohibition was seventy-five percent of my problem. I had gambling and prostitution under control, but I could not enforce this unpopular law.'"

Owney's arrest in January of 1924 for riding in the booze truck stolen from broker Charles Mayer had not been forgotten by the authorities. At the time, he explained to state troopers that he had given a false name because he was an innocent bystander afraid of being accused of bootlegging. He was hitch-hiking home when this truck loaded with five men had pulled up and offered him a lift. New York County District Attorney Joab H. Banton, however, was not impressed with his story. A few months later, in April, he tried to curb the Duke's widespread activities by writing to James L. Long, the State Superintendent of Prisons, complaining that Madden had broken his parole. Banton argued that, in view of his two arrests in the company of men with long criminal records, he should be immediately sent back to Sing Sing. "If the parole means anything to the community," he wrote, "it must mean that those on parole cannot associate with criminals." Long declined to take any action because he possibly was persuaded against it by Owney's old pal, Jimmy Hines, who by now was a figure of immense political power in the city.

The warning made Owney less reckless in his dealings, or at least ensured that he was not directly involved, unless a job was so big that it required his personal supervision. On the other hand, it was impossible to completely take a back seat. The 1920s were tough years, and there were times when leadership could only be maintained by setting an example.

Frank Costello, for instance, had put away his gun but still managed to retain an iron-hard reputation. After serving a year in prison, he told his lawyer, George Wolf: "That's when I realized it was stupid. Carrying a gun was like carrying a label that says: 'I'm dangerous. I'm a criminal. Get me off the streets.' I made up my mind that I would never pack a gun again and I never did." As with Owney, no one considered it to be a sign of weakness. Indeed, many years later, when Wolf announced to one of Costello's friends that he intended to write his client's biography, the man grinned and said: "If you're writing a book about how nice a guy Frank was, don't put too much in there about the Twenties."

Frank and Owney were perhaps closer to Jimmy Hines than anyone in the New York underworld, but there was a limit to their influence. Under the conditions of his parole, Owney could be returned to prison to serve out his ten-to-twenty-year sentence for an offense as slight as just mixing with known criminals.

The risk was brought home to him one night when he was strolling down Broadway with a girl on his arm. She had a criminal record and was recognized by a veteran detective who had known Madden for years. "I suppose I ought to pick you up," he told Owney, "but I'm not going to. Listen, you'd better watch your step." The incident made him take stock of his position again and, as his bootleg empire grew, he began to take more of an administrative role.

Arrest was a constant threat but, with Jimmy Hines's campaign manager, Joe Shalleck, as his lawyer, his confidence remained undiminished. One of the recurring problems of the era was that not everyone in a police uniform was who he appeared to be.

"He was afraid of being framed, either by the police or by enemies in the underworld," Stanley Walker recorded when he worked on the Herald. "He knew a great many policemen and it implies nothing discreditable to anyone to say that he was on good terms with many of them. He was glad always to run as fast as he could to police headquarters when he was wanted for anything. If possible, he liked to be accompanied by veteran detectives who he knew would not double-cross him for whatever fleeting fame there might be in it. 'No strange cop is going to arrest me,' he said once. There was good sense working behind that decision. He knew how easy it was for gunmen to pose as policemen, force a man into an automobile, and take him for his last journey on earth.

"Fakes and liars annoyed him. Many a time a silk burglar or a jewel robber would tell the police that Owney had lured them to do the job, which would throw Madden into a terrible rage. He was forced to submit to all manner of petty shakedowns. His largesse, merely to appease the army of harpies who thought he had all the money in the world, was tremendous. It wasn't the most comfortable life in the world."

Big Frenchy had extensive nightclub interests, and, as Owney's power extended, he took him into partnership.

"I guess I'll have to cut you in before you start tearing the town apart," Frenchy would say.

"Aw, I wouldn't do that for all the tea in China," Owney would say.

Frenchy was impressed by the way Owney conducted himself and thought that an aura of impeccable politeness would go down well with wealthy patrons. And so began a partnership which became legendary on the New York nightclub scene.

6.

The Great White Way

One evening in the early 1920s, a limousine pulled up outside Harlem's Club Deluxe and a group of well-dressed men strolled through the front door and asked to see the owner. Jack Johnson, the former world heavyweight boxing champion, was a hero to African Americans and was well known to Owney, a connoisseur of the fight game. Jack, a huge, amiable fellow as handy on the cello as he was with his fists, was a familiar figure in Harlem nightlife. After retiring from the ring, he had invested in an old, run-down property on the corner of Lennox and 142nd Street and turned it into a supper club.

The two-story building originally had a theater on the ground floor and a dance hall upstairs, but patrons had deserted it in favor of the fashionable Renaissance Casino on West 133rd Street. In the lean years of early Prohibition, Jack's place had failed to prosper. Success in the club business required good liquor connections, and Jack, despite knowing Owney, was not into the rackets. The Duke, on the other hand, most definitely was.

Johnson was delighted with Owney's offer to buy out the Deluxe, especially as the deal included retaining him as part of the management. Big Frenchy was cut in as an operating partner, and Arnold "the Banker" Rothstein, who had capital tied up in countless bootleg outlets, invested in a slice of the action.

Harlem had once been a fashionable area where professional people, both black and white, retired to their grand homes—many designed by architects—after a busy day in the city. Housing prices began to tumble, however, around 1900 due to an influx of migrant workers from the South. Many houses were turned into rental properties which became overcrowded and caused wealthy families to move out. Harlem was still an exciting place to visit for jazz, dancing, and the blossoming of black artistic talent. Everyone was calling it the Harlem Renaissance. By day, there may have been poverty and violence, but at night Harlem came alive, glittering with creative talent, music cellars, and tiny restaurants.

The year Owney and Frenchy shook hands with Jack Johnson, a young musician arrived in New York. He was penniless but full of talent. Duke Ellington, fresh from Washington, had heard through the grapevine that Harlem had work for musicians. He found the engagements less than promising, but the Renaissance charged the atmosphere with creative excitement and a new optimism. Langston Hughes and James Weldon Johnson were writing there. Singers like Ethel Waters and Florence Mills could be heard performing in dimly lit cellar clubs. The dance craze, which had swept America with the Bunny Hug and Turkey Trot in the First World War, had lingered on, attracting musicians from all over the country. Ellington liked Harlem because any style of music went down, leaving endless scope for experiment and improvisation. Kid Lippy found work playing at "rent parties" thrown by impoverished tenants to raise money and stave off eviction. James P. Johnson, a favorite piano player of the Duke's, raised the roof at parlor socials, along with a gangly kid named Fats Waller.

"They were smoke-filled rooms filled with conversation and laughter, flowing with bad booze," Jim Haskins recalled in *The Cotton Club*. "Some were furnished with oddly assorted chairs and white porcelain tables, others with linen-covered tables and velvet-smooth floors. In many, the entertainment consisted of one piano and one female blues singer, her hoarse voice rising vainly over the babble. Larger establishments usually featured a small band or combo, whose size often depended on the volume and economic status of the audience. The common arrangement between musicians and club management was to place a bowl or cigar box in a central location so that patrons could make donations for the entertainment. At the end of the evening, the contents were then divided equally. Often, the accessibility of the box or bowl caused difficulties. Willie 'the Lion' Smith played at a place called LeRoy's in those days. He recalls having to keep a mirror on top of the piano in order to keep an eye on the cigar box and the singers, musicians, and waiters, who were prone to dip into the till for themselves."

The people in Harlem were proud of the way their neighborhood had blossomed into a breeding place of African-American culture. White people often made the trip uptown to "slum" and soak up the lively atmosphere, but their presence was resented. On more than one occasion, police had to deal with knife fights and brawls, triggered by patronizing strangers who were hanging out in Harlem nightclubs. Surprisingly, many of these newer establishments were Irish-owned but catered to a black clientele.

Jack Johnson had inadvertently brought the situation about after his barnstorming victory over Jim Jeffries, the so-called "Great White Hope," in 1910. The fight had been less of a boxing contest than a focus of racial rivalry and tension. When Johnson, one of the greatest black athletes of the era, beat his opponent, riots broke out all over New York. Outraged whites overran Hell's Kitchen and surrounding neighborhoods, burning and wrecking black clubs. When trouble died down, many clubs reopened in the "safer" black area of Harlem.

Owney, with his Irish connections, was familiar with the uptown entertainment scene long before he opened the Cotton Club. His passion for listening to street talk, underworld gossip, and sifting through newspaper columns kept his finger on the pulse of things. Harlem, he felt instinctively, was ripe for "development." A nightclub was the perfect outlet for the beer that rolled hourly from the Phenix Brewery and the cargoes of King's Ransom and House of Lords scotch smuggled by his ships from Scotland. At the time, Harlem, more than anywhere else in New York, had a distinctive atmosphere and electric energy which wealthy white society would love to take in. Those already smitten with the romance of rubbing shoulders with gangsters in downtown speakeasies would love the added attraction of good jazz and non-stop dancing, he believed.

Somehow, the old Deluxe had to have a name which summed up the new fare it was offering. The Cotton Club, with its carefree, Southern undertones, seemed to be the answer. No one knows exactly who coined the name, but Owney, with his meticulous attention to detail, may well have been a likely candidate.

Madden and DeMange walked around the empty Deluxe, working out the best way to overcome their first problem. In order to make enough money, they needed to pack the customers in yet also retain a feeling of exclusivity about the place. Owney's suggestion was to increase the seating capacity by raising the floor onto two levels. More tables could be brought in without losing the intimate cabaret atmosphere they wanted to achieve.

Along the way, Owney had picked up a few tips by studying the approach adopted by Larry Fay. "Mr. Cabs" applied great care to his clubs and, while Owney did not wholeheartedly approve of his rather tacky approach, it was essential that even the smallest detail should not be overlooked. Frenchy had his own club, the Argonaut, as well as interests in many others and, between them, the plan began to take shape.

Josef Urban, the fashionable interior designer, was brought in to surround the peninsular stage with jungle decor and motifs. Dancers and singers were auditioned in a search for exceptional talent. They had to be good because the clientele Owney was hoping to attract would probably drop in at the Cotton Club for supper after seeing some of the best shows on Broadway. There was a wide selection of cuisine, from Chinese to Creole, priced in line with Manhattan nightspots of comparable size. Booze, the main attraction rivaling the floor show, was cheap and plentiful.

Before the establishment of the crime syndicates, the New York underworld was a complex and interlocking jigsaw puzzle. It was almost impossible for a legitimate operator to set up in business. Every aspect of commerce was tied to one racket or another, and the discretion of a diplomat was required to ensure that the right deals were struck with the right people.

Jim Haskins mentions in his history of the Cotton Club that Owney brought in all his staff from Chicago to ensure loyalty. In practice, this would have been an unthinkable affront to gangland protocol. "Strangers" were never employed at the Cotton Club because the unwritten rules of protection and corruption were quite inflexible. Owney would first have consulted with his associates, Bill Dwyer and Frank Costello, out of courtesy, to tell them what he had in mind, just as they would have done for him. The next move was to open discussions with Tammany Hall, which arranged and controlled police protection. Politicians also enjoyed the privilege of sending along friends, relatives, or constituents who might have been looking for work as doormen or waiters. As much as possible, Owney wanted to keep all his business within the "family."

Other City Hall departments had to be considered, too. "Health Department inspectors, to make sure the kitchen of a nightclub was clean, had to be catered to," Thompson and Raymond noted in their study of New York crime. "Inspectors from the Buildings Department, who were supposed to make sure the building was structurally safe, and those from the Fire Department, who were supposed to see that no extraordinary fire hazards existed, also came in for a share of the total fix."

In other clubs, these overheads were covered by adjusting the prices of drinks. Whisky, for instance, often went up from a standard 15 cents a shot to something approaching 75 cents in order to pay for the protection. Owney, however, as a major bootlegger, could afford to keep his prices low and still maintain the right flow of customers. The web of corruption woven by Tammany Hall was so wide that every item of club equipment had to be checked for vested political interests before purchases could be made. Light bulbs, for example, could only be bought from the Monroe Lamp and Equipment Company on West 14th Street because two Democratic district leaders had stakes in the firm. Fire extinguishers had to be supplied by the Croker National Fire Prevention Company, run by the nephew of one of the Tammany Hall bosses. Fire Department inspectors, upon seeing Croker extinguishers hanging in the club kitchen, were inclined to overlook minor violations.

"When it came to putting in the furniture and decorations for nightclubs, it was a good thing for the gangster proprietors to find out from the district leader who gave the approval for opening the place, if he had any relatives or friends in the furniture or equipment supply business," Thompson and Raymond added. "Such equipment was a little higher priced generally than it might be elsewhere, but it helped promote a warm and friendly feeling."

Owney's own laundry business took care of supplying clean linen, but other fittings such as paint, carpet, drapes, and stage lighting all had to be purchased through the appropriate racketeers or the right political channels. Other clubs, in turn, had to approach Owney for their linen service, drink supplies, and permission to open rival ventures. Sins of omission were not lightly overlooked. Someone once made the grave mistake of opening a chic club called the Plantation farther down Lennox Avenue at West 126th Street without the appropriate consultations. At the time, Duke Ellington's orchestra had been temporarily released from its contract to play in Hollywood. Cab Calloway and his band filled in at the Cotton Club until their return.

Calloway, an eccentric, exuberant performer, was a tremendous draw with hit songs like "Minnie the Moocher" and "Hi-De-Hi." When Ellington took over the stand again at the Cotton Club, the Plantation immediately booked Calloway as a rival attraction. Owney had been patient with the new owners for opening their club without his permission, as well as their choice of another "Southern" name for it. Poaching stars, however, was considered beyond the bounds of reasonable behavior.

A few days later, "some of the boys," as they were subsequently described, paid a visit to the Plantation. They reduced every single item of furniture to kindling and smashed every bottle and glass in the place. Their parting gesture was to tear out the Plantation's showpiece bar, a huge and elaborate affair, and dump it outside in the gutter. No one, of course, ever came forward to identify those responsible and no charges were ever leveled. Cab Calloway and his band happily accepted an offer to return to the Cotton Club.

The genius of Duke Ellington proved to be a major attraction of the club, and Owney promoted him heavily. Lady Mountbatten, a friend of Joseph P. Kennedy who had interests in Haigh and Haigh whisky, visited the club one evening and enjoyed the atmosphere so much that she christened the Cotton Club "the Aristocrat of Harlem."

The Cotton Club was Owney's flagship. Billboards promised unforgettable nights of style and excitement, and its neatly printed theater cards circulated among the rich and famous:

See This After Theater, Wow!
The New, Sparkling, Lightning Fast Cotton Club Show.
BLACKBERRIES OF 1931
Brown Sugar—Sweet, But Unrefined
—Produced by Dan Healy
*Plus Duke Ellington and his Famous Cotton Club Orchestra
Reservations—Bradhurst 2-1687
COTTON CLUB
"Aristocrat of Harlem"
Lennox Ave. Corner 142nd St.

A new Cotton Club floor show, with fresh Ellington numbers, became a major New York attraction. On one occasion, before the new season opened, there was a mix-up in bookings. It was discovered that Ellington and the band were honoring a prior engagement at Gibson's Standard Theater in Philadelphia. When an anxious Jimmy McHugh, one of the Cotton Club's production crew, broke the news, Owney took it calmly. He picked up the telephone and called Boo Boo Hoff, a life-long friend and much-feared mastermind of organized crime in the City of Brotherly Love. Owney explained that he had a small problem and, because of the distance involved, wondered if Boo Boo could put a word in the right ear on his behalf. Boo Boo said he would be delighted to oblige and promised to delegate one of his best men, Yankee Schwartz, to unravel the delicate contractual tangle. Schwartz, not a master of sub-tlety, paid a visit to Clarence Robinson, the theater impresario.

"What can I do?" Robinson shrugged helplessly when the problem was outlined.

"Be big," Yankee advised, "or be dead."

Ellington and his band were on the next train back to New York.

Weekly radio broadcasts were made from the Cotton Club, and Ellington's career was given an enormous boost. Most of the patrons were white, not from any strong policy of racial discrimination as some have suggested, but possibly due more to a combination of high prices and a desire by management not to develop a reputation for trouble. Blacks were no more responsible for fights than whites but, in the Harlem of the 1920s, Owney and Frenchy thought it prudent to avoid the kind of bloody confrontations other clubs had suffered. Mixed au-diences became more common as the Cotton Club established itself as a center for high-class entertainment. Ellington himself was responsible for bringing some of the barriers down when he remarked to Owney that many of his friends wanted to see his band in action.

"If one thing hallmarked Owney's clubs, it was an absence of fear," remarked attorney Jack Reuben, a regular patron from opening night. "Anyone could visit the Cotton Club without the slightest worry of vio-lence or intimidation. Everything, from the show to the food and the quality of the service, was of the highest standard. Believe me, there were other places you felt lucky to get out of alive."

Big performers, such as Ellington and Calloway, looked back with affection at their times at the Cotton Club. After the show, Ellington would linger until breakfast, playing cards with Big Frenchy, who always came to life when he had a deck in his hands.

Louis Sobol was one of many newspapermen, along with gossip columnist Walter Winchell, who dropped in at the club to pick up tidbits. Sobol, like Frenchy, was an avid player of pinochle—a card game rather like bezique that had been invented in America thirty years previously.

"They were serious battles," he recalled in his memoirs, "and Frenchy would get apoplectic when he lost, though the stakes were minimal. But once the session was over, he became a good-natured host and it was difficult to conceive that this big, burly man had been on the Public Enemy roster."

Frenchy had mellowed a lot under Owney's influence and improved his manners in order to fit in with the Cotton Club's exclusive image. He had a big heart but, despite attempts to polish his social demeanor, could do little to disguise his appearance. Big Frenchy was a bull of a man, with a pock-marked face, broken nose, and bullet eyes set deep beneath thick, black brows. Trapped in a tight-collared evening suit, with his hair gelled and parted into uncontrollable tufts, he seldom looked comfortable. Most nights he could be found with Owney, sitting at their favorite table at the back of the club. From this vantage point, they could observe the flow of business, take in the show, and receive visitors.

Curiously, once Owney became established in bootlegging, he never drank. He remained a teetotaler for the rest of his life. On social occasions, the only bottle to be found in front of him held Mountain Valley water, which was bottled in Hot Springs. Similarly, when he branched into gambling after Prohibition, he was never known to lay a bet. His lifestyle, despite an inclination to generosity, remained simple to the point of frugality, and he chose his tiny circle of friends with caution.

When the Cotton Club became hot and raucous toward the middle of the evening, he would go up onto the roof in the cool air and listen to his prize pigeons cooing in the loft he had built there. One of the few privileged visitors invited up to admire them was a dazzling, dark-eyed young songwriter named Dorothy Fields. She was slim with bobbed hair and extremely feminine, but with an air of innocence that worried her comedian father, Lew Fields. When Dorothy was offered a job writing lyrics for the Cotton Club floor shows, Lew Fields took Owney aside and expressed his concern about her working in a nightclub. Owney put the word around to his managers. Dorothy recalled later: "The owners were very solicitous of me. They grew furious when anyone used improper language in my presence."

Dorothy's pride in the work she had put into her opening show turned to hot embarrassment on the first night. The Cotton Club had a reputation for producing risqué cabaret. Unknown to Dorothy, one of the singers had spiced up the lyrics of her opening number, thinking it would go down better with the audience. For her big celebrity premiere, which opened on Sunday evening, the young songwriter had invited her parents and columnist Walter Winchell to sit at the front tables. When the singer launched into the number, which was laced with innuendo, Dorothy blushed tearfully and explained to her outraged father that she had nothing to do with it. Lew Fields stormed over to Owney's table where he was sitting with Frenchy and complained bitterly. The Duke stepped up on stage and saved Dorothy's tender reputation by publicly announcing that she was not responsible for the lyrics. Owney's solicitude gave Dorothy the confidence to continue writing more beautiful songs. One of her most memorable was "I Can't Give You Anything But Love," a song said to have been inspired after listening to a pair of down-and-out young lovers as they gazed longingly into the window of Tiffany's, the elegant department store. She also wrote the classic song "The Way You Look Tonight." Later, she and her brother Herbert wrote the Broadway musical, "Annie Get Your Gun."

Walter Winchell, her father's dinner partner that night, was one of the most powerful and influential columnists in America. He was feared despite the fact that he seldom got his facts right and perhaps because of it. Winchell enjoyed being a celebrity and loved the sycophantic respect paid to him by performers and their agents. He also regarded himself as gangland's self-appointed public relations man. Mobsters were, after all, as famous as movie stars, but Winchell had a disturbing weakness for those who moved in such precarious circles as organized crime. His ego was, at times, greater than his sense of self-preservation. He believed that underworld figures were fair game for gossip columns and the big names were flattered by his attention. It was all harmless trivia, largely concocted in fashionable clubs over bootleg whisky, but a dangerous game nonetheless.

Broadway, the Great White Way, reached up through Manhattan like a multi-colored ribbon to the so-called "Mason-Dixon Line" of 110th Street on the edge of Harlem where it then became the Great Black Way—a grid of streets and avenues pulsating with jazz, cuisine, and culture. The 1920s was an era when Manhattan hitched up its skirts and abandoned itself to the wholesome madness of the Jazz Age. To underworld figures, who enjoyed the celebrity status afforded them for supplying New York with booze, Broadway meant glitter and lots of girls. In the clubs and shows playing nightly along the strip it became fashionable for gangsters and glamorous showgirls to be seen in each other's company.

The Lords of Broadway, searching for new investments for the enormous fortunes made from bootlegging, became the unlikeliest of "angels." They began backing new productions and showing up at rehearsals to ogle the show girls as they went through their paces. Underworld involvement in Broadway became so widespread that, at one time, it was unlikely that any girl without gangster connections could find work in the theater. Waxey Gordon, New Jersey bootleg baron and hotel owner, highlighted this bizarre situation when he backed two shows, "Strike Me

Pink" and "Forward March." Waxey liked to spend an hour in the mornings with his chums, reclining in the orchestra seats and watching the girls at rehearsal.

According to one report, "Waxey noticed a particularly strapping wench in the chorus, tossing her legs with healthy abandon.

"'Who's gal is that?' he asked the director.

"'She ain't nobody's gal,' was the answer.

"In view of all the requests that had been made on him by the gang to put their molls on the company payroll, Waxey was startled.

"'If she's nobody's girl,' he said, 'how in hell did she get in the show?'"

Waxey was later to make his name as the first gangster to fall before the might of a powerful new prosecuting machine, poised to cut a swath through the underworld. But, for the moment, the Twenties roared on with the momentum of an endless party, and there was little to worry about apart from how to dispose of the profits. A popular place to spend money was in a string of clubs along Broadway owned by a boisterous blonde woman named Texas Guinan and her silent backer, Owney Madden.

Owney's network of nightclubs had grown to become the biggest and most prestigious in New York but, despite paying for the right political protection, there still was no guarantee that some errant judge would not impose a padlock order for peddling illicit booze. Closures became so routine as to be almost tedious but seldom affected the smooth operation of his empire. Some clubs even went to the length of installing up to a dozen doors, all with different address numbers. When an order to padlock one door was carried out, patrons simply used one of the others. Tammany Hall's worst administrative slip-up occurred when someone made a mistake and blinked, and the Cotton Club was put out of business for three months. Club closures were so commonplace at this time that the *New York Times* afforded the story only a couple of paragraphs in 1925:

Dry padlocks Snapped on Nine West Doors;
Owney Madden's Club is One of Them

"Owney Madden, a notorious gangster and gunman, who was paroled from Sing Sing in 1923 after serving seven years for manslaughter, turned up again yesterday in a liquor case. He was named in the Federal Court as secretary of the Cotton Club at 644 Lennox Avenue, between West 142nd and 143rd Streets, which Judge Francis A. Winslow padlocked yesterday for three months.

"Frederick C. Bellinger, Assistant United States Attorney, said that there had been forty complaints of violations of the Volstead law against the place. The prosecutor pointed out Madden's record to the Court, and said that Sam Sellis, president of the 'club,' had been arrested many times, especially for picking pockets. Madden and Sellis both told Judge Winslow that they had tried to 'make good' since their last prison sentences..."

Clubs could avoid padlocking by putting up a $1,000 bond against future good behavior, but most just took a chance and soldiered on. Texas Guinan's clubs had been closed so many times that she wore a necklace of gold padlocks and sported a miniature gold police whistle on her rattling charm bracelet. On one of her many rides to the local precinct house, an admiring officer had presented her with his own police whistle which she adopted as her trademark. Whenever business flagged and the drinks were not moving quickly enough, Texas would stride onto the dance floor and give an ear-splitting blast. "Come on, suckers," she would shout. "Open up and spend some jack." At the signal, cheering patrons would obligingly dig into their wallets.

She was the undisputed Queen of the Nightclubs. "If Mayor Jimmy Walker runs the city by day, Texas Guinan runs it by night," one newspaper said of her. Owney and Texas were close friends and, in many ways, the perfect business partners. Like Big Frenchy, she had a burning urge to be up in front, haranguing the patrons and granting audiences with more verve than DeMange could ever muster. Owney was content to take a back seat and loved her company, as well as that of her elderly

father, who hung around the tables. Owney enjoyed business partnerships with women, especially those of strong character and spirit, and
was content to let them take the helm.

Guinan's showgirls had a theme song which always brought loud
applause and whistles from the audience:

> "The judge says, 'Tex, do you sell booze?'
> I said, 'Please, don't be silly.
> I swear to you my cellar's filled
> with chocolate and vanilly.'"

The girls were all chosen for their startling good looks but were carefully chaperoned. Fraternizing with customers was strictly forbidden, and
any drunken patron who tried to pull a passing girl onto his lap ran the
risk of being thrown out onto the sidewalk, after paying his bill, of course.
Nights at Guinan's clubs, such as the Three Hundred, were noisy, raucous
affairs, with many famous faces often to be seen at the tables.

"The first number is called 'Cherries,'" Allen Churchill wrote. "A
group of almost naked girls prance out from backstage to group themselves on the big dance floor. One carries a basket of fruit. She starts
singing a song called 'Cherries' and two things immediately become apparent. One is the zany aspect of the Three Hundred Club for, as the
girls sing, the waiters begin to yell 'Cherries' in time to the music. So,
shortly, does the audience, until it is all wild, fetching, and very, very
funny. The other notable aspect is the extreme youth of the girls...There
is a vague sinfulness about such dewy-eyed innocence in a nightclub.
Ruby Keeler, for instance, who does a tap dance at Guinan's clubs, was
only fourteen when she began. At seventeen, she married Al Jolson (a
movie star whose earnings in 1927 were $350,000) to create one of the
great lullabies of Broadway."

The man responsible for the floor shows was Nils T. Granlund who,
after surviving a kidnap attempt by gangster Vinny Coll, lived to see four
of his employers gunned down in gang wars. He believed in quick-fire

entertainment with a sledgehammer approach designed to permeate even the most drunken patron. Owney, at this time, was fond of lending a helping hand to up-and-coming young entertainers, many of whom always remembered his paternal assistance. Any opportunity to pull strings for his childhood pal, George Raft, was seldom overlooked and work was always available for him in the Guinan clubs.

George often followed the Cherry dancers or a procession of torch singers, adagio teams, or boy-and-girl dancers. According to Churchill: "Among the last is a slick-haired jellybean doing a whirlwind Charleston. It is such a spectacular dance that columnist Mark Hellinger has been moved to call it 'the weirdest, maddest dance that anyone has ever seen.' The customers sit in silence as he fixes his eyes on one spot and whirls. Faster. Faster. It is fascinating—almost uncanny.

"The whirling dancer finishes, panting proudly and Tex shouts, 'Give the little guy a great big hand.' Next, she tells the room that the young dancer, who looks like a callous Valentino, is George Raft. The ambitious Raft works hard these days and makes a neat one thousand dollars a week as a result. After doing his dance at the Three Hundred Club, he dashes up the street to Tommy Guinan's Playground Club, where he does it again. After which, he races to the Parody or Silver Slipper and does it there, too. Weary, but still ambitious, he hastens back to the Three Hundred in time for the second show. Such heroic activity, it has been noted, gave him scant time to return the affections of a sixteen-year-old Guinan kid named Hannah Williams, who later married famous boxer Jack Dempsey, and was the inspiration for the song, 'Hard-Hearted Hannah, the Vamp of Savannah.' At the Three Hundred Club, Hannah worships George Raft from afar and, as in a thousand backstage movies, watches adoringly as he dances. 'You work too hard, Georgie,' she tells him when he finishes, but the preoccupied Raft pays no attention, only rushes off to his next appearance."

George's transport on these hectic evenings was Owney's high-speed Packard. In exchange for the use of it, he toured Broadway between performances, collecting box office receipts from shows in which Owney had investments. The arrangement suited them both—Owney because he trusted George implicitly and Raft because he enjoyed the heady atmosphere of Broadway theaters and their stylish stars. George became a familiar face along the Great White Way and, as he usually went about Owney's business between club spots, he gained a reputation for being the sharpest dresser in town.

One of his favorite styles—a black shirt with a white tie and a grey fedora pulled low over one eye—was borrowed from Owney. Others he absorbed with a constantly roving eye for new fashion trends. "Come wintertime, he'd either be in a black form-fitted coat with a velvet collar or a sporty brown camel wrap-around," fight manager Maxie Greenberg noted. "He wore fifty-buck shoes with pointy toes, shined so bright you could see your face in them." George and Owney shared a similar taste in clothes. Madden had a preference for hand-tailored, double-breasted suits with wide lapels and gleaming shoes. In summer, his fedora would be replaced by a smart straw hat which he wore with everything. Only after his exile to Hot Springs did he hang up his smart wardrobe and adopt a vest and woolen cap. "Sometimes," said his friend, Q. Byrum Hurst, "his wife Agnes would get him to wear a suit, but she would have to nag, nag before he would change."

One of Raft's regular Broadway ports-of-call in April 1926 was Daly's Theater where he collected the takings from an outrageous play by Janet Mast called "Sex." Mast was a pseudonym for its leading lady, Mae West, with whom Owney had a long-running, though not exclusive, relationship. George would often drop by her dressing room to chat, and Mae took a liking to him. Later, they appeared together in the 1932 Hollywood movie *Night After Night*. ("She stole everything but the cameras," he remarked admiringly.) For the moment, however, George was not yet ready for acting. "I liked his style and dark good looks," Mae said, "and I wanted to use him in *Sex*. But, somehow he seemed nervous and felt he couldn't do any serious acting."

Owney had known Mae years before she hit big-time Broadway. Among his many property ventures, he ran the Harding Hotel on 54th Street—next to Texas Guinan's club—in partnership with Mae's tough-minded German mother, Tilly. Legs Diamond and boxer Kid Berg were among the many residents. Battling Jack, Mae's Irish father, ran a private detective agency and was a well-loved figure among both police and the underworld. Mae loved Owney's quiet English manners. She was intensely proud of a coat-of-arms which traced a branch of the family back to Long Crendon, Buckinghamshire, and also treasured a slim volume of family history. She was fond of reading the preface aloud to visitors: "The Wests were an ancient family of knightly rank connected by ties of marriage and descent with royal lineages, and other families of peerage, and among the landed gentry of the oldest type throughout the kingdom."

Owney's attraction for her, however, was not as that of a knight in shining armor but as the toughest man she had ever met. Mae was very physically minded, with a penchant for muscle men, but Owney had a certain style which placed him apart from the other gangsters of her acquaintance.

She kept their affair secret for most of her life and never referred to it in her autobiography since her memories for Owney evoked deep emotions. Kevin Thomas, the Los Angeles Times film critic and a personal friend of Mae for many years, believes "there was no doubt that it was a hot affair." Throughout their lives, they always retained a great affection for each other. Owney, even in old age, would never discuss Mae. If friends tried to ask about her in a relaxed moment, he would simply throw back his head and roar with delight at their inquisitiveness.

It was many years, shortly before her death in 1980, before Mae mentioned Owney. After unveiling an image of herself at a Los Angeles wax museum, she left for dinner with some old friends, including Thomas and the actor Rock Hudson. As they sat around the table, their talk drifted back to the old days and some of the celebrated characters around at the time. Also at the table was Jack La Rue, one of Mae's leading men in Diamond Lil, a show in which Owney had a fifty percent stake.

His presence probably led her to remark, out of the blue: "Do you re-member a lot of talk about the blonde Owney Madden was backing in a Broadway show? Well, that blonde was me."

"That evening," said Kevin Thomas, "and on many other occasions, Mae referred to Madden in a way that suggested the Cotton Club owner had something more than a monetary interest in her and that she recip-rocated the attention."

Owney first met Mae when she moved into her mother's hotel, and it was soon clear to everyone that there was a strong chemistry between them. Among the hotel guests was Allan Dwan, the pioneer film direc-tor, who died in 1981. When Madden was away on business, she talked about him incessantly, sometimes referring to him affectionately as the "clay pigeon" because of the number of times he had been shot. Mae was a girl who was easily impressed, but she had never met anyone quite like her soft-spoken tough guy.

"He musta' taken twenty-six bullets," she told Dwan. "Every couple of months, he'd have to go to the hospital and have another one dug out."

When she took her shows on tour, Owney made sure that she was amply looked after wherever she appeared. Word of her arrival was al-ways sent ahead so that a suitable reception could be prepared. Whenever she played Chicago, she told Kevin Thomas, Al Capone and his boys always turned out and decorated her dressing room with flowers. In Detroit, it was the same with the Purple Gang. "They always behaved like perfect gentlemen," said Mae proudly. "They all knew I was Owney's girl."

Mae was later to repay his attention by hiding him in her Hollywood apartment when he was wanted for questioning. It was clear that the flame between them never completely died. Many years later, in 1949, Owney risked the legal complications of leaving Hot Springs to see her in a touring revival of *Diamond Lil*, which rekindled memories of their time together. The show's stage manager was Herbert Kenwith, later a Los Angeles TV director, who recalled their reunion:

"I think it was in St. Louis," he said. "There were always small knots of people waiting to see Mae after the show. She was very kind about meeting everybody, but always wanted them announced.

"This man started in, and I said: 'You can't just go in like that. You have to be announced.'

"'But she knows me.'

"'You still have to be announced,' I insisted.

"When he said, 'tell her it's Owney Madden,' I blurted out, 'Owney Madden—aren't you the gangster?'

"I was so embarrassed—I was barely out of my teens—I don't remember what he said, but I remember he smiled and seemed amused, and I took him in to Mae.

"They started in right away talking about all those bullets, and then I left to give them some privacy. He was formally dressed. As I recall, he had rather a full face and wasn't terribly tall. He was very pleasant and had a very pleasant voice, too. Mae said he was one of the few gangsters she knew who truly was a gentleman—and she knew them all."

Owney's stake in *Diamond Lil* stemmed from the runaway success of *Sex*, the first show Mae wrote herself. It had an inauspicious opening night when the curtain rose in New London, Connecticut. Only eighty-five seats in the auditorium were filled. The play Mae had agonized over, writing dialogue on scraps of note paper and the backs of envelopes, seemed doomed to failure. She had created the starring role for herself—Margie Lamont, a Montreal hooker who followed the British fleet from port to port only to fall victim to a suave blackmailer. The tart with the heart of gold was the perfect vehicle for her natural aptitude for comedy. With a title sensational even for the Roaring Twenties, she had been convinced the show would be a huge success. After the first performance, the producer was so discouraged that he offered to pay the theater management to use the stage for rehearsals in order to cut their losses. Fortunately for Mae, a lot of money had been spent on advertising and the management refused. She gritted her teeth and hoped that something would turn up.

By matinee time of the next day it did. Unknown to Mae, the fleet had arrived in town and hundreds of sailors, lured no doubt by the title, were already queuing around the block to see the show as she made her way to her dressing room. Was it simply coincidence? Mae West's biographer, Fergus Cashin, noted that she naively thanked the Navy for saving the day, but there is every certainty that Owney had telephoned to inquire how the first night of his new investment had done.

Cashin is convinced that Madden "papered the house with paying customers," as he is reputed to have done on opening night on Broadway. According to her memoirs, Mae always believed that she became "a star in the legitimate theater" when Walter Winchell first mentioned her in his column. Who put him up to it is not recorded. Owney came to the rescue a second time in New London when some locals made powerful protests about the nature of the show. He introduced Mae to his lawyer, Joe Shalleck, and instructed him to iron out the difficulties with the city authorities.

Sex ended up being one of the great Broadway success stories, billed in the *New York Times* as "The Biggest Sensation Since the Armistice." After a month, receipts were running at $14,000 a week and, after two months, had risen to $16,500. By the end of an eleven-month run, Mae was slipping risqué ad-libs into her nightly performance to relieve the boredom. Eventually, they reached the attention of City Hall and police officers were dispatched to watch the show. As a result, she was charged with obscenity in a prosecution brought by acting mayor Joseph "Holy Joe" McKee, while New York's fun-loving mayor Jimmy Walker was on vacation in Cuba.

"For her court appearances, Mae changed costumes daily, favoring a variety of black satin numbers—some with georgette tops and satin lapels, others with bugle heads—modish, fur-trimmed, wrap-around coats and cloche hats or turbans," biographers George Eells and Stanley Musgrove reported.

The outcome of the case was a $500 fine and eight days in Welfare Island Reformatory. Mae, true to form, made the most of it by writing an "inside" story for *Liberty* magazine.

Her short incarceration was cushioned by the familiar touch of Owney's Tammany Hall connections. The warden allowed her to wear silk underwear instead of the regulation cotton. She was given a private cell and allowed to go horseback riding in the evenings. The story made headline news and established her Broadway reputation. As Mae herself was fond of saying: "I used to be Snow White, but I drifted."

Madden with his gang, the Gophers, and a flock of pigeons on a New York rooftop. (Madden is on the back row, fourth from left.)

Madden was captured here by a studio photographer during one of his trips to Hollywood to see Mae West.

Film star Mae West, whose career was bankrolled by Madden, said he was "so sweet yet so vicious."

Madden (second from left) sitting on the beach at Atlantic City with his lifelong pal George Raft (third from left) and boxers Maxie Rosenbloom (far left) and Kid Francis (far right, front).

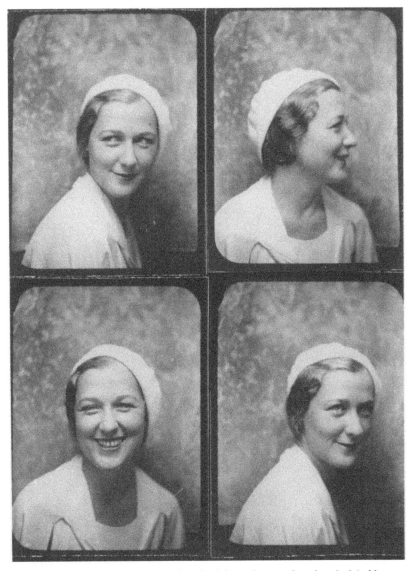

Agnes Demby, the postmaster's daughter, had these photographs taken for Madden soon after they met in Hot Springs, Arkansas.

The Duke of the West Side, Madden, with Agnes Demby, the woman who stole his heart.

7.

Phoenix Rising

Owney had ambitions to boost his bootleg activities by making huge financial investments. His first aim was to get a slice of the sea-going smuggling business and, secondly, to cover all his options by moving into liquor manufacture and brewing.

By the mid-1920s, Owney was one of three figures who dominated the import of booze through what smugglers called Rum Row—a stretch of the Eastern seaboard which had rapidly extended from Florida up to the farthest reaches of Maine. The other two were Frank Costello and Big Bill Dwyer. The U.S. Coast Guard, hopelessly outmaneuvered, advertised for new recruits on billboards all over New York: MEN OF ACTION REQUIRED WHO LIKE ADVENTURE. A CHANCE FOR ADVANCEMENT—ONE YEAR ENLISTMENT. Men of such caliber were hard to find. Costello, Dwyer, and Madden had already recruited most of them.

A lawyer once noted, in all seriousness, that some of the greatest sea battles in history took place off the Eastern seaboard in the 1920s. Risks were high but the incentive was great. Only one boatload in five needed to offload safely in order for these three bootleggers to break even. They operated side by side in a loose partnership and were all formidable strategists.

Journalist Henry Lee recalled their ingenuity:

"One of the most notable examples was the British schooner *Rosie M.B.*," he wrote. "When she was caught off Montauk Point, Long Island, raiders found a $300,000 cargo and a dozen hollow steel torpedoes each carrying about forty gallons of liquor. These were to be fired from Rum Row, then picked up and dragged underwater by small craft, according to the story. Even submarines were pressed into action against sea-going forces. Operating off Cape Cod, a big U-boat of the commercial grade was known to have flooded the Cape area with deliveries of wine, ale, and beer. And this wasn't a journalistic 'pipe.' The Feds themselves said so."

The bootleggers used fast sea-going vessels which could outrun anything in the Coast Guard fleet. Among their investments were surplus U.S. Navy submarine chasers and torpedo boats, laden with booze. Even the most unlikely craft were pressed into service. The Coast Guard once pulled alongside a slow-moving New York City garbage scow and uncovered $90,000 worth of liquor. The twenty-one crew members atop this "floating garbage" were all arrested.

Madden, Costello, and Dwyer, unlike the vast majority of New York's trigger-happy hoods, had the common bond of being astute businessmen who enjoyed the shifting challenges of the bootleg market. Costello had honed the rum-running business to an exact science by the time Owney was investing in his own private navy. Freighters pitched and tossed through heavy seas with tough-looking men in overcoats and fedoras standing on the bridge alongside the captain. Hijacks were as common on the high seas as on land, and anyone who tried to board Frank's vessels with grappling irons was met by a hail of machine-gun fire.

His business strength lay in the fact that he learned quickly from each setback, changing his methods with quite amazing rapidity to fit the circumstances. According to his attorney, he appeared at one time to have bribed most of the U.S. Coast Guard. He would pay one man who then would make an offer to the man next up on the ladder of seniority. This went on up to the highest level. Coast Guardsmen loyal to Frank directed his shipments to safe landfalls and even helped unload them. "Everyone gets his share," was Uncle Frank's motto. When one of his ships hit an iceberg and sank with a valuable cargo of spirits, he observed wryly: "Too bad we can't buy the icebergs."

One of the rum-runner's biggest enemies was a teetotaling, incorruptible Coast Guard skipper named Commander Thomas Backer, the scourge of Eastern seaboard smugglers. Backer commanded a powerful destroyer which had awesome firepower. He had no qualms about blowing "rummies" right out of the water.

All of Frank's crews were hand-picked and in constant touch with a string of radio stations he had established along the coast. These were linked directly to his New York headquarters at 405 Lexington Avenue. This nerve center, incidentally, was a tribute to his administrative genius. "Let me point out that Frank's operation," George Wolf recalled, "was organized exactly like a corporation, with departments and staff for all phases of the business.

"There was a traffic department, a distribution department, a corruption department to handle bribery, a defense department employing gunmen to cope with rivals, and even an intelligence department to keep an eye on what Prohibition agencies were doing." Frank later added his own wire-tapping department, manned by electronics experts, to bug government offices. He ran, in effect, his own FBI.

Commander Backer had little notion of what he was really up against on the misty morning he gave the order to pursue Costello's rum-runner, the *Elise*. The destroyer put a shot across its bow and instructed it to hove-to. When the *Elise* ignored the warning, Backer ordered a "full speed ahead." Through his binoculars, he could clearly see the liquor stacked on deck, ready for unloading, and a man on the bridge distinctly thumbing his nose at the destroyer. The incensed commander shouted to his gun crews to put a shot through the bows but, even as they were taking aim, there was a deafening roar.

A seaplane from Costello's private air force was skimming the water alongside the destroyer, about ten yards from its deck rail. Behind it billowed an impenetrable cloud of black smoke, emitted from special canisters fitted under the wings. By the time the dense smoke cleared, the *Elise* was astern of the destroyer. Then, as Backer swung to starboard to blast it from the water, to his absolute astonishment, a submarine surfaced fifty yards away. Seconds later, there was an explosion and all engines stopped. Someone had blown off the destroyer's twin screws.

All this duly emerged, to Backer's embarrassment, at a federal inquiry. The punch line, which Frank later confessed to his lawyer, was that the commander had sent an urgent radio message for assistance. Back came the reply: "Pull yourself together. Positively no submarines in your vicinity. Positively no aircraft in your area. What's the commotion? Full report required when you return to base." What the commander did not realize was that no messages were either sent or received. Even the radio operator on the destroyer was one of Frank's men.

Although Owney had begun his bootlegging enterprises by hijacking Big Bill Dwyer's trucks, the two decided to team up later to import whisky from Britain and rum from the West Indies. Two whisky brands began to flood New York—House of Lords and King's Ransom—imported directly from the distiller, J.C. Turney & Sons of Leith, Scotland. According to Turney's board minutes, Costello imported so much of their whisky during Prohibition that, as a gesture of thanks, he was appointed their United States sales consultant on an annual salary of $5,000. His function, according to the company, was to visit New York outlets to inquire if they stocked the two brands. "And," as one reporter waggishly added, "heaven help them if they didn't."

King's Ransom, in those days, was the world's most expensive twelve-year-old whisky. It had a raffish, roguish history which would have appealed to Owney and Frank. It was perhaps not by chance that, in shipping the aristocrat of scotches and its eight-year-old stablemate, House of Lords, the bootleg barons teamed up with an equally adventurous distiller. William Whiteley, who created the brands, was a fearless Scottish entrepreneur with a healthy contempt for bureaucracy. He hit on the name House of Lords because he considered it had the right image for the blend on which he had lavished so many years. Whiteley's idea of obtaining official approval for the name was to travel to London in the early 1920s and persuade a superintendent at the House of Lords to sign a "letter of authority." Legend has it that £500 changed hands, and the employee, when found out, was hastily dismissed. Their Lordships still have inches of correspondence on the subject.

"Whiteley was asked to refrain from using the name," said Paul Hick, export marketing manager of the House of Campbell, which produced the two blends. "He totally ignored them and sold the whisky in 94 countries around the world, except the UK where it was banned. William Whiteley loved to invite his overseas agents to London. He would take them down the Thames, opposite the Palace of Westminster, where, by remarkable coincidence, a barge loaded with crates labeled 'House of Lords' would chug into view. Whiteley would remark in an offhand way that this was merely the Palace's regular weekly supply. As he gently turned his visitors around to take them for lunch, the barge would execute a u-turn and return to the warehouse."

During Prohibition, New Yorkers knew King's Ransom as the "Round the World Scotch." Whiteley spent many years trying to create the perfect blend. Once all the constituent malt and grain whiskies were blended, he offered casks to shipping companies as free ballast so that the gentle rocking would assist the "marrying" process. Thus, he was able to confidently boast that every drop had been around the world, while also saving him a considerable sum in warehousing costs.

No financial records exist of Owney's partnership with Dwyer. Big Bill was notorious for failing to record business transactions. The year he joined forces with Owney, he owed the authorities $800,000 in unpaid taxes. The Duke, for his part, also preferred to commit as little as possible to paper. Their lawyer, Joe Shalleck, privately estimated their expenses in wages, bribes, shipping, storage, and distribution at $10,000 a day. They commandeered ships big and small—new ones as well as those rescued from the junkyard—to ferry their whisky from freighters waiting at anchor beyond the twelve-mile limit. Many were proud of their tough image. One European schooner proudly carried its name on a plaque on the bulkhead: SS *Newton Bay, Rum Runner, Rum Row.*

For some crew members, the temptation of carrying such an appealing cargo proved too much and, from time to time, remaining sober was a problem. Owney, mild-mannered and of a quiet disposition, lost his temper when he was given news of one of his schooners, the *Allegro.* It appeared that the entire crew, hopelessly drunk on William Whiteley's twelve-year-old scotch, became incapable of navigation. The *Allegro* drifted across the path of a Coast Guard vessel, which promptly impounded its $120,000 cargo and threw the crew into jail in Philadelphia.

Unknown to most of the Coast Guard Service, the Madden-Dwyer booze ships running the gauntlet on Rum Row had not freshly arrived from Europe or the West Indies. They came from the inhospitable, wind-blasted island of St. Pierre in the Miquelon group, way beyond anyone's territorial waters in the North Atlantic off Newfoundland. The remote community of three hundred people had been transformed into a boom town by Frank Costello. In 1921, he had written to the mayor and made an epic voyage there, wrapped in his tailored overcoat, on the bridge of a rusty freighter. He arranged with the mayor to have all his imported liquor stored on the island for a commission of two dollars per case. By the time two million cases—most of it King's Ransom—had been off-loaded on the lonely outcrop, the residents of St. Pierre were very wealthy people indeed.

Frank applied himself to the task with characteristic efficiency. "The men who came in those ships were rough customers," George Wolf recalled. "Grey fedoras instead of sea caps (the fedoras usually held with both hands in the icy North Atlantic winds), shaky sea legs happy to hit shore, guns in holsters, and very business-like actions when they started to work. Warehouses had to be built, piers strengthened, loading equipment brought in, and workers ferried to the island."

Soon, Owney Madden and Bill Dwyer's ships were moored alongside Uncle Frank's navy—a motley collection of coasters, schooners, ex-service vessels, yawls, and tramp steamers. "If you were to believe the figures," the *Herald Tribune* reported, "a scandalous drinking problem had broken out in all the British and French possessions surrounding us.

"In the five-year period ending in 1929, Canada gravely reported that declared exports of its whisky to the British West Indies had more than doubled and those to British Honduras more than tripled. But, the ninety-three-square-mile French isles of St. Pierre and Miquelon were the worst problem. Canadian whisky exports to these barren crags almost quadrupled. In just one year, of the more than 4,800,000 Canadian gallons declared for export to all places, more than 1,000,000 were marked for these truly tight little isles."

While Costello and Dwyer involved themselves more heavily in bulk imports, Owney assumed control on dry land. By 1925, there was no aspect of bootlegging in which he did not have a major interest. He dominated illicit beer brewing and ran the cream of the big nightclubs as outlets for his beverages. He even operated a laundry racket, washing table linen under contract from all the other clubs in New York. Initially, the business provided an ideal cover for transporting King's Ransom and House of Lords in laundry baskets to speakeasies all over the city. Door-to-door deliveries could easily be made without attracting any attention. As a respectable business venture, however, he considered it to be the worst mistake he had ever made.

After buying up three laundry chains across the city for more than a quarter of a million dollars, he found that they demanded more of his time than he realized. Despite a $2,000,000 turnover, the business returned only modest profits. Against his enormous margin from bootlegging, it seemed a disaster.

"I'd like to get out of it," he told a friend in dismay. "I like an investment where you can put your money in this week, and pull it out double next week, or the next. But these legitimate rackets—you have to wait for your money."

The philosophy of the businessman and gangster has seldom been summed up so succinctly. It has been estimated that not even his closest friends, such as Bill Dwyer and Frenchy DeMange, could have made a list of all the enterprises in which Owney had interests. While racketeers tended to specialize in fields which they knew well and had experience in, Owney had interests, big and small, in almost every possible aspect of New York life. Even clubs with which he had no connection came to him for advice on decor or ways to increase their business. He always gave a straight opinion and kept confidences. He was never known to gossip or have wild nights out on the town.

Owney's whole life revolved around improving and perfecting his business interests. Outside that, his time was devoted only to pigeons. However, those who knew him could not help but notice that his closest women friends—speakeasy queen Texas Guinan and sex goddess Mae West—were the most sensational girls in town. Owney's huge, maroon, bulletproof Duesenberg, a personal gift from Cuban president Fulgencio Batista, was often seen outside their apartments. Despite his hard reputation, he always visibly melted in the company of children. When he drove home, kids would run the length of the street shouting, "There's Uncle Owney." It was rare that he did not pause to hand out candy from a bag he always carried in his glove compartment.

In the Roaring Twenties, he became synonymous with the Jazz Age. Around New York, he was regarded as a multimillionaire in the great American tradition of hard work and business flair. The fact that it was achieved largely through bootlegging served only to enhance his popularity in an era when millions of people flouted the unpopular law. It has been said that he was the only gangster who fulfilled everyone's image of a gangster. He was lean, good-looking, tough, and always well-dressed in the way that George Raft and the rest of the movie industry were to portray mobsters for years to come. Alongside Owney, the overweight boys bursting out of their collars were little more than thugs in fancy dress. "If Hollywood has been looking for the perfect gangster," a reporter once said, "they would have hesitated about Owney Madden. He just looked too good to be true."

George Raft's lifelong association with gangsters finally caught up with him when his social life began to attract the attention of the authorities. George, like Owney, was conditioned by the world in which he grew up and he never apologized for his friends.

"If you were an entertainer on Broadway in those days you would have to be blind and lame not to associate with gangsters," he would say. "Look, they owned the clubs. That's where the work was. Besides, all of those people—including Owney, Larry Fay, Frenchy, people like that—were looked up to by everyone. Christ, Owney ran New York in those days. They had a kind of glamour about them. They were more important in those days than a Jimmy Durante, Milton Berle, Ruby Keeler, Ted Lewis, George Jessel, and others who worked the clubs. Maybe I got into some things at times a little over my head. But, in those days, the things I did weren't that unusual. Liquor and speakeasies were big business. Everybody drank, even though it was illegal."

Owney protected his business interests by drawing up strict territorial agreements with other gangland figures. These were typed contracts, signed by all parties, to which he insisted they adhere. Only Dutch Schultz gave him any real trouble, arguing over an agreement until Owney was forced to put him in his place.

When someone once asked him how he justified his rackets, he replied with heavy cynicism: "What's the matter with rackets? They're a real benefit to the small tradesman. Take laundries, for instance. Why, I'll bet all the tea in China that half the little guys in the business would be starving to death if it wasn't for the racket. They get protection from independents. If someone opens a laundry where he isn't wanted, the boys tell him to get the hell out of the neighborhood. And they see that he does. You've got the rackets all wrong. They are a genuine benefit to people."

The Madden bootleg empire was always busy, working around the clock at a frenetic pace to slake the thirst of dry New Yorkers. To operate smoothly, Owney had to have trusted lieutenants and helpers he could depend upon implicitly. Raft, through his long association with Owney, was an obvious choice. Owney, as always, enjoyed an opportunity to give him a helping hand.

George's "getting into things a little over his head" included riding shotgun on Owney's booze convoys which rumbled through the empty back streets of New York under cover of darkness. Before Raft was assigned to active service, the Duke ensured that he first serve a suitable apprenticeship. He sent for one of his best drivers and gunmen, "Feets" Edson, and told him to give "the kid" a few lessons. Edson, a man of deadpan expression and a veteran of ferocious gun battles in the course of protecting Owney's liquor, took his teaching role seriously. "Feets" held the view that, if George was going to work alongside him, then showing him everything he knew might prove to be a life-saver.

He arrived in a big, black Packard and drove George uptown to a quiet spot near Bloomingdale's Department Store where he parked under the 3rd Avenue El—the elevated railroad which snaked through the East Side on steel pillars. The Packard was a beast of an automobile, favored by gangsters both for its power and its seating capacity. They were notoriously heavy on steering and appalling on corners, but they had an impressive rate of speed when necessary. In the right hands, with a little sweat, they could be made to do almost anything.

"Feets" tutored George in the basic elements of the fast getaway—gunning the engine and holding back the car until it leapt forward like a panther on amphetamines. He demonstrated the highly skilled art of rounding a corner on two wheels and how to master a U-turn at high speed. By night, they accelerated down dimly lit streets no wider than alleys. These routes were used by the liquor trucks but also presented ideal spots for an ambush. After sending many a garbage can spinning, George gradually became a master of the technique. The tricks "Feets" taught him did indeed help save his life—not in the dangerous wastelands of the East Side—but in the more comfortable confines of Hollywood.

"Feets" finally gave his student a grunt of approval when George proved that he could drive beneath the El with the car's wheels locked to the trolley rails. Further, he had learned to get around road repair sites and abandoned cars without slackening speed for almost half the length of 3rd Avenue. Few actors could have received such intensive coaching to play future roles.

His main purpose was to drive the Packard either ahead of or behind the booze trucks—driven by men armed with shotguns—and keep a keen eye out for any possible attackers. Men had died with regularity in such deserted back streets, but George appeared to thrive on the adrenalin. Owney liked to move his liquor in the early hours of the morning when neighborhoods were empty and any suspicious rival activity could easily be detected. George, at the time, was working as a dancer in clubs owned by Owney's business associates, Larry Fay and Texas Guinan. Just before dawn, he could finish his act and, still in his tuxedo and tap shoes, climb into the waiting Packard to face the unknown perils of the booze run. Once the convoy reached the limits of Owney's territory, it would then head to a distribution depot, escorted by relief guards working for other bootleggers such as Dutch Schultz.

Some years later, George was playing the role of Joe Fabrini, the tough trucker in the movie, *They Drive By Night*, produced by Mark Hellinger, another old friend of Owney. In one scene, George was behind the wheel of a truck alongside his brother, played by Humphrey Bogart, and Ann Sheridan was cast as his girlfriend. He told this story to biographer Lewis Yablonsky:

"Some people say I got nothing from Owney Madden but a bad reputation—but the driving skill I acquired when I worked for him in New York, years before, undoubtedly saved my life and those in the picture with me. In this scene, Humphrey Bogart, Ann Sheridan, and I are high-balling down a long hill in an old beat-up truck. Halfway down, the brakes really went out—a situation that wasn't in the script. Bogart saw me press the pedal and when nothing happened he began to curse.

"'We're going to get killed,' he yelled.

"Ann screamed and turned her eyes away from the road as I fought the wheel. I couldn't have been more scared myself. The speedometer hit eighty when I saw a break on the right where a bulldozer had started a new road. I pulled hard on the wheel and the truck went bouncing up the embankment. Thank God—it finally stopped.

"Ann was too upset to talk, but Bogart said: 'Thanks, pal,' with definite appreciation.

"'Don't thank me,' I thought to myself, because I didn't have the breath to answer. 'Write a letter to Owney Madden or Feets Edson.'"

New York's seriously undermanned Prohibition Bureau made valiant efforts to uncover the city's large-scale bootlegging operations but made little ground against the corruption that was sweeping the authorities. Between June 1923 and March 1931, the annual graft collected by federal agents and police was conservatively estimated at $59,840,000. Patrolmen on the beat, regardless of their duties, were paid a dollar for every one of the 4,800,000 half-barrels of beer delivered each year to the speakeasies. One of Owney's establishments, near Grand Central Station, paid the sum of $31,200 a year just for the privilege of staying in business. A large proportion of the money was collected on behalf of the political machine. "Speakeasy owners regard the average Prohibition agent as an insatiable grafter," the *New York Herald Tribune* reported. "He has reduced collecting to a science."

Journalist Denis Tilden Lynch painted a picture of the figure with whom New Yorkers were familiar: "Most Prohibition agents live extravagantly, and it is amusing to see one on his day off having a good time. He is usually drunk when he reaches a place where he intends to play the role of a sport, and all at the bar must be his guests. He orders round after round of drinks and, marvelous to relate, pays for them. No one else may buy. Everyone humors him, even those who despise him. There is no choice, for he is a coarse fellow, a gangster, irresponsible... And, he has a revolver."

Owney, despite an income estimated at $3 million, never completely settled into the comfort of executive life. He could often be found taking seemingly enormous risks for a man in his position, hustling new sales in speakeasies and even along the curb from his car. Life on the streets still exerted a strong excitement and appeal.

He was so sure of police protection and the powerful political support of Jimmy Hines that he was once seen selling beer from the steps of the New York Public Library at 42nd Street and 5th Avenue. Owney had a black Cadillac parked at the roadside, curtains pulled tightly around the windows, and loaded with cases of beer. The story was told by the man who made the purchase. It was an undercover Prohibition agent posing as a speakeasy owner. Such was Owney's influence that nothing came of the offense.

To illustrate how widespread corruption had become, the same agent told the *Police Gazette* that even squeaky-clean U.S. Treasury agents were on the take. "When arranging a major raid, he asked the officer in charge of the T-men's New York office how many completely trustworthy men he had. 'Only one,' the official replied. Even that one man turned out to be a shakedown artist."

One unverified story from the period claims that Owney took a wicked delight in walking into speakeasies run by his biggest rivals and asking for a beer. He would hold the glass up to the light before taking a long swig, as though he had been deprived of the pleasure for years. Then, with his face contorting in disgust, he would spit the mouthful on the floor and demand of the bartender:

"Who are you buying this dishwater from?"

When the quaking barman told him Dutch Schultz, which was usually the case, Owney would shake his head and smile gently.

"Well, from now on, you're buying from me."

Schultz was renowned for selling "needle beer," an adulterated brew so unpalatable that patrons drank it only out of desperation. Speakeasy proprietors bought it only out of fear of the consequences. At its worst, it had a distinctly green hue when examined closely.

Owney's beer—"Madden's Number One"—rolled off the line at the rate of 800,000 half-barrels a year, bringing in an annual profit, according to one expert, of $7.4 million. His partners in Manhattan's biggest illegal brewery, the Phenix Cereal Beverage Company, were Big Bill Dwyer and an anonymous Tammany Hall member of Mayor Jim Walker's cabinet. The previous occupant—Clausen and Flanagan Brewery—vacated the sprawling building on 10th Avenue when Prohibition took effect in 1923. The owners could see no legal future for the place and were happy to offload it. In the first few years of Prohibition, former breweries became "cereal beverage plants." They produced "near beer," which was below the legal limit of 0.5% alcohol. Demand proved insufficient to keep these companies in business.

Sean Dennis Cashman's study of Prohibition brewing points out that one large company—Anheuser-Busch—spent $18 million converting its $40 million plant to produce a near-beer called "Bevo," but nobody wanted it. As Will Rogers said: "After drinking a bottle of this near-beer, you have to take a glass of water as a stimulant." Prohibition, for all its good intentions, radically changed American drinking patterns. Bootleggers, who were always searching for new ways to cut their liquor with other substances to make bigger profits, popularized the cocktail. Mint juleps, highballs, and orange blossoms soon became national favorites. Scotch distillers, too, pinpoint the Dry Era as whisky's launchpad into world markets.

Owney's plans for the Phenix were applauded by every New Yorker who remembered good beer. He rightly calculated that speakeasy drinkers were heartily sick of the concoctions masquerading as beer which passed nightly over the counters. On the theory that quality would create its own custom, he set about producing the finest beer in New York, and demand soon outstripped supply. The Phenix, towering above 10th Avenue, emitted mouthwatering smells of malt and hops and was seen as a monument to Madden's power and influence. Through its stone portals, barrels rolled onto delivery trucks while the authorities turned a blind eye. "Madden's Number One" was the pride of the West Side.

It also became a prime target for a group of federal agents who appeared increasingly obsessed with closing it down. Officially, the Phenix still had a Treasury Department permit to produce near-beer. Still, everyone knew that, behind securely locked doors, Owney's brewers were making a highly alcoholic beer with a fine head and a distinctive, almost British, creamy texture. Thanks to the vigilance of the New York City Police, who were protecting the Phenix on Owney's behalf, few of the federal raids were successful. Prohibition agents closed the building and seized trucking equipment on a handful of occasions, but each time, Owney's lawyers obtained court rulings that the raids were illegal.

The missions were led by H. J. Simmons, special agent in charge of the Department of Justice's undercover team—a man who showed unbridled enthusiasm for his work. After watching the Phenix brew illicit beer for nine unhindered years, Simmons felt he had a personal mission to nail Owney. His first raid was instigated on the tip-off of a friend who had been driving down 10th Avenue and had seen fourteen trucks parked between 25th and 26th Streets outside the brewery. Each was loaded to capacity with 120 half-barrels of Madden's Number One. Half an hour later, a convoy of cars, crammed with fifty federal agents, screamed around the corner. The trucks were still there but not a soul was in sight, and the three reinforced steel doors of fortress Phenix remained firmly closed.

"The whole affair became a farce," Thompson and Raymond wrote. "The agents, it seemed, had nothing to offer the court as information on which to base the issuance of a legal search warrant, except their own statements that beer could be smelled in the neighborhood of the brewery. This was not regarded by the jurists on the federal bench as sufficient evidence. And so, on four separate occasions, the agents conducted raids, closed the plant, and seized the trucks. On all four occasions counsel for the brewery went into court and obtained a complete release."

Cheated of convictions, Simmons ordered his men to place the brewery under close surveillance and make themselves ready for raids at a moment's notice. It was war—the kind which Owney, as a strategist, particularly enjoyed—and Special Agent Simmons labored under the disadvantage of not completely knowing who the enemy was. On the first day of surveillance, a car full of plain-clothes special agents picked its way through the back streets toward the brewery and found themselves flagged down by a patrolling policeman.

"What do you fellows think you're doing around here?" he demanded.

It was standard procedure for federal agents not to reveal their identity. When they invented an excuse, the officer told them: "You're violating the traffic laws, don't you know that?"

To avoid arrest, they were forced to show their badges, thereby exposing their cover. The same scene was enacted again and again. When individual agents tried to approach the brewery on foot, they were stopped and asked to prove that they had means to support themselves.

"One agent told an accosting policeman that he was a peaceful, law-abiding citizen, and had a right to walk the streets without hindrance," journalist Denis Tilden Lynch recalled in 1932. "The policeman replied that the undercover man was a suspicious-looking character; that gunmen frequented the neighborhood; and that if he did not give a better account of himself, he would be arrested. By this time, the special agents were fed up with police interference. This one insisted on standing on his rights as an American citizen, only to learn that these rights did not exist in the beery atmosphere of the Phenix. At the station house, the special agent was freed after he showed his shield and other credentials."

Everyone, with the exception of native New Yorkers, seemed astonished at the lengths to which the police went to protect Owney. New York's Finest, of course, were being well paid for their services in an elaborate protection system organized and directly controlled by Tammany Hall leaders. As Frank Costello was fond of saying, "Everybody gets their share."

To his great discomfort, Owney was becoming a celebrity—the savior of a thirsty city—and was feted wherever he went. He was a shy man who loathed publicity and went to great lengths to remain out of the news headlines. Being hailed as a notorious underworld leader, he also believed, was setting himself up in order to be knocked down. There were many ambitious figures of authority looking for just that opportunity. He avoided press photographers but, by word of mouth, became one of the city's great attractions. Millionaires and their ladies made Owney's nightclubs their favorite meeting places. Suddenly, there was something smart and exciting about rubbing shoulders with gangland personalities. "They were thrilled when Owney Madden was pointed out to them," the *New Yorker* reported.

Part of Owney's attraction was that he looked every inch the part. He was clearly an urbane, intelligent man with an accent that charmed everyone he met. To Westsiders, however, he was still simply "the Duke," and the cops, with a little extra in their back pockets, loyally ensured that federal agents were kept from fingering him.

One harassed federal law-enforcement officer told the *Police Gazette*: "If you merely parked your car near 26th Street on 10th Avenue, where the brewery was located, New York policemen would appear from several directions and order you to leave, 'or else.' Just driving through a side street after midnight made the place sound like a bird sanctuary. Whistles blew and doors slammed and, I suppose, machine gunners took their stations."

Life was tough trying to uphold the law. Undercover agents regrouped and tried another tactic by attempting to rent rooms overlooking the Phenix for surveillance. However, they found their progress blocked at every turn. The nearest apartment they managed to rent was two blocks away and, even then, it was only a short time before Owney's intelligence network picked up the news. "One evening, the superintendent of the building told them to leave," Denis Tilden Lynch reported in the *Herald Tribune*. "They could have remained, as the lease

was binding, but they would have been wasting their time, their useful-
ness passing with the disclosure of their identity."

The problems met by Special Agent Simmons were nothing new.
Years earlier, Maurice Campbell, New York's Prohibition Director, had
a similarly frustrating lack of success with the Phenix. "There was no
question policemen were in league with the brewery," he complained.
"My agents could not rent a room in the neighborhood of the plant without being spied on by the police, and their movements reported to the
men in charge of the brewery."

Throughout the 1920s, the Prohibition Bureau made extensive efforts to put Owney's partner, Bill Dwyer, behind prison bars. Bruce
Bielaski, an abrasive attorney, was paid $1,100 a month solely to bring a
watertight case against rum-runners, and Dwyer was the obvious target.
Big Bill was ostentatious and enjoyed his high social profile. Bielaski succeeded in "turning" one of Dwyer's former employees to testify against
him. It is remarkable that, in the harsh spotlight of such a rigorous investigation, Owney himself was completely overlooked by the authorities
and escaped prosecution. Big Bill was sent to Atlanta Penitentiary, convicted as much on what the judge considered to be his contemptuous
attitude in court as on the evidence of the informant.

Dwyer attracted great attention during his trial. "There was a diamond stickpin in his tie," according to one report, "and a dazzling ring
on his finger that was made in the shape of a swastika, with a ruby in
the center, and diamonds forming the four bent arms." Whenever the
judge addressed him, he appeared to sneer disrespectfully. Few people
realized that, shortly before the trial, Big Bill had been sitting in the rear
seat of his limousine when his chauffeur, Crim, completely wrecked it.
As a result, Dwyer's jaw had been broken and incorrectly set, leaving it
sagging at one side. When he spoke, his mouth twisted into what appeared to be a contemptuous smile, which did not help his case.

While Big Bill went off for a term in "college," as a jail sentence was
euphemistically known, Owney continued to run the brewery with his

usual aplomb. Apart from taking on the entire New York City Police Department, federal agents could do little to breach its defenses. On one memorable occasion, thwarted by landlords and threats of parking tickets, they tried to storm the citadel in force, only to be sent retreating by a hail of warning gunfire from New York's Finest.

Perhaps Prohibition Director Maurice Campbell knew the extent of Owney's influence even more than Special Agent Simmons. Fresh from Washington, Campbell had tried to close the brewery down in its early days. Soon afterward, he was visited by a "prominent New York Republican politician" who offered him $200,000 in cash to "call off the heat." When he declined, he was then ordered by a superior to discontinue the raids.

Federal agents, however, did make a successful raid on a corner of the Madden empire in 1929. Special agents William Thibadeau and Carl Dodd received a call from a Mrs. Anna McLain complaining about the comings and goings of a band of bootleggers near her home. They arranged to meet her at 8:00 one morning on the corner of 49th Street and 9th Avenue to gain more information. Mrs. McLain knew the names of the leaders—Alfred Handel and John Sheanan—and, perhaps having a domestic axe to grind, immediately identified one of their helpers as a certain George McLain, known to everyone in the neighborhood as "Pops." The rest sounded as though they had stepped straight from the pages of a story by Damon Runyon. There was Pat the Harp, Spotty Doyle, Happy Malloy, Little Arthur, The Judge, The Black Irishman, and The Necker. (The latter, incidentally, was a nickname sometimes given to Owney by friends in the Irish community.)

The agents discovered that several of the men were wanted for various offenses, and Sheanan had a murder charge outstanding against him. Their liquor was stored at the Amos Garage on West 50th Street, two doors east of 12th Avenue. Inquiries also revealed that anyone in the neighborhood requiring a delivery of bootleg booze could call Columbus 0080, 1849, or 6713 to get the supply they wanted.

The telephones were traced through New York Telephone Company records to an office building at 211 West 61st Street. Two teams of agents, accompanied by police who had been ordered to arrest Sheanan on the murder charge, raided the premises. At the Amos Garage, they found a Pierce-Arrow truck ready and loaded with 83 half-barrels of beer. Nearby were 4,818 bottles of Gordon's Gin and 110 five-gallon drums of alcohol. Nine men were subsequently arrested at the garage.

The fifth-floor offices were closed, but a nervous-looking man was apprehended for acting suspiciously in the corridor outside. It was Pops McLain, the man who may or may not have been related to Anna. In his pocket was a set of keys which opened the door. Pops was paid sixty dollars a week to take down telephone orders, and the phones were already ringing when the doors were opened.

Pops was ordered to carry on his work as usual and had accepted eighty orders for cases of gin by noon. The agents hid behind the door and seized everyone who walked in. Now feeling confident of a conviction, they arrested Owney at his home on 10th Avenue and released him on a $5,000 bail. Some of those caught red-handed received jail sentences, but Owney's case, once again, was never brought to trial.

The Duke felt that he had worked hard to attain his seemingly unassailable position and, in many ways, he undeniably had. He also considered himself lucky. With his early track record of hijacking and muscling in on rival operations, he had survived where others in gangland had been cut down in their prime. "This is the man," stated the *Police Gazette*, with more than a trace of admiration, "who—from the standpoint of color and excitement—towers over today's underworld figures the way Babe Ruth and Ty Cobb stand out above the ordinary ballplayers of this or any other era."

New York encapsulated the mood of America in the 1920s, and Owney was seen as the spirit of New York. They called it the Whoopee Era. It was a decade of abandon that featured hip flasks, raccoon coats, well-heeled gangsters, and pretty flappers dancing to tunes like "Bye, Bye

Blackbird" and "Doo-Wacka-Doo." Bootleg soaks were crooning "Show Me the Way to Go Home." Most of those who remember New York in the 1920s remember it with affection, and the anthems of the day summed up their feelings.

Despite the trauma of the Crash and the looming Depression, New Yorkers had a warmth and fondness for characters like Jimmy Walker, their handsome, party-going Mayor, and Owney Madden, the quiet Duke who supplied their booze. There were times when wisecracks, cockiness, and optimism bubbled like bootleg beer. Perhaps the window cleaner on Broadway best summed up the spirit in 1926. When the very regal Queen Marie of Romania arrived for a grand tour, Jimmy Walker rolled out the red carpet and drove with her through the crowded streets in the back of his open limousine. As the cavalcade, with outriders and mounted policemen, passed beneath his ladder, the window cleaner called down: "Hey, Jimmy. Did you lay her yet?" The crowd, and the Mayor, roared with laughter. An observer recalled: "Queen Marie, whose knowledge of English was of a formal variety, waved upward in friendly response."

Owney survived this age of wonderful nonsense in his own style. With the exception of the Patsy Doyle slaying, to which he always pleaded innocence, he had beaten every rap—genuine or fabricated—that the authorities had thrown at him. Encouraged by this, he wrote a personal letter to Governor Franklin D. Roosevelt in 1929, petitioning him for a full pardon from his manslaughter conviction. The petition was flatly rejected. As the greatest madcap decade in American history drew to a close, Owney had little inkling that storm clouds were gathering ahead. Prohibition's endless, uninhibited party was to present dangerous gangland enemies, and a new breed of ambitious lawmen and politicians were out for his blood.

8.

Fighting Chance

As a gangland diversion, showgirls and actresses were eclipsed only by the raw excitement of the fight game. Owney had maintained an interest in boxing since boyhood, and many of his close friends were professional fighters. To some, he freely gave large sums of money to assist with training and promotion. He also held lucrative investments in others. Throughout the 1920s and 1930s, he maintained controlling interests in five world champions. At least two of them—Max Baer and Rocky Marciano—remained lifelong chums. Big Frenchy joined Owney as a business partner in many ring ventures and took exceptional pleasure when he knew that the opposing fighter was backed by rival gangsters. This intense competition was perhaps never more vividly demonstrated than in the 1933 World Heavyweight Championship.

Primo Carnera, a powderpuff giant known as "the Ambling Alp," was jointly owned by Owney, Frenchy, and trainer Bill Duffy, an old Madden crony. Jack Sharkey, his opponent for the title, had an erratic, mob-sponsored career. Hundreds of thousands of dollars in side bets were riding on the fight. Owney and Frenchy arranged the best training camp they could find—Dr. Biers Health Farm at a New Jersey lakeside resort—and made sure that their fighter was in perfect shape. Sharkey was undergoing similar treatment in the hands of his own backers, and, by the time the two came together, the rivalry had reached fever pitch.

It was perhaps one of the few World Heavyweight Championships in which the "sidemen" of the two contenders provided almost as big an attraction as the fight itself. In "Da Preem's" corner, Owney and Frenchy leapt up and down throughout the bout, bawling instructions. In Sharkey's corner, the Purple Gang from Detroit yelled themselves hoarse. Finally, as the *New York Times* put it, "Da Preem took out Sailor Jack in six with a punch that has yet to be seen, probably owing to gangsters Owney Madden and Big Frenchy DeMange in Carnera's corner."

"Everybody loved to watch Owney at the big fights," said trainer Ray Arcel. "They seemed to change his personality. He would stand up at the front, shadow boxing, throwing punches, and shouting instructions. He used to get beside himself until somebody pulled him back into his seat. He just loved boxing. All the big fighters were personal friends."

The Ambling Alp, who came from the era of hungry fighters, was brought to the United States in 1928 with little education and no command of English. He stood six feet, seven inches tall and tipped the scales at around 260 lbs.—the biggest boxer America had seen. The media went wild. Carnera became a sensation wherever he went, pursued by packs of photographers and frustrated reporters determined to coax a few words of English out of him.

Before his fight with Leon "Bombo" Chevalier at Oakland, California, Carnera's Los Angeles hotel was besieged by newsmen. A radio reporter managed to get through to see his tiny French trainer-manager, Leon See.

"I am," he said, straightening his tie, "the announcer of the most important radio station in the city. I would like to have Carnera and his manager say a few words into the microphone tomorrow evening."

"Your intention is kind," See replied, in his engaging French accent, "but I think Carnera is obliged to excuse himself. Primo, if he must speak, could do it only in Italian or French."

The announcer became visibly agitated: "That's too bad, because the air audience will be listening for Carnera. Can't he pronounce a few words in English? This is all I want—I'll ask him three questions which he can reply to in a few words."

See looked doubtful: "What questions do you count on asking him?"

"Okay. Here they are. I'll ask, 'Primo, how much do you weigh?' I suppose he could easily answer 275 lbs.—I think that is his weight."

"We'll get him to do his best," See conceded.

"Then I'll ask, 'How old are you?' If he just answers twenty-three, that will be fine. Finally, I'll say, 'What is your height?' And all he needs to say is 'six feet seven.'"

Leon See was still unsure but he promised: "I will not guarantee Primo's English, but you can count on his willingness."

After intensive coaching between training sessions, See and Carnera took the elevator to the thirty-sixth floor of the radio building for the live interview. "Primo," the announcer began, "how old are you?"

"Two hundred and seventy-five," the Alp beamed.

Carnera became loved by the American public despite allegations that many of his one hundred fights were fixed. With Owney and Frenchy managing him, it is not surprising that many were, but in fairness to the man-mountain, he was probably unaware of it.

Primo made a total of two million dollars for his backers and saw little of it for himself. Only after retirement from boxing in 1946, when he took up wrestling, did he become really wealthy. The Alp mainly had brought a circus atmosphere to boxing. He was always an attraction rather than an outstanding heavyweight. For this reason, Madden invested in him as he would have in any quick-return racket. But, despite all the stories, he was always straight in his financial dealings.

Carnera, in various accounts of his career, is said to have been swindled out of his earnings by the mobsters who ran him. As this was principally assumed to be Owney Madden, I tried to pursue these allegations. From what I heard of his code of honesty, bilking a fighter seemed strangely out of character. I tracked down Ray Arcel, who trained most of Owney's fighters, including Carnera. Ray prepared Primo for his bouts while Duffy took a more managerial role. When I tracked Ray down, he was living on Lexington Avenue in New York and could clearly recall the fights from decades ago. His story reversed many of the claims made about Carnera's earnings.

"To me," said Ray, "Owney was a wonderful fellow because he never took advantage of the situation he was in by bulldozing people, you know. He paid his way. When he managed Primo Carnera, he made a deal with Leon See, who took a lot of money for him. Owney didn't shoulder See out of the picture—Mussolini did that. Right in the beginning, Primo returned to Italy after some success in New York, and his father threw a party for him in his village. In the course of the evening, the family gathered around, and the father asked:

"'You made a lot of money over there, Primo. What did you do with it?' All Primo said was: 'Ask Leon See.'

"When his father did, See told him he had bought property here and property there, but what he was doing in fact was playing the stock market with Primo's money. Now, at the party, there was a village official who was a personal friend of Mussolini, and he told him the story. Mussolini cabled the Banca d'Italia in New York and instructed the vice-president, Louis Cerissi, to make good the money Carnera had lost. Cerissi took an interest in Primo and approached Owney and Duffy to join him in managing the fighter properly. Owney drew up a proper deal and bought a fifty percent interest in Primo. Carnera's share was paid to Cerissi, but what happened to that I don't know. Owney stuck to his part of the bargain, like he always did. Leon See was the real culprit of all those stories."

Owney never became as friendly with Carnera as he did with other boxers, possibly because of the keen interest the New York Immigration Department began to show in the Italian and his associates. There were endless legal wrangles over Primo's status and his work permits, which were intensified when the Italian government applied pressure for him to return and enlist for military service. Owney considered such matters a little too close for comfort and took a back seat in the fighter's affairs.

Compared to some of the boxers Owney helped with gifts and no-strings loans, the Alp was an ungainly fighter with a bone-crusher approach. Nevertheless, he hammered some of the best men in the world into submission—albeit in some of the roughest fights the ring has witnessed. Carnera finally lost his World Heavyweight title to Owney's pal, Max Baer, in an eleventh-round knockout. The bout still ranks as one of the toughest and bloodiest on record.

No quarter was given and none asked. At one stage, both men lay sprawled flat out on the canvas, which led to Baer's much-quoted remark: "The last one up's a sissy." From then on, Owney's association with Baer bloomed. Max visited him often in Hot Springs to tell stories and play golf. In his absence, he always wrote to Owney, keeping him in touch with underworld gossip in letters which fondly began, "Dear Champ."

Curiously, all the champions in whom Owney had a stake were offered parts in Hollywood films. He had extensive contracts and, it was rumored, financial interests in certain studios. He used his influence on behalf of pals at every opportunity. The most colorful and closest of his boxing friends was World Light Heavyweight Champion Maxie Rosenbloom, who went on to become a Hollywood celebrity with his own nightclub, "Slapsie Maxie's." Rosenbloom was a wild, witty character with a weakness for gambling which cost him a quarter of a million dollars at racetracks around the country.

He was discovered as a teenager, brawling in a fight over a curbside dice game. George Raft, who was gaining a toehold in Owney's clubs at the time, happened to be passing on an errand when he saw an Irish policeman breaking up the rumpus. Rosenbloom handled himself well and George called him over.

"'You can fight, kid,' Raft remarked, according to an account of their meeting in *Everybody's* magazine. 'Ever do any boxing?'"

"Rosenbloom looked up to see a slim, dark young man, dressed in Broadway style, regarding him quizzically.

"'Come and have coffee,' he invited.

"In the small cafe the dark young man, his glossy hair carefully parted, told Maxie that he had done a bit of boxing himself and that, if he liked, he'd introduce him to an amateur club and give him a few wrinkles in fighting science. A little overawed by the magnificence of his newly found friend, Maxie accepted the offer and shook hands with the other as he rose to go, having made a date for the next day. Just as he reached the door, Maxie suddenly remembered something and yelled:

"'Hey, mister. What's your name?'

"'Raft,' came the reply. 'George Raft.'"

Owney financed several amateur boxing clubs on the West Side and funded countless boys' clubs in the hope that young men might achieve a good start in life without turning to crime. It was a belief he held sincerely. He often warned wayward youngsters to keep on the right side of the law despite his own experiences. On one occasion, he financed a trans-Atlantic tournament and sent young amateurs to box against boys in his hometown of Liverpool to broaden their experience. Owney's fondness for both prizefighters and youngsters surfaced many years later in Hot Springs. Local historian Mark Palmer recalled that one day, as a boy, he had crept through the shrubbery of the local golf course to spy on two of his great heroes—Owney Madden and world heavyweight champion Rocky Marciano. They were carrying their own clubs and seemed deep in conversation. Owney, someone once said, always had a habit of staying close to the cover of the trees when he walked the course. Little Mark, clutching an old box camera, crawled out of the bushes and asked if he could take Mr. Marciano's photograph. Owney laughed and called someone over. He sandwiched the wide-eyed kid between himself and Rocky and ordered the man to take a picture. Mark ran all the way home, clutching his camera, in case by some terrible misfortune it all turned out to be a dream.

After meeting Rosenbloom, George enlisted Owney, and the two set to work supervising his training. Maxie was a talented fighter and soon proved his worth in a grueling schedule of amateur fights, often as many as half a dozen in a single evening. On one occasion, he amazed his mentors by scoring five knockouts in the short space of two hours.

Between dancing engagements at Owney's clubs, George began to take an intense interest in Maxie's training, helped by money and advice from the Duke. To push him into a professional frame of mind, they told him that, in view of the poverty his family was living in, he should turn pro and go out and fight for them. Maxie thought it over and agreed. George and Owney had ringside seats at his first professional contest, and Maxie wanted to justify their belief in him. His sense of responsibility placed him under great mental strain and, for the first few rounds, he took more than his share of punishment. At the sound of each bell, George leapt into his corner, whispering advice:

"Feint him, kid. Watch his left hook. He swings it wide. You can nail him with a right hand when he lets go."

By the sixth round, the message had sunk home and an impressive right from Rosenbloom dumped his opponent on the canvas for the full count. When the referee raised his hand, Maxie turned to his corner and broke into a war dance of delight. After the fight, Raft took him to a cafe where they discussed plans and ambitions until the early hours of the morning. As a grey-yellow dawn crawled over the Hudson River, George gently broke some news:

"Listen Maxie," he said, as kindly as he could. "I've something to tell you. Texas Guinan has offered me fifty dollars a week to dance in her floor show. It looks like the break I've been waiting for and I can start next week. The only thing is—well, it means you and I can't be around together in the same way. I won't have the time to manage you." Rosenbloom looked saddened but understood. "I've got a friend of mine to take you under his wing," George added. "He'll look after you all right."

Raft did indeed have a dancing offer, but he omitted to mention that a brief, impassioned fling with Mae West had kept him from devoting all the time necessary to Maxie's training. George and Mae both had strong sex drives, and some of the occasions on which he called to collect box office takings were spent making love. Mae and George enjoyed their affair in the back of the Packard, her dressing room, and even in a broom closet. It was "love on the run with half the buttons undone," Mae was to laughingly recall years later. Owney presumably knew nothing of their fleeting diversion.

George parted company with Maxie, but they remained in close touch, often taking trips with Owney to Atlantic City to unwind and relax on the beach. Maxie soon discovered that the links between the underworld and the fight game were too powerful to ignore. After turning pro, he fought an old neighborhood pal, Joe Scogny, whom he beat in six rounds. In the dressing room after the fight, they arranged to meet for a game of pool the following afternoon. As Maxie approached the pool hall, he saw police holding back a crowd and had to push his way inside. Scogny was lying on a floodlit pool table with blood seeping into the felt from a fatal bullet wound to his head. Rosenbloom was told that the hit man's bullet was meant for someone else, although the identity of the intended victim was never made clear.

Around this time, Owney kept a friendly eye on Rosenbloom's affairs but kept his distance. George continued to offer enthusiastic advice at every available opportunity. Even after he had gone to Hollywood, Raft insisted on giving pre-fight tips by telephone, and Maxie always accepted them with good humor. When Tony Loughran gave up his World Light Heavyweight title, the boxing commissioners scheduled a title bout between Rosenbloom and Jimmy Slattery. Maxie felt a psychological disadvantage when the city of Buffalo, Slattery's home town in New York State, was selected as the venue. Nevertheless, it was the chance he had been waiting for.

"George Raft was more excited than I was when I wired him the news," Maxie recalled. "He telephoned long distance from Hollywood, and we stayed on the phone an hour while George told me how I should box Slattery. That call cost him over a hundred dollars—expensive advice. He promised to come with a party on the great night."

Raft was as good as his word and turned up with Clara Bow, Harry Richman, and Jack Oakie to boost his friend's confidence. They met up in Maxie's hotel a few hours before the fight for a reunion which certainly succeeded in taking his mind off the impending contest.

"To while away the time," Rosenbloom recalled, "we started a dice game and, to my annoyance, Jack skinned me of a hundred and fifty dollars within an hour. At last, we taxied to the ball park which had been crammed since early in the evening, mainly with Slattery's home town supporters. With George and the others, I went to the dressing room. We started to play dice again and then I changed and put on my old red dressing gown."

It was a much tougher contest than Maxie ever imagined. Slattery was a classy fighter but had a roughhouse approach when cornered, and this left dangerous openings in his style. Before the first round was over, it was clear that neither fighter would give any quarter. Each inflicted considerable damage in illegal holds and, by the fifth round, Slattery had become vicious. He caught Rosenbloom in the eye with a right hook and almost fell over his opponent when the second punch went wide.

"At that instant," Maxie recalled, "my sight cleared and I looked full in the face of George Raft. George, crazy with excitement, had jumped from his ringside seat and was up at the ropes.

"'Right hook,' he yelled at me. 'Right hook.'

"Blindly, I pivoted around and lashed out with my right glove. All my weight was behind the punch. My fist seemed to sink up to the wrist in Slattery's solar plexus."

It was the turning point in a fight which was bitterly fought and went the full distance. After the final bell, the referee raised Maxie's arm, signaling a celebration party which went on for a total of forty-eight hours. In the midst of all the revelry and celebration, Owney was treated to a blow-by-blow account from George by telephone, despite having already sat through the radio commentary. Maxie earned his title, but Raft's psychological help undoubtedly carried him through.

It was not the first time he had intervened in a fight in which Owney had a keen interest. According to Raft's biographer, the actor always denied a story that he had once helped Owney with a pre-fight favor involving Carnera. Owney had eased trainer Leon See out of the picture and booked Carnera for a tour against fighters who were paid to establish the Ambling Alp's reputation by taking a dive. "After his whirlwind national tour and over twenty victories," Yablonsky wrote, "Carnera was set for his first fight in Madison Square Garden against a pretty good fighter, 'Big Boy' Eddie Peterson. Peterson was untrustworthy as a 'fall guy,' especially after he let it be known that he felt he wasn't being paid enough. Owney wanted no slip-ups. If Peterson got lucky, the potential million-dollar proposition with Carnera could go down the drain.

"One report alleges that several hours before the fight, on January 24, 1930, Raft, as a favor to Owney, called on 'Big Boy' Peterson at the Claridge Hotel. George carried a bottle of champagne and suggested that a few drinks would help Peterson calm down. There is no record of how much 'Big Boy' drank, but Peterson seemed to be feeling no pain when he went to Madison Square Garden that night. Primo Carnera knocked him out in the first round and began his climb to the Heavyweight Championship of the World."

Fight fixing was commonplace in the Depression era of the 1930s. Maxie Rosenbloom, thanks to the right connections, relied solely on his talent to rise to the top but not without a few close calls. Mobsters in every major city had their own protégés, and Chicago, under Al Capone, was no exception. When Rosenbloom was selected to fight against a formidable African-American boxer named Theodore "Tiger" Flowers, he realized that he was up against more than a pair of lightning gloves. Seats at the Windy City stadium had sold out. Rosenbloom was happy with his road work and was sitting in his dressing room waiting for the summons when five men walked in.

"The last closed the door behind him, after motioning my seconds to leave, and then locked it," he recalled. "I took one look at them—then

I knew what was coming. They were racket guys all right, with the usual pearl grey hats, shiny shoes and the usual bulge under the left shoulder. The spokesman discussed the weather, the fights, and what I thought of my chances with Flowers, and who did I think might beat Gene Tunney. His pals ranged themselves along the walls, smoking and silent. Then he asked me if I couldn't use a little extra cash—$10,000 for instance.

"'It's this way, Rosenbloom,' he continued. 'Me and the boys kinda like the Tiger. We figure he'll take you this time. But it's close—too close for our money. The boys and me bet a lot of money on fights and we'd feel more comfortable if we had your cooperation. Ten grand's a lot of money.'

"'Get the hell out of here,' I yelled before I realized what I was saying.

"The men by the wall moved forward angrily, but their leader held them back. 'All right, Rosenbloom. Do what you want. But it'll be too bad for you if you win. And now there isn't ten grand in it.'"

The incident, so close to the opening bell, shook Maxie, and he worriedly discussed what to do with his trainer Frank Bachman. Someone is then reported to have made a telephone call to Owney in New York. After a short interval, the Chicago boys returned with a change of heart.

"'Listen, Rosenbloom,' the spokesman said. 'We've changed our minds. We're switching our bets and we're taking you.' At the door he paused to save face. 'And if you don't win, it will still be too bad for you.'"

Both boxers put everything they had into the fight, which fortunately ended in a draw. Flowers was taken to the hospital with an eye injury which later became infected. Tragically, he died five days later on the operating table.

9.

Birth of the Businessman-Gangster

Toward the late 1920s, Owney's star had risen high over New York's grimy skyline. The Cotton Club, the Stork, and the Silver Slipper were among the best and most stylish nightclubs in the city. His ships steered a fairly uninterrupted course to Rum Row, laden with King's Ransom and House of Lords whisky. The Phenix Brewery was working, as usual, at full capacity. In addition, he had extensive real estate interests in hotels, apartments, and office buildings and heavy investments in world champion boxers and top Broadway shows. By any standards, it was success in the greatest American tradition. The lad from Liverpool, via Hell's Kitchen, had cemented powerful connections with the Democratic machine, the New York City Police, the U.S. Coast Guard, the judiciary, and the underworld. But the wheel of events seldom turns smoothly. A single bird can ground a plane like a Boeing 747 and a bee in the engineer's car can stop an express train. As Owney discovered years earlier with Patsy Doyle, it requires only one rogue gunman to rock the equilibrium of an empire. If life, as they say, runs in circles, then Vincent Coll must have given Owney Madden a disturbing sense of déjà vu.

Coll, like Doyle, was of Irish descent and was imbued with a wild, Celtic spirit that prompted him, in his worst moments, to strike out at whatever stood in his way. When New Yorkers called Vinny Coll crazy, they meant that even Owney Madden, Frank Costello, and Dutch

Schultz looked over their shoulders. Coll was a tall, gangly youth with a grin that exposed inches of upper gum. He had blue eyes that roamed unpredictably as he talked.

Prohibition had made millionaires of New York's big-league gangsters, but there were always those beneath them looking for an opportunity to wrest control from their hands. At times, power struggles were waged for a block of territory at a time and occasionally whole neighborhoods. The greedy, who had the cunning to survive, became greedier. Dutch Schultz, who was earning $5,000 a day, was one of them, and his empire gave wildcat operators like Coll a reckless urge to take over. The bottomless thirst of New Yorkers bred coups and counter-coups. By the end of the 1920s, Owney became concerned that the escalating, bloody squabbles would spill over into all-out war. He continued to expand at a steady pace but was increasingly wary of certain associates. On the surface, the city went about its business, but the bootleg barons became engaged in a war of nerves. Schultz constantly pushed and tested the strength of other gang leaders. A 1931 newspaper report gave an indication of the trouble dangerously bubbling:

"Schultz was nearly done for by Madden gangsters in January. Owney and Dutch have been at loggerheads for some time, and there is a silent understanding between them that the Bronx gunmen keep discreetly on the upper side of 54th Street. But it was the Christmas season, and Dutch decided to celebrate in a unique way. Not only did he cross the dividing line, but he and a few of his gangsters stamped into the very bosom of the enemy, the Club Abbey, which is owned by Madden, right on the boundary line.

"The bored playboys and their Broadway butterflies were treated to something unusual in the way of entertainment. Instead of the usual floorshow, the patrons were favored with an advertisement that had an unexpurgated Dan McGrew motif just as the party was beginning to go flat. Dutch and his boys pulled out their gats and began shooting up the joint. Some of Madden's boys retaliated in a like manner, and the lights that hadn't been shot out suddenly went out. In the free-for-all that followed, Dutch was seriously wounded. Mr. Schultz steers as clear away from the Broadway sector now as Mr. Diamond does from the East Side."

It was the kind of warning that would have no impact on Vincent Coll. Schultz was playing a dangerous hand because he knew his actions threatened to incur the displeasure of the entire organized crime community in America. Less than two years earlier, the big names had decided internal disagreements must stop. By 1929 a group of saner, wiser underworld figures sensed that public opinion was turning against them. Police officers, newspapermen, and innocent bystanders had been hurt or killed in gang shoot-outs, and the time had come to call a truce.

One incident which prompted the decision was the murder, on November 4, 1928, of Owney's Cotton Club partner, Arnold Rothstein—the man who bankrolled early bootlegging operations and funded some of the country's biggest crime operations. Rothstein was an underworld legend.

Tales were still told of how he fixed major league baseball's 1919 World Series by bribing eight of the Chicago White Sox star players. The team stunned the nation by losing, five games to three, against the Cincinnati Redlegs, a bunch of self-confessed losers. Shortly before his death, Rothstein lost $320,000 in a single poker game with two tough characters, Nate Raymond and Titanic Thompson (no relation to Thompson and Raymond, the New York criminologists). Uncharacteristically, Rothstein was reluctant to pay up. Despite real estate interests estimated in the millions, he tried to cover his losses by ordering a table at Lindy's Restaurants and taking bets on the 1928 presidential election. Rothstein, a compulsive gambler but a good one, laid out a total of $100,000 on Herbert Hoover to win against Al Smith. He never lived to collect his winnings. Two hours later, he was gunned down in New York's Park Central Hotel, leaving a financial vacuum in the underworld.

In Chicago, meanwhile, Al Capone had shocked the nation with the St. Valentine's Day Massacre. He was never brought to trial for the slaying of six rival bootleggers in a garage, but there was little doubt who was responsible. In New York, war was about to break out between Mafia leader Joe "The Boss" Masseria and Salvatore Maranzano, who appeared bent on unseating him. In an attempt to track "the Boss" down, Maranzano had even kidnapped and slashed Lucky Luciano, and it was clear he would stop at nothing.

With all these troubles in mind, the senior executives of Gangland USA decided that it was time to meet and settle their differences. Luciano, a close friend of Owney, visited Joe the Boss and put the idea to him. Masseria took one look at Lucky, who was badly disfigured from his kidnapping, and believed that the whole thing might be a plot to overthrow him.

"No deal," Masseria growled.

Lucky talked over the problem with Frank Costello. Italian interests would have to be represented at any summit, but no one wanted to risk offending Joe the Boss. The biggest meeting in the history of American crime would either have to be called off or proceed without him. Frank voted to go ahead.

To avoid invoking Masseria's anger and suspicion, they hatched a plan. Absurd as it seemed, the simple answer would be to pretend to be on vacation. No one knows who first proposed the Atlantic City Crime Convention but, by mutual consent, it was agreed that Owney and Frenchy—perhaps the two most neutral and trustworthy gangsters in the country—should organize it. Frenchy sent out the "holiday" invitations— any invitation from Frenchy was considered above suspicion—while Owney tied up the arrangements.

Atlantic City in 1929 was under the control of Enoch "Nucky" Johnson (the nickname was a corruption of "knuckles"—the brass variety). The meeting place was a wide-open holiday resort, famous for its board-walk, sea bathing, and single people out for a good time. Atlantic City was also a popular venue for conventions, and the booking at the Hotel President aroused little attention. One by one, the most formidable names in America arrived in town, swept from the railroad station in convoys of black, bullet-proof limousines packed with bodyguards. The New York contingent was the biggest, followed by Al Capone and his boys from Chicago. Al had brought his generals, Paul "the Waiter" Ricca and Jake "Greasy Thumb" Guzik. Boo Boo Hoff breezed in from Philly. Also arriving were Moe Dalltz, the stone-faced Cleveland mobster, John Lazia from Kansas City, and Joe Bernstein with his big delegation from Detroit. The list was endless. With the notable exception of Joe the Boss, every major criminal in America was present.

Capone ordered one of his aides to contact the local newspaper to get a picture of himself and his host, Nucky Johnson, strolling arm in arm down the boardwalk. But behind the smile there was trouble brewing. Big Al, convinced that the entire convention was somehow aimed at him, almost checked out before proceedings started. With personal annual earnings of $10 million, he was wary of any moves to take over his domain.

Eventually, they all sat down beneath crystal chandeliers around the Hotel President's enormous mahogany conference table for the historic meeting. No one was anxious to be accused of manipulating events, and there was a tense silence before anyone spoke. Johnny Tomo, the dapper and respected New York Mafia member, finally broke the ice and, in his thick accent, spelled out the theme:

"The reason we are all here," he said, blowing cigar smoke at the ceiling, "is that we have to get organized. Everybody is working on his own—we have independent gangs muscling in—and that's got to stop. What we need is a combination around the country where everybody in charge of his city is the boss but we all work with each other."

Frank Costello complained about the Chicago shootings and how they had alienated public opinion: "We've got a thing where millions of dollars can be made just by getting people what they want. When I was on trial three years ago on the whisky deal, all the people were behind me. And I was able to stay in business." They agreed to form a confederation of twenty-four major gangs, molded for solidarity into a National

Crime Commission. Under its rules, no one could be killed without a majority decision and no policemen, newsmen, or members of the public were to be assaulted.

In keeping with the mature philosophy of Costello, Lansky, Madden, and others, the objective was to attract as little attention to themselves as possible. Everyone around the table knew that the decision was a collective disapproval of Capone's working methods. In the eyes of the new National Crime Commission, he was wayward and in danger of turning both the public and politicians against their activities. Big Al, everyone was beginning to realize, needed to be seen as penitent.

The events of the next few minutes were later relayed by Costello to his lawyer, George Wolf Torrio. The elder statesman of the convention rose to his feet and gazed calmly down the length of the table at Capone:

"'You're going to jail, Al.'

"'To what?' Capone was smiling.

"'To jail. We have to smooth this thing over right now. You go back to Chicago after that Valentine Day shoot-out and the heat will go higher and higher. We think you need a vacation, Al.'

"Capone said to Torrio: 'Tell me when I'm supposed to laugh.'

"But the answer came from Frank Costello.

"'This isn't a joke, Al. We've got too much invested for you to ruin the gravy train. Make it easy on yourself. Think of a way. But we need you off at college until things cool down.'"

Capone rose angrily and, followed by his entourage, swept out, slamming the door behind them.

Two days later, after lengthy negotiations between his lawyers and the police, Big Al walked out of a Philadelphia cinema and was arrested by a waiting detective for carrying a gun. He was sentenced to a year's imprisonment, and the power of the National Crime Commission was established.

The rest of the meeting was devoted to discussing future plans. There was talk of investing legitimately in distilleries and breweries after Prohibition and branching into nationwide gambling. All members asserted that, if the agreements worked out, the next logical step would be to form a National Crime Syndicate.

Before the proceedings broke up, there was a formal presentation. Owney was asked to step up and receive a commemorative watch as a gesture of thanks and as a token for running an exemplary operation. Big Frenchy was deputed to make the presentation speech, a function he clearly had never been called upon to perform. He lumbered awkwardly to his feet and made his way to the head of the table. The incident later reached the ears of a New York detective, Barney Ruditsky, who once related the story as part of his testimony to the Senate's Kefauver Committee.

"Now Big Frenchy had never made a speech in his life," Ruditsky recalled with a trace of a smile. "He got up onto the dais and he said:

"'Owney, have you got a watch?'

"Owney said yes, and took it off and showed it to Big Frenchy. Big Frenchy didn't quite know what to do. So he dropped Owney's watch on the floor and stepped on it.

"And he said: 'Gee, Owney. I'm sorry I broke your watch, but here's another one for you...'"

Frenchy clumsily presented Owney with the watch and shook hands to a ripple of applause from the assembled meeting. Owney, by all accounts, was speechless—uncertain whether to express his gratitude or beat Frenchy over the head with it.

Around 1930, there was an atmosphere hanging over New York rather like that of the long, hot summer which preceded the First World War. It was a feeling that the world was changing beyond recognition. The first warnings had rung out a year previously. On Black Thursday, October 24, 1929, everyone decided to ignore economists who were insisting that the declining market would recover. Financial experts tried to spread calm like officers on the deck of a sinking ship, but those aboard were seized by an uncontrollable urge to save themselves. Amid scenes of unprecedented hysteria, thirteen million shares were traded until the ticker machines could no longer cope—the sheer weight of business left the tapes limping 104 minutes behind. Panic-stricken small investors stampeded the Stock Exchange like residents locked out of a besieged city and surged onto the floor. "It was like a madhouse or a menagerie," Andre Maurois reported. "There were the roars of lions and tigers: lunatics seized one another by the throat shouting 'Steel' or 'Radio' as they rolled together on the ground."

For a day, it seemed as though the very foundation of American enterprise was tottering like a tall building rocked by an earthquake. Then just five days later, on October 29, the Stock Exchange collapsed. More than sixteen million shares changed hands, precipitating losses in the billions. Share values plummeted by forty percent, and overnight the princes of Wall Street became paupers. Some even committed suicide rather than surrender to the prospect of poverty. A tidal wave of depression swept the land like some medieval pestilence. Banks folded in its path. Factories closed, and the unemployed wandered the country like hopeless refugees. In New York there was a joke that hotel receptionists were asking, "Do you want the room for sleeping or jumping?"

Curiously, much of Owney's business went unaffected. Those who could still afford it had a desire to lose themselves in the warm cocoon of his clubs where jazz, fast dancing, and good booze would keep the outside world at bay. In many ways, they were experiencing what he himself had felt as a boy when he sat in the plush gilt and velvet glow of Liverpool music halls to escape life's harshness for a few brief hours. Owney understood their mood and supplied what they wanted. To his great discomfort, however, the Depression also brought a hardening of attitudes. A new power structure was emerging which viewed the lush, uninhibited gangster life with puritanical disapproval.

By December 1929, the Depression was making the gulf between New York's old rulers and its new poor more apparent. Corruption no longer had its air of healthy abandon but was seen increasingly as the city's rotten core. By an oddly American yardstick, racketeering was acceptable to the man on the street when times were fat but appeared gross and unseemly in an era of deprivation. In the Bronx, meanwhile, plans were being made for a presentation dinner which, under normal circumstances, would have attracted little attention. Overnight, it became a focus for new demands for political change.

Magistrate Albert Vitale was invited to the Roman Gardens restaurant at 187th Street and Southern Boulevard by the executive committee of the Tepecano Democratic Club for a dinner in his honor. It was a thinly disguised "thank you" from Tammany Hall and the underworld for services rendered. Vitale's links with the mob went back a long way—Arnold Rothstein had once loaned him $20,000, and the Tepecano, of which the magistrate was president for life, had an estimated ten percent of its members heavily involved in organized crime.

The banquet was a lavish affair. The tables groaned under an abundance of good food and drink, and the air was thick and heavy with cigar smoke. Among the guests were politicians, detectives, gunmen, and senior members of the local Italian crime combination. All were relaxing and enjoying themselves in familiar company. After midnight, Vitale rose to his feet at the head table to give a speech of thanks. He was barely in full flow when the doors opened and seven gunmen walked in. Five of them, in a prearranged plan, fanned out to cover the guests and exits. The remaining two walked up to Vitale, disarming a tuxedoed member of the New York Police Department on the way, and told him to turn out his pockets. All the other guests were instructed to do the same. The gang walked out with $2,000 in cash, including $40 from the guest of honor, and $2,500 worth of jewelry.

News soon reached reporters who, in the changing political climate, were less interested in the robbery than the relationship between the dinner guests. Allegations of links between the judiciary, politicians, and gangsters began to make headline news. Vitale was investigated and found to have $100,000 in his bank account which could not be satisfactorily explained. He was removed from the bench, and the spotlight then swung over to Mayor Jimmy Walker with calls for a clean sweep of the city's magistrates' courts. Everyone knew, of course, that they were asking the wrong man. When Walker tried to pull the rug from beneath any possible inquiry, he himself became the target of a press campaign.

Owney followed the developments with a sense of foreboding. On Broadway, the great party continued unabated, but he detected the first signs of the enormous pressure which was to be applied to him. He read the indications as clearly as a needle rising up the graduations of a steam gauge and felt a growing need to take a break from New York.

The Duke began to lay plans for short trips out of town to expand his business activities in ways which were less easy to detect. Manhattan was acquiring a certain claustrophobia. Prohibition, the ingredient which had given life its edge of reckless excitement, now seemed likely to disappear, leaving New York to slip into the doldrums. In addition, powerful new underworld combinations were emerging, particularly among the Italians. Owney's relations with Frank Costello had always been sound, but now many were vying for elbow room in the teeming world of rackets and attracting too much attention.

The next turn of the screw came in 1930 when Mayor Walker bowed to pressure and Judge Samuel Seabury was appointed to investigate the city courts system. In one three-day hearing, the eminent, grey-haired figure unearthed evidence of corruption beyond anything even the imaginative press had visualized, and several magistrates resigned. For a time, it seemed that Jimmy Walker might topple and take down a barrel of rotten apples which editors could pick over for months. His power, however, was legendary. When Walker's actress girlfriend Betty Compton appeared in a show called "Fifty Million Frenchmen," for instance, she complained about her dressing room. City Hall inspectors descended on the theatre and promptly pointed out no less than fifteen safety violations. They could have closed the building down if management had refused to cooperate on repairs.

The Seabury Investigations continued, leading to a further inquiry by Senator Samuel Hofstadter into links between the judiciary, the political machine, and the mobs. The net began to close in on Tammany Hall, and news pages were crammed daily with fresh accounts of indiscretions. Owney worried constantly about the shift of authority, but, in fact, his own troubles were only just beginning.

March 15, the deadline to file income tax, was an annual fact of life to which millions of Americans reluctantly applied themselves. It also became an important day in the life of twenty-eight-year-old Thomas E. Dewey, who was sworn in as Chief Assistant U.S. Attorney for the Southern District of New York. There was almost no limit to Dewey's ambition, and, like many who later climbed the career ladder via the relentless pursuit of criminals and communists, he recognized an opportunity when he saw one. Elmer Irey, head of the Treasury Department's Intelligence Unit, had just scored a notable success in curbing Al Capone's activities in Chicago. With the "big guy" behind bars for tax evasion, Irey thought it might be profitable to apply similar treatment to criminals in New York. Thus, the stone-faced "T-men," as they were known, came to team up with the Boy Wonder who would stop at nothing to secure a prosecution. A ripple of nervous apprehension ran through the New York underworld, but nothing, for the moment, gave anyone cause for lost sleep.

Behind the scenes, however, the Treasury Department's heavy guns were being brought up to the front line. Irey contacted his New York bureau chief High McQuillan and decided to reinforce the operation with three crack agents—Ellison Palmer, who was brought in from Atlanta, Paul Anderson from Washington, and Cliff Mack from Boston.

After a council of war, they decided to concentrate on bootlegger Waxey Gordon as their first target. Waxey had a good operation running in the New Jersey cities of Paterson, Union City, and Elizabeth. His three large breweries worked day and night to produce legal near-beer. It did not take a shrewd Prohibition agent to notice that despite the frantic, non-stop production, only a handful of delivery trucks rolled out of the gates each week. The key to Waxey's empire lay beneath the city streets.

All his profitable bootleg beer was pumped through pressure hoses running through the sewage system to bottling plants in garages half a mile away. The fortune he made was estimated at two million dollars. Officially, he claimed to be earning an annual salary of only $8,125. When the three Treasury agents got to work, Waxey was indicted for tax evasion, and it took the jury just forty minutes to find him guilty. The stocky, heavy-jowled bootlegger was sentenced to ten years in prison, fined $20,000, and ordered to pay court costs. It was a warning to everyone, and, in Waxey's case, he did not see the lights of New York again until 1941.

Slowly, the Treasury Department worked down its hit list and, aided by Dewey's courtroom technique, achieved impressive success. Only Dutch Schultz wriggled twice from their grasp. By the time papers were being prepared for a third prosecution attempt, he was gunned down at a restaurant table. Irey was impressed by Dewey's performance: "He was the perfectionist to end all perfectionists," he said. "He left nothing to chance, including a man's promise. Most guilty pleas came as no surprise because the defendant's lawyer, looking for all the possible favors, will tip off the district attorney of his intentions. Most D.A.s then stop working on the case and turn to something else. Not Dewey.

"If we learned a guilty plea was coming up, we would tell Dewey. He would look off into space, flash his controlled smile, and say: 'That's fine. But go on digging up evidence. We want to be ready if he changes his mind.'

"Dewey recognized work well done, but he never mentioned it until the case was won. Then he meted out praise gingerly and briefly. The only thing wrong with Dewey was his youth. I explained to my men that he feared no lawyer, no crook, and no judge and jury. But he was frightened to death that anybody might accuse him of being a boy on a man's errand. Man or boy, he was certainly quite a trial lawyer."

Irey did not perhaps remember his faults as others did. Among Franklin D. Roosevelt's mail one morning was a letter from a woman who had been raised in Dewey's home town of Owasso, Michigan. She recalled him only as "a nasty, bad-tempered bully" who had grown a moustache to hide a lip split in a fist fight. The force of his ambition, nevertheless, propelled him eventually to the governorship of New York.

Owney began to consult more closely with Joe Shalleck, his lawyer and a friend since the days of the Gophers. Shalleck had always been a reliable buffer against official pressure. He had a knack for fending off trouble which made him worthy of his large fees. As his reputation grew, he had tried unsuccessfully to distance himself socially from his underworld clients, but they shared too much genuine affection for each other to completely sever the ties. Joe was a dedicated Democrat, and Owney's political heart was squarely in the same place. There was an understanding between them, and, when official hostility loomed, the Duke could always pick up the phone and dial Shalleck's practice in the Knickerbocker Building.

Joe was a small, decisive Polish immigrant with soft, deep-set eyes which could light up fast with his sense of humor. His opulent suite was situated at 152 West 42nd Street, a building which formerly housed the Knickerbocker Hotel, where Caruso the famous singer was fond of staying. The inner office was lined with legal tomes in antique cabinets and furnished with a heavy mahogany desk and deep leather armchairs.

Joe sat and listened impassively to the stream of movie stars, businessmen, and gangsters who had been caught in the riptide of justice and were now looking for a life raft to save them.

Beneath the immaculate silk tie and hand-made shirt, he carried a bullet scar across his ribs, a souvenir of the days when he managed the 1921 election campaign of Jimmy Hines for Borough President of Manhattan. Hines had incurred the displeasure of Tammany Hall over a business deal and was passed over for nomination. Jimmy, undeterred, ran for the plum Democratic post as an independent candidate. It was a bitter campaign, with Tammany Hall throwing all its weight into crushing the rebel and Hines dragging his opponent's effigy through the streets. By election night, feelings were running high, and

Joe, monitoring the votes, received a tip-off of ballot-rigging on Second Avenue. He raced over by taxi to see what was going on and found himself confronted in the polling station by district leader William P. Kenneally and two bodyguards.

"Who are you?" Kenneally demanded. "What do you want here?"

"I'm Joe Shalleck, Jimmy Hines's campaign manager," said the diminutive lawyer, standing his ground.

"How do we know that?"

"Here's the stationery," Joe answered, digging into his pocket. "That's my signature. There. I'm Joe Shalleck."

The district trio exchanged glances.

"So," said Kenneally, "you're Joe Shalleck, then?" He instantly threw a punch which sank the attorney to his knees.

At the first sign of the attack, a police patrolman who had been standing next to them turned his back and ambled out of the door. One of Kenneally's associates then pulled a gun from his overcoat pocket and aimed at Joe, who was doubled up on the floor. The man next to him, realizing there were lots of witnesses around, knocked his hand away shouting: "Are you crazy?" The bullet creased Joe's ribs and blood began to seep through his shirt. Kenneally, cheated of satisfaction, landed a few heavy kicks into the man at his feet. Joe spent election night in the hospital and, in the tradition of many of his clients, steadfastly refused to identify his attacker.

He remained one of Hines's closest friends until the politician's imprisonment in 1936. Joe, said one reporter, had a loyalty to Hines which "burned in him like an altar flame, never to be extinguished. He was Hines's man without deviation and even, so far as was ever known, without dissent. Shalleck was not alone in his devotion. Hines was a greatly loved figure throughout the West Side. He was revered among older residents for his help and generosity despite his dubious dealings. The least that can be said of him is that old political cliché. He was "a man of the people" and, like some of his constituents, was not averse to bending the law if he thought he could get away with it.

Shalleck's allegiances understandably gained him as many enemies as friends, and there were those in his own profession who would not have passed up an opportunity to participate in his downfall. They almost succeeded just at the time when Owney was in great need of his services. Joe arrived to represent the Utah Lead Company in a 1930 fraud case, full of tales about an outing with Owney the previous day. The Duke had taken him to see Primo Carnera, and Joe had found it hard to forget the enormous size of the giant boxer. When Owney handed him a handful of tickets for a Carnera fight, Shalleck was delighted.

Joe took a back seat in the Utah trial, compiling summaries of evidence while two other lawyers defended the case. Toward the end of the long hearing, a Puerto Rican juror named John Cruz collapsed from malnutrition—a condition not uncommon in the Depression—and had to be examined by a doctor. While Joe had slipped into another court, arranging a trial date for another client, the juror was ordered home by car. One of Shalleck's colleagues handed a bailiff five dollars and told him: "See that the poor devil gets a plate of hot soup." Later, out of sympathy, the two defending lawyers sent some more money to his home. Cruz eventually returned, looking a little less pale, and Joe, who had missed the donations, handed the bailiff ten dollars to slip into the emaciated juror's pocket. He was immediately reported for attempted bribery.

When the charge was heard, Joe, to his disbelief, was disbarred but eventually managed to have the decision reversed on appeal. It was only later that he remembered that he was out of court at the time most of the money was handed over, offering a neighboring judge tickets for the Carnera fight—a point which might have gone a long way to establishing his innocence.

The case, which made front page headlines in the *New York Law Journal*, left him unable to practice for a period and placed Owney in a dilemma. While Joe was trying to ease back into courtroom life and restore his practice, the Treasury Department was finally moving down to Madden's name on its long list of tax targets.

10.

The Mad Dog

Organized crime was a claustrophobic occupation. As more contenders and recalcitrants rose in Manhattan's crowded 22.7 square miles, the less pleasurable gang life became. Owney, in particular, a man as hard as the best of them but with sensibilities and refinements lacking in most of his contemporaries, began to live on his nerves. He smoked heavily during this upheaval and began to express worries about the changing political structure. All the portents told him that the vultures were gathering but, perhaps for the first time, he felt unable to bring even his powerful influence to bear.

His recurring stomach problem also began to badly affect his general health. Late in 1930, Owney was chauffeured to Sing Sing where Dr. Sweet performed surgery on his ulcerated bullet wounds. To add to his troubles, recovery was slow and painful. Owney, along with other senior New York gang leaders, was unprepared for the exploits of renegade gangster Vinny Coll. Coll was born in County Kildare and immigrated to the U.S. where he grew up an orphan in a Hell's Kitchen tenement with his brother Peter and sister Florence. His crime career was marked by an arrest at the age of thirteen, followed by years of burglary and robbery punctuated by spells in a reformatory. Even as a teenager, no institution wished to cope with him and no one on the streets felt safe when he was free.

Coll soon began working for Dutch Schultz, protecting his beer trucks from hijackers. He proved himself a valuable gunman but was too much of a liability. "Coll was undoubtedly a cold-blooded and efficient triggerman," one observer noted, "but Schultz soon learned that he couldn't be kept under control. He was too ambitious, too resentful of taking orders, too dangerous to have around."

The Dutchman was furious when Coll began attracting attention to his bootlegging operations by staging freelance robberies on the side. When Coll held up the Sheffield Farms Dairy in the Bronx and escaped with $18,000, Schultz called him into the office. Dutch paced the carpet, roaring with anger and, when he had cooled down a little, demanded an explanation. None came. Instead, Coll arrogantly told Dutch that he wanted a partnership. Coll was barely shaving at the time, and his proposal was taken as a serious affront. According to historian Richard O'Connor, Schultz was staggered by the proposal:

"No more hundred and fifty bucks a week salary, Dutch," the presumptuous youth said. "I want a piece of all your beer sales and a cut on all the new joints we take over. Take it or leave it."

"I don't take in nobody as a partner with me," Schultz said. "You're an ambitious punk, but you take a salary or nothing. Take it or leave it."

"Okay. I'm leaving it," Coll said.

The grinning young hitman casually walked out, leaving Dutch Schultz with a very uneasy feeling. Coll, like Jack Diamond, wanted the spoils but lacked the business acumen to run an empire of his own. He may have been short on intelligence, but he was possessed with an abundance of cunning. Even the biggest names in New York crime would have to cast an eye over their shoulders.

Coll appeared to be leading something of a charmed existence. By May of 1930, he had evaded four robbery charges and was happily rampaging over Schultz-Madden territory. If the situation had been left unchecked, it might well have given the dangerous impression that anyone else could do the same. Schultz sent a messenger to Coll with a tough ultimatum—either he stayed out of bootlegging or he would be killed. The young Irishman took the hint but instead began to vent his annoyance on the men whom he felt were curtailing his business expansion. He decided to make his enemies subsidize his tiny empire by digging into their own pockets. Owney, well known for his generosity, was the obvious target. Coll carefully began to put together an ambitious plan to kidnap Big Frenchy in the certain knowledge that the Duke would pay anything for his friend's safety.

It was not an original idea. Kidnapping was becoming increasingly popular in the underworld, despite being frowned upon by major criminals. In 1931, there were an estimated 2,000 specialist kidnappers at work in the criminal community, and only sixty-five had been convicted. One gang in the Midwest netted an average of $50,000 a month in ransom demands. It was becoming a burgeoning business. Police calculated that in 90 percent of these cases, the authorities were not notified of kidnappings but heard of them through other sources. Kidnapping was fast becoming an unpleasant fact of life.

Among the offenders was the notorious Purple Gang of Detroit, which made a practice of kidnapping bootlegging rivals and releasing them when they received enormous sums. By the time Vinny Coll hatched his idea, the crime was so common in New York that one newspaper reported: "Nightclub owners are snatched early in the morning and delivered safe and sound to their friends the same evening on a strictly C.O.D. basis."

The late Arnold Rothstein had acted as a go-between when the owners of a Kentucky distillery were kidnapped on a business trip to New York and held for $500,000 in a Brooklyn apartment. Coll's prime motive, however, was revenge, and he was undeterred by the sixty-year sentences handed out to each member of a four-man gang convicted by Judge Joseph Colligan at New York's Court of General Sessions.

If Vincent was nervous, it was not about the law. Challenging Owney Madden was the biggest step in a hitherto undistinguished career, and only someone mad enough to disregard the consequences would have attempted it. Frenchy was, in fact, his second try. A previous attempt to kidnap Owney's friend Nils T. Granlund, an entertainer, had failed when news leaked out and someone tipped off the police. Coll decided instead to play for higher stakes.

His bold insanity was earmarked for the evening of June 15, 1931. Frank Giordano, his best gunman and most trusted lieutenant, had been watching Big Frenchy's movements. DeMange had few enemies and was a man of habit. Soon after dusk each day, he made his way up to his Club Argonaut on West 50th and 7th Avenue. As Frenchy approached the club entrance, ambling heavily along the sidewalk without a care in the world, Coll approached him with a wide grin. It did not occur to the Frenchman that it was odd the young man was wearing an overcoat on a balmy June evening.

"Hiya, Vince," Frenchy said amiably. "How's tricks?"

Coll dropped the smile abruptly and Giordano emerged from the shadows to join him. Vincent opened the front of his overcoat just enough to show Frenchy the barrel of a gun, and the big man knew he meant business.

"Why, men, this is silly," Frenchy spread his hands in protest. "If it's money you want, you can have it. You don't have to try this gun stuff."

His captors' expressions did not change. Frenchy exuded rough charm but, as one commentator later remarked: "You can imagine how much impression that made."

Coll kept his hand in his pocket and waved the front of his overcoat. "Get in the car," he ordered. "I ain't here to argue."

Frenchy shoehorned his bulk into the back of the waiting limousine, and the driver roared away in the direction of Riverside Drive.

DeMange, from his conversations with Owney, knew how reckless Coll had recently been. It was now clear that he was mad enough to stop at nothing. As the car bounced along toward Westchester County, Coll outlined his intentions to the Frenchman and asked him how much he considered his life was worth.

Frenchy looked thoughtful but, before he could answer, the Mad Mick, as he was known, set the ransom at a six-figure sum. Frenchy considered it ludicrous. This was, after all, the Depression, he said. A more realistic sum, taking all into consideration, would be around $10,000. Coll grinned. As the car sped along, figures were bandied back and forth. Coll tried to increase the stakes while Frenchy tried to lower them without antagonizing his captor.

By eleven that evening, Owney realized something was wrong. Frenchy's favorite seat at his Cotton Club table was empty. A phone call quickly established that he had also not arrived at the Club Argonaut. The answer was provided within the hour when Owney was told that there was a telephone call for him in the club office. When he picked up the receiver, Coll wasted no time getting down to business.

"I've got Big Frenchy," he said. "The tab is fifty grand. If you want to see him alive, you'll get up the money."

"Too steep," Owney replied, playing for time.

"Get it up or something is liable to happen to him," Coll sounded irritated. "I'll be down in half an hour, and I'm coming alone."

"Come ahead," said Owney and hung up the phone.

Madden confessed later that his first thought was that Coll was bluffing, and he decided to call him on it. Exactly thirty minutes later, Coll pushed open the door of Owney's office and stepped inside, grinning. Owney remained behind his desk and watched him in silence.

"Got the dough?" Coll demanded. There was an excited edge to his voice. "I left word with the boys that if they don't hear from me in half an hour, they give it to Frenchy."

Owney did not answer him. He rose to his feet and walked over to a wall safe from which he pulled $35,000 in bills.

"Take that, you maniac," he said, tossing it to Coll. "Now get out of here."

At the sight of money, Coll appeared to be in no hurry. He put the bundle on the desk and began to count it.

"It's all I could raise at short notice," Owney said.

Coll shrugged, then picked up the phone and dialed a number.

"Okay boys," he said. "I got the stuff. Keep him on ice."

Coll scooped up the cash and, at the door, turned and gave Owney a grin.

The Duke looked at him and said, "That was very unwise, Vincent."

In the early morning hours, Big Frenchy was dumped from a car unharmed outside the Club Argonaut. He freshened up and drove to the Cotton Club where he was swamped by well-wishers. One of the first to hear of the reunion was Walter Winchell but, in accordance with his agreement with Madden, he omitted to mention it in his column. The band struck up, and a celebration party was soon in full swing. Frenchy bear-hugged his partner in gratitude but, as the champagne corks popped, the expression on Owney's face suggested that the incident was far from over. Winchell, for his own part, had similar feelings. Gossip ran in his blood, and his urge to publicize the incident bubbled in him like a corked volcano. The time would come when he could no longer contain it. It would prove to be the biggest mistake of his career.

When the news reached Dutch Schultz, he immediately went into hiding. Coll, he knew, was crazy enough to try the same thing again. Dutch lay low for several days in the perfumed luxury of Polly Adler's exclusive whorehouse, guarded round the clock by his best gunmen. Both Schultz and Madden summoned out-of-town gunmen to discreetly search all Coll's favorite haunts, but the wily Irishman had gone underground.

After a few days, Coll surfaced with renewed determination to step up his war against Owney and Dutch. A little more than a month after the kidnapping, on July 28, 1931, he issued Schultz with a warning that he intended to take over more of his empire. To drive the message home, he filled a car with men and cruised the streets of Spanish Harlem looking for Joey Rao, the man who ran the Dutchman's gambling rackets. Somehow, news often leaked out about Coll's plans—he and his gang members were notoriously careless talkers—and his latest escapade was no exception.

Some sources claim that Rao received a tip-off that an attempt was to be made on his life. "Knowing he was marked for slaughter, Rao was said to have kept a pocketful of pennies for distribution to the children on the block around his headquarters, the Helmar Social Club in East 107th Street, so that he was always surrounded by swarming children and Coll's gunmen couldn't open fire on him," O'Connor mentions. Rao need not have taken such precautions, as the streets of Harlem on a sunny afternoon were always crowded with playing children and families sitting on the steps of their brownstone tenements.

It was a typical July afternoon in New York, hot and muggy with little breeze, and the air languid with dust and exhaust fumes. Rao, like most of the neighborhood, was sitting outside his headquarters in his shirt sleeves, chatting with two bodyguards.

A few feet away, on the edge of the sidewalk, fourteen-year-old Frank Scalesi had set up a penny lemonade stand, and a group of children was milling around it. Among them was five-year-old Michael Vengali and his seven-year-old brother, Salvatore. A fourteen-year-old girl, Florence D'Amello, was helping at the stand, serving little Samuel Divino, aged five. Nearby, dozing peacefully in a wicker baby carriage, lay three-year-old Michael Bevilacqua.

No one noticed a huge, open touring car nose quietly around the corner at walking speed. It was filled with hard-looking men. When it was almost level with the Helmar Social Club, the men produced weapons and began to rake the frontage with gunfire. Rao rolled from his chair and down the steps of an adjoining basement, followed by the swearing figures of his two bodyguards, their revolvers already drawn. The deafening noise of the shooting was finally drowned by the roar of the car engine as the driver accelerated away. In its wake, Michael Vengali lay dead in the gutter, the baby lay seriously wounded in its baby carriage, and the other children screamed and rolled on the sidewalk clutching bullet wounds.

Rao and his companions gingerly poked their heads above the basement steps, unharmed. By early evening, both the police and the newspapers were placing the blame squarely on Coll. Outraged head-lines called him the "Mad Dog" and "Baby Killer." Overnight, he became the most wanted man in New York. The Helmar, where the shooting took place, was a Democratic social club, run by Vincent Rao, Joey's cousin. Despite the tragedy, the political machine showed only cautious cooperation. Gangsters hanging around the building identified Coll as the killer but declined to identify the target. Early statements suggesting that it was Joey Rao were quickly changed. The man outside, said witnesses, was a minor criminal called Anthony Trobino.

Rao, it seemed, was too close to political boss Jimmy Hines to get drawn into the affair. Later, when Joey was serving a term in the House of Correction on Welfare Island for pushing cocaine and heroin, Hines expressed his thanks for the gunman's silence. Rao was allowed to virtually run the prison and preside over kangaroo courts, safe in the knowledge that, under Hines's orders, wardens would lose their jobs if they interfered.

Owney passed the word around the underworld that he was prepared to pay $25,000 to anyone who could track down Coll and kill him. Schultz followed suit with a similar figure. Once again, however, the Irishman had gone underground. Ironically, it was the police who found him, hiding in a West 23rd Street hotel where he had grown a moustache and darkened his hair.

Coll and his gunman Giordano, amidst headline publicity, were indicted with the murder of the five-year-old boy in a case which became known as the Harlem Baby Killing. Their lawyer, Samuel J. Leibowitz—later to become one of New York's toughest judges—proved to be worth every penny of his considerable fee. The main prosecution witness, George Brecht, who was outside the Harlem club at the time of the shooting, seemed strangely familiar to the defendants. Some reports suggested that he had a habit of talking out of the side of his mouth, a trait common among ex-convicts. In any event, his appearance was considered worthy of further investigation. Leibowitz had his background checked out, and it was discovered that he had given perjured evidence at a murder trial in St. Louis.

The discovery was enough for the astute lawyer to successfully appeal to have the case dismissed.

Outside the court, Coll stumbled over the words of a statement which he had prepared for reporters: "I have been charged with all kinds of crimes," he said, "but baby killing was the limit. I'd like nothing better than to lay my hands on the man who did this. I'd tear his throat out. There is nothing more despicable than a man who would harm an innocent child."

And, with that, he drove away with his girlfriend Lotte Kreisberger on his arm to celebrate by getting married.

Coll was not a man to learn readily from his fortunate escape from justice. Soon after his release from custody, he made plans to kidnap Owney's brother-in-law, a local bail bondsman. Again, he talked too much and too loudly, and the scheme had to be abandoned. After spending a few days mulling over his next move, Coll redoubled his efforts to strike back at Schultz and Madden, this time with the boldest plans he had yet conceived.

To all appearances, Owney seemed the less aggressive of the two gang leaders. Coll wrongly deduced from this that it meant Owney was the weaker. On the basis of this error of judgment, he decided to challenge Owney head on. Schultz had a reputation for throwing fits of anger when crossed and was known to retaliate with guns blazing. Owney, as Coll had noticed during the ransom episode, was quiet, almost withdrawn, and apparently easy to push around. Experience had unfortunately not yet taught him that first impressions can be deceptive. The Mad Dog, whose funds had been seriously depleted by the hefty legal fees of his trial, tried again to force Owney to subsidize his war against Schultz.

This time he decided to go for the big one and kidnap the Duke and, in view of his leaky operation, actually rang him in advance to tell him so. Vincent's message was simple: if Madden did not pay $100,000 by a certain deadline, he would be snatched from the streets and held for ransom. Owney found the idea so incredible that he hung up the phone without speaking. Events, from then on, moved quickly. Gang leaders, including Schultz and Costello, were invited to a council of war at one of Owney's quiet mid-town hotels to talk over the Coll problem. They voted to concentrate on one of Coll's bodyguards, whom they knew to be susceptible to bribery, in order to obtain information. In the meantime, according to O'Connor, the city was divided into equal zones, manned by gunmen who would cut Coll down the moment he was pinpointed. It was unanimously decided that, until the trouble died down, Owney should take a holiday in Florida—"not exactly scared out of town, perhaps, but finding a change of climate essential for reasons of health."

Those at the meeting felt a responsibility to curtail Coll's madcap activities without breaking the Atlantic City agreement and triggering an open war on the streets. It was to prove harder than they ever imagined. Owney found himself unwillingly in the eye of a storm which he had striven for years to avoid. Open conflict could still result in a violation of his parole on any number of charges. To distance himself further from the trouble now bubbling dangerously on the West Side, gunmen were imported from the Midwest. These were highly professional killers who were almost completely unknown in Manhattan. They proved so efficient that, to students of gangland murder, the slaying of Vincent Coll was regarded for many years as a textbook operation and, in detective circles, a classic underworld assassination.

After days of inactivity, Coll was sighted and discreetly followed. His hiding place and activities were carefully noted and reported back to Schultz and Madden, who had returned to the city. Between them, they decided on a plan of action and set his execution date for February 8. A message was relayed through Coll's bodyguard that Owney was ready to talk business about the $100,000 ransom. The intention was to lure him to a place where he felt safe to discuss terms with Owney by telephone, thus removing from his mind any thought of an ambush. Owney selected a drugstore on West 23rd Street and 8th Avenue in Hell's Kitchen, around the corner from the tenement where Coll had grown up and only a short distance from the hotel where he was hiding. The young Irishman knew the neighborhood well and everyone there knew him. In all Manhattan, it was perhaps the one place where he felt on home ground. What he perhaps failed to realize was that the drugstore was also only a block and a half from Owney's penthouse apartment.

Walter Winchell had been monitoring events on the underworld grapevine, picking up gossip in clubs and speakeasies and piecing the story together. He was the most awesome one-man information industry in America. On Sunday evenings, his radio broadcasts were networked around the world. On Monday mornings, his gossip column appeared in 165 newspapers across the country. He built up those who courted his favor and demolished those who offended him. One hint from Winchell could make or break a reputation, and he reveled in his power. Despite accusations of being "one of the most inaccurate reporters in the history of journalism and also one of the most unscrupulous," by St. Clair McKelway of the New Yorker, he still commanded enormous fees. After taxes, Winchell's estimated income was $285,000 annually. His inaccuracy, incidentally, was notorious within the trade. McKelway trawled a random 259 items from five Monday columns one month and found 103 of them either unverifiable or simply wrong.

It was hardly by chance that Owney struck up an acquaintanceship with Winchell, "the friend of gangsters, the pal of the police, the intimate of G-Men, and J. Edgar Hoover's 'Man Friday.'" It was even less of an accident that Winchell never used his columns to the Duke's disadvantage. Among the gifts he received for services rendered were an impressive automobile and a personal bodyguard. Under Owney's patronage, "Mrs. Winchell's little boy," as he termed himself, looked just like a real gangster as he was chauffeured around town. Walter, however, through a disastrous slip of the typewriter, was to discover to his horror who really had the upper hand in the relationship.

Winchell always appeared brash and sure of himself but apparently was not too sure. He packed two automatic revolvers, with full police permission, for personal protection—presumably from his army of readers. Owney considered Damon Runyon, another of his small circle of writer acquaintances, a "likeable guy," probably because they both shared a genuine affection for New York characters. Winchell tended to treat people as column fodder and a means of enhancing his own reputation—a trait which had always made Madden wary of most newsmen. As he was a British passport holder, they were a threat to his continued existence in New York. Careless gossip and indeed any coverage of his activities could easily lead to jail for parole violation and ultimately to deportation. With characteristic cunning, he remained sociable enough to deter curiosity while ducking out of range of sniping city editors. Owney maintained his low profile by leading a quiet, almost tedious existence, conducting his affairs with propriety and generous persuasion.

He first ran into Walter Winchell, less by accident than design, in the columnist's favorite barber shop. Owney sat down for a haircut in an adjoining chair and, within minutes, Winchell was talking about himself. His first question was whether Owney realized who he was:

"When Madden flattered the jet-propelled columnist by conceding that he had heard of him before, the odd pair got along well," the *New York Post* reported in one of its many muckraking stories about Winchell's social life.

Owney cultivated Winchell but had little respect for him. "He's anybody's dog," he would warn friends behind the columnist's back. "Watch him. He'll hunt with any pack that comes along." Later, in retirement, Owney would sit in his lawyer's office in Hot Springs listening to Winchell's radio broadcasts with his fox terrier on his knee. When a particularly unreliable item tumbled from the radio among the torrent of "informed" snippets, Owney would look skeptical. "I'd check that out," he would say to anyone within earshot.

It appeared that the whole West Side criminal fraternity knew that there were new faces in town, quietly asking questions about the Mad Dog. Winchell, in deference to Owney, had kept Frenchy's kidnapping out of the newspapers. Suddenly, right in his lap, he found a sequel too tantalizing for any newspaperman to resist. Walter, however, overlooked the essential point that most newsmen were not handsomely paid to suppress their stories. Eventually, his love of dropping tidbits of inside information overrode his better judgment. Winchell pulled a chair up to his battered typewriter in the *Mirror* office and hammered out a paragraph for his column. As far as he knew, Owney was still in Florida and Coll would be dead anyway by the time it appeared in print. The implication that he had received a prior whisper about the biggest secret in New York would be a further boost to his reputation. "Five planes brought dozens of machine guns from Chicago Friday to combat The Town Capone. Local banditti have made one hotel a virtual arsenal and several hot spots are ditto because Master Coll is giving them a headache."

Winchell's piece was inaccurate as usual. That would have mattered little but for the fact that, by a grave miscalculation, it hit the streets two hours before the attempt on Coll took place.

Winchell's blood presumably ran cold when he read the piece in print. Thumbing through the news pages, he quickly learned that the killing had not yet happened. "Mrs. Winchell's little boy" could only imagine how Owney and Dutch would react when they read the column. It was not a prospect he readily savored.

Coll, it appeared, did not read the *Mirror* that evening because his suspicions were not aroused. The weak link in his gang—the bodyguard—proved a valuable asset. Enticed by the promise of $50,000 for his master's head, he offered to convince Vincent that it was quite safe to make the call from the drugstore.

Late on the night of February 8th, Coll and his bodyguard strolled from the Cornish Arms Hotel on West 23rd Street, between 8th and 9th, and walked to the London Chemist's Shop on the other side of the street. It was a small neighborhood drugstore with a soda fountain and a friendly atmosphere. Unknown to Coll, however, this was about to change dramatically. Pharmacist Morris Kantrowitz had just served drinks to two customers—Dr. Edward Pavner, a local practitioner, and a friend who had dropped by from Chicago, Dr. Leo Latz. As they were chatting quietly, Coll ambled in with his bodyguard and looked around the room. When everything appeared to be to his satisfaction, he stepped into the telephone booth at the back of the store and pulled the door behind him. The bodyguard settled down on a stool to wait. Unknown to anyone, two Manhattan detectives had been shadowing Coll to ward off any further bloodshed when his enemies caught up with him.

The officers, for some mysterious reason never explained, had not reached the drugstore when a large car pulled up outside. Bo Weinberg, one of Dutch Schultz's best men, was behind the wheel, and a stranger sat beside him. Coll had been engrossed on the telephone for eight to ten minutes when the stranger walked into the drugstore looking relaxed, with a machine gun tucked loosely at waist height under one arm.

At the sight of him, Coll's bodyguard slid off his stool and hastily made his way out. Weinberg, waiting outside, recognized him and allowed him to go. Inside the store, the pharmacist and his customers were in a state of near panic.

"Just stay where you are. All keep quiet. Keep cool now," the gunman told them calmly.

He then clicked off the safety catch and aimed a short burst of bullets through the glass of the booth. After a second or two, he paused. Unhurriedly, he corrected his aim and continued the job until Coll crashed through the shattered door onto the glass-strewn floor.

Reporters later filled in the details with relish: "Never nicking the wood outside that glassed-in target, the marksman raked a zone from head-high to knee-low, straight down the side of the window at the left, and across to the right, then up the right side. He stopped firing and saw that the job was done. The Mad Mick, riddled, was on his knees on the floor. The gunman ran out to find his partner already at the wheel, and the car shot away toward 8th Avenue, picking up speed.

"Two detectives, who had been assigned to trail Coll, came running up, and one of them jumped on the running board of a taxicab, prodding the driver to get into high. The detective started firing at the car ahead, but he never had a chance to catch it. It swung up 8th Avenue and dashed away at better than sixty miles an hour, so was soon lost from sight."

Vincent Coll was twenty-three years old. When detectives searched the Cornish Arms Hotel, where he had been staying with his wife Lotte, they found his entire savings of $101 pinned inside one of her brassieres. Lotte, fearing that something had gone wrong, had raced to the drug-store in the red dress she had worn the day they married. When police arrived, she was bent over her husband's body, screaming. The officers were anxious to ask her many questions. The most puzzling being how did she know that her husband had been shot? And, more importantly, who had been on the other end of the telephone receiver, now swinging like a pendulum in the empty booth?

"I don't want to be stubborn," Lotte replied, "but I'm not going to say any more about Vincent and me."

Reporters besieged Commissioner Mulrooney's office at police head-quarters demanding answers. He shouldered his way through a pack of newsmen and exploding flashbulbs, fending off questions about Madden and Schultz like a boxer. His only comment was that the killing was "a positive defiance of law and order." Hardly powerful stuff under the circumstances.

Vincent Coll's shattered body was taken to the morgue with more than sixty holes torn in it by steel-jacketed bullets. Fifteen of them were found lodged in his brain, heart, and limbs.

Lotte, a willing accomplice in her husband's affairs, returned to a life of crime and ended up serving twelve years for robbery in Bedford Reformatory for Women. With the exception of his wife and sister, no one mourned Coll's passing. Unlike the lavish, flower-strewn funerals of other gangland characters, no one turned up to pay their last respects at St. Raymond's Cemetery in the Bronx. The Mad Dog was lowered into his grave in a tin coffin while Walter B. Cooke, the undertaker, read the Lord's Prayer. No priest attended the brief ceremony, and the undertaker's men left quickly as the drizzle turned to rain. Behind them, on the coffin lid, was a single wreath of red and white carnations—the English working-class symbol of death—and a black-edged card which simply read: "From the Boys."

Owney's immediate problems were over, but Walter Winchell's were only just beginning. Terrified of what might befall him, he asked for police protection and his column lost a little of its usual bravado. When it next appeared, on the following Monday, Winchell expressed his nervousness in a paragraph which read: "If only when my epitaph is readied, they will say: Here is Walter Winchell—with his ear to the ground—as usual."

In another item he remarked: "If I had any moxie I would chuck the whole thing and go somewhere with Mrs. Winchell and the children and laugh a little." Unfortunately, he was given little opportunity. District Attorney Crain summoned the terrified columnist before a Grand Jury called to investigate Coll's death and demanded an explanation. Winchell lapsed into uncharacteristic silence and claimed that the information had come to him as an anonymous tip through the mail.

Soon afterward, the *Mirror* announced that Walter Winchell had suffered a "nervous breakdown," and the column would be discontinued until further notice. Walter took himself off with his family to California, presumably still finding it difficult to "laugh a little." Six weeks later, he eased himself back into work, restricting his column mainly to show business gossip.

"By then," his rival paper, the *New York Post*, observed, "the party, or parties, most seriously distressed by his extraordinary foresight in the Coll murder, cooled off." It was seven years before Walter Winchell attempted to cover a serious organized crime story again.

11.

The Postmaster's Daughter

It was time to take a vacation, and the safest place to which a man in Owney's position could turn was Hot Springs, Arkansas. The "Baden Baden of America," as it styled itself, was a spa in the grand tradition. It attracted millionaires, movie stars, and members of high society from all over the world. Andrew Carnegie, F. W. Woolworth, John Barrymore, or Douglas Fairbanks Sr. were faces visitors might encounter in the marbled lobby of the Arlington Hotel or the imposing Majestic. They could listen to the finest singing at Hot Springs Opera House, dance to famous bands, and play the tables at the Belvedere or Southern Club. Hot Springs had a certain style. At a time when Las Vegas and Miami were wastelands, it glittered like a jewel in the heavy mountain dusk and clattered to the sound of cash registers. Bath houses sprouted along Central Avenue, offering warm, natural spring water to the aching and infirm.

Many casual visitors were unaware of its other attraction as a safe haven for members of the underworld, including the likes of Meyer Lansky, Frank Costello, and Benjamin "Bugsy" Siegel. Mayor Leo Patrick McLaughlin, a dictatorial lawyer of Irish descent, did not invite them there, but, once he had approved their presence, they were free to lay low, plan campaigns, pursue local business opportunities, meet up with old friends, or simply avoid being arrested. Visiting hoods in the late 1920s and early 1930s would alight from the train at Hot Springs station and tell the cab driver: "The Cigar Store." Everyone knew where they wanted to go. The White Front Cigar Store, run by an amiable tough called Dick Galatas, was a casino, pool hall, bookie shop, and underworld clearinghouse rolled into one. There, they could discover who was in town or arrange to buy a gun from the thin, stooped Chief of Detectives, Dutch Akers.

Hot Springs was the last meeting place of the old Wild West and the new urban cowboys of Chicago and New York.

The underworld nicknamed it "Bubbles" after its sparkling waters, and the spa became a favorite watering hole of Al Capone. He first arrived in town, they say, to buy liquor for his Windy City speakeasies from the stills which sprouted like conifers in the wooded hills. Much of the booze was manufactured by three families—hillbillies according to local historians—who made as much as $25 million a year during Prohibition. Capone would arrive in town with a huge entourage and always demand Room 442, which overlooked the Southern Club across the street. From the hall, Capone could step into an elevator, lined with beveled glass and shining brass, and ride down to take the waters. Later, he bought one of the town's old stately bath houses and equipped it as a gym for his boys.

McLaughlin, who held the office of mayor unopposed for twenty years, did not mind the big names of crime strolling the boulevard with their bodyguards. Anyone who brought money to Hot Springs was welcome—on the condition that they never attempted to take over. The mayor and his cabinet of wealthy racketeers—known as the "Little Combination" or "the Partnership"—ruled the town with an iron hand.

When the summer visitors had departed, Hot Springs embarked on its dazzling winter social season of balls and banquets, attended by high rollers and their beautiful women. By 1931, however, even the "Karlsbad of the South" was succumbing to the rigors of the Depression. The annual street pageant, with floats, marching bands, and floral slogans announcing "We Bathe The World," had been discontinued. Horse racing at Oaklawn Park had fallen victim to the puritan rod of Prohibitionists. The winter season waltzed valiantly on, but the number of visitors had noticeably fallen. For the first time in living memory, small businesses began to close, praying that the onset of summer would revive their fortunes.

Along the picturesque avenues, the trees were already in bud, ready to paint neat gardens with pink and white blossoms. But even the first smile of spring could do little to alleviate the gloom the town was undergoing.

After sitting all day in the Provincial Coffee House and Gift Mart without seeing a single customer, Agnes Demby closed up shop in the late afternoon. Her receipt pad, headed "We Appreciate Your Custom—Thank you," had lain beside the till without recording a sale for days. She walked dejectedly home to the pretty, white family house on West Grand Avenue. Her father, James Demby, a wiry, outspoken veteran of the Spanish-American War, ran the Hot Springs Post Office. Her mother, who looked old and unwell of late, sat near the fire and brightened when she walked through the door. Agnes was thirty, an attractive, single woman with energetic tastes for riding, golf, and endless dinner dates with friends. Her bright eyes danced with spirit and humor when she spoke, and she had no shortage of suitors. It was boredom, as much as the lack of business, which made the cold opening of 1931 seem intolerable.

Agnes spent the evening at home sewing with her mother, discussing the news, or lack of it, and debating over which male visitor to town might take her out to dinner. She hoped it would be Joe Diamond, a thoughtful, good-looking young man from East St. Louis, who had taken a liking to Hot Springs. Later, Agnes lay in bed in her room, which overlooked the orchard, and rested her new five-year diary against her knees. The publishers, the Fan-C Pack Company of New York, had printed an uplifting foreword on the title page: "From the everyday medley there is an event that should re-echo down the years. Happily it is usually a bit of sunshine: sometimes it may be a bit of disappointment—even a trace of sorrow. But, whatever it may be, jot it down in THE BOOK OF ECHOES and in after years you will find the

Happy High Lights setting up a musical harmony—and even the disappointments and the sorrow bits shall be mellowed and ease gracefully into the general medley of "ECHOES."

If Agnes read the foreword that evening, it provided her with little inspiration. She unscrewed the top from her fountain pen and wrote:

"23.1.31 Business still punk. Finished my black dress. Mama says I look like a dashing widow in it with my black tri-corn hat."

Flicking back through the handful of pages she had filled showed no lifting of the heavy atmosphere hanging over town.

"5.1.31 Business at the store quiet. I am sewing tonite. Making myself a new black woolen dress. Mama is so glad to have me home.

"7.1.31 Business still very poor. Mrs. Leviston is also very discouraged with the tearoom business. This is an awful year.

"19.1.31 Business still poor. Given a bad check today for $35. Came home early tonite to sew some more on my dress..."

Agnes closed the book and went to sleep, hoping that some friendly face would soon drop into town to brighten up her life.

When Joe Diamond arrived, her jaded social life began to look up. He arrived with a pal, Jack Becker, and immediately called to invite her to dinner at the Belvedere, a sumptuous gambling club in the old tradition on Highway Five North. The Belvedere had high ceilings, crystal chandeliers, and a cavernous fireplace blazing with winter logs. Up to 1,500 diners could eat in comfort, listening to the dance music of Paul Whiteman and other big orchestras. By 1931, the club, with its distinctive arched windows, had been remodeled and largely rebuilt and was the most fashionable place to be in Hot Springs for an evening out.

Joe was very attentive. He sent her a dozen roses, bought her new riding breeches, and led her on a whirlwind tour of golfing and dinner parties. One Saturday evening in February, they stayed at the Belvedere until 3 a.m. and then talked around the dying embers of the fire at her home until 5:30 a.m. Agnes began to think seriously about Joe, but her mother's failing health prevented her from giving the future too much consideration. At dawn, after listening to Joe talk of his plans, she climbed into bed, pausing only to fill in her diary:

"I've had the blues terribly all day. Don't know why, but I feel like something is going to happen..."

A few days later, her mother's condition worsened, and the family doctor called James Demby from the post office and Agnes from the gift shop to be at her bedside. Joe spent his last night in Hot Springs with Agnes, keeping a vigil in the old-fashioned bedroom with its hand-made rugs and sanded floors.

"Joe and I sat up all night with Mama," Agnes wrote. "She seems a little better today. Joe brought her out candy and roses and told her he would come back for me. She smiled and said, 'alright.'"

Agnes missed Diamond when he took the train back to East St. Louis but welcomed the opportunity to devote her time wholeheartedly to her mother. Hot Springs seemed desolate again. Business at her shop was fifty percent below that of the previous year. Mrs. Leviston, struggling with similar problems at the neighboring teashop, returned home one evening to find that her husband had walked out, claiming in a note to her that he had gambled away all their savings.

Night after night, Agnes stayed at her mother's bedside, sometimes praying for her health to improve. On the morning of February 19th, Mrs. Demby woke at 8 a.m. Agnes kissed her, then washed her face and combed her hair before lying down for a while beside her. At 10:45 a.m., Mrs. Demby died, leaving her daughter heartbroken and wondering if she could ever fill the vacuum in her life. After a funeral befitting the wife of one of the town's leading citizens, the rambling, old frame house seemed empty. Agnes found fulfillment more elusive than ever. The bright spring days, fresh and full of promise, dragged along interminably as she sat in her gift shop waiting for customers.

As the weeks went by, the breeze from the Hot Springs mountains grew warmer and the hills turned green. A few familiar faces began to drop in, lifting Agnes's spirits. Summer drew closer and the town stirred to life again, as though emerging from a long hibernation. Joe Diamond returned, as he said he would, with candy, flowers, and another pal. By the end of his short stay, when work and St. Louis beckoned, he claimed to feel sick. Agnes began to wonder if he genuinely wanted to stay on or, as she suspected, he was simply lazy.

Sometime later, as she sat in the back of her shop, something in the street outside caught her eye. An enormous Duesenberg convertible, grander than anything she had ever seen, pulled up, covering the entire length of the front window. Two men climbed out and stretched themselves. The driver, casually dressed for the country, glanced up at the sign above the shop and strolled inside. He was slightly built, with a shy, boyish smile and a soft accent which intrigued her as soon as he spoke. As they stood facing each other across the counter, neither could have ever imagined how, from that moment on, their lives were to radically change.

It was no accident that Owney had walked into Agnes's shop that day. Dutch Schultz is said to have told him to look out for "the good-looking dame" in the gift store when he reached Bubbles. It was his first trip to Hot Springs after hearing so much about it from the New York crowd. Joe Gould from New Jersey, who managed one of his fighters, was already in town on doctor's orders, taking the waters for his arthritis. Owney looked him up at the Arlington, and they drove around together. Joe was a good friend, but he would have preferred someone prettier than an ex-pro boxer to show him the sights.

Agnes smiled impishly when she recalled that spring day at the coffee shop more than half a century ago.

"I sold gifts and costume jewelry in the front of the shop, and you could take coffee and cake in the back. A friend was with me, and she pointed him out." Agnes gave a wry chuckle. "I told her, 'You stay here. I'll take care of him.' I noticed he was a good dresser. He just looked around the place and talked. I think he bought about a thousand dollars worth of stuff. Then, he asked me out to dinner, but I said 'No.'"

Agnes locked up the shop at the end of the day and walked home along Central Avenue, past the baths and gambling joints and oyster houses, filling up a little now as summer approached. When she took the key from her handbag and opened the front door, the emptiness of the house hung everywhere.

"Papa was out somewhere," she recalled. "He was often away since Mama died. I felt so blue and lonely."

Her thoughts went back to the handsome New York visitor who had asked her out with his friend. Agnes walked through the rooms, footsteps echoing on the wooden floor, and made up her mind. She changed, fixed her hair and makeup, and walked back into town to the Arlington, where they said they were staying. Agnes found them sitting together in the lobby and said: "Hello. Do you still want to go to dinner?"

"Owney gave a broad smile and said he would love to," Agnes recalled years later, sipping her glass of iced water as we visited. "We went out to a place that cooked chicken dinners and talked and talked."

What was it about Owney that set him apart from the long line of suitors who wined and dined her on their visits to Hot Springs? Agnes thought about it for some time, parting the years of familiarity in order to recall the days when they were almost strangers.

"He was interesting," she finally said. "He kept my interest all the time. That was one of the biggest reasons, I suppose. In those first days, I could have married several times, but with Owney I was never bored. After meeting him, I asked myself, what could anyone else offer?"

Owney stayed for more than two weeks, spending most of his time going out with the attractive proprietor of the gift store. They dined out, played golf against Hot Springs's backdrop of forests and mountains, and went for drives together. It was an idyllic setting for romance, but the city huddled in the hills receded as they became absorbed in each other. Toward the end of his visit, Owney told Agnes that he and Joe had to get back to New York for a big fight that one of his boxers was preparing for.

"Before he left, he handed me an envelope," she said. "When I opened it, I found a train ticket to New York. He said he wanted me to visit him after the summer. This time, I didn't say no."

In Owney's absence from New York, the vise had tightened. His business affairs began to attract wildly inaccurate stories. And anyone connected with him was now considered fair game. It was open season on the city desks, and fight manager Bill Duffy, Owney's partner in the Carnera circus touring the country, was one of the first to be lined up in their sights. Duffy had served time in Sing Sing, but the New York State Boxing Commission appeared to have overlooked his record when it issued him—quite illegally—a license. The *New York Evening Post* was the first with the story, illustrating a bloodthirsty spread by Milton Mackaye with a list of Duffy's convictions. The *Post* also produced figures which suggested that the diminutive manager had made $200,000 from the first four months of Primo's tour. Strangely, neither the boxing commission nor City Hall paid the slightest attention to the information. It served, however, to swing the spotlight further onto Owney. The war raging between Dutch Schultz and Mad Dog Vincent Coll was also drawing more attention to what was seen as lawlessness on the streets.

Owney's business activities were almost "legitimate" compared to the drug-running, prostitution, and contract killings in which some gang leaders were immersed, yet powerful forces were gathering to put him back into Sing Sing. In the eyes of ambitious prosecutors, the Cotton Club, the Stork, and Madden's No. 1 Beer had become a familiar part of city life. To break the man behind them would be considered a coup, though how much popular support it would receive from New Yorkers was another question.

By May of 1931, Judge Samuel Seabury was still collecting evidence about corruption in the courts. Stirred by his success, the law-and-order-minded Citizens' Union staged a conference demanding a closer look at graft within the police, the law courts, and the political administration. Undeterred by the fact that only nineteen citizens turned up, it was grandly called the New York Committee of One Thousand. There were police raids on Democratic district clubs, which had long sheltered illegal drinking and gambling, and Senator Hofstadter's committee began to look more closely at how they were run.

The downfall of Jimmy Hines, Mayor Walker, and the infamous underworld leaders who kept them in office was being played out square by square on the political chessboard. On one side, whole empires were at stake. On the other, was the promise of careers to be made. New York's governor, Franklin D. Roosevelt, watched nervously from the wings. There was less than a year to run before the Democratic National Convention in Chicago when the next candidate for the U.S. presidency would be nominated. To succeed in his ultimate ambition, he would have to be seen to throw his weight behind the crusade against crime and corruption. At the same time, he would not even be considered for office without the support of the very Democrats under investigation.

Costello, Luciano, Hines, Walker, Dewey, Roosevelt, Seabury, Hofstadter—men who wielded immense power—were inexorably drawn into combat. Everything each of them had worked for was at stake. For a while, on the battlefield of New York in 1931, there were no good guys and bad guys, just raw ambition and an insatiable drive for supremacy. Owney had made his own decision years earlier. All he ever wanted was an opportunity to survive unrecognized and intact. For the moment, however, his plans had taken an unexpected turn. He did not consider it a setback but it looked quite strongly as though he had fallen in love.

Just a few weeks earlier, Agnes had been the unlikeliest candidate for a headlong romance. She seemed destined, if anything, for marriage to some fine young man with prospects. Owney, approaching his fortieth birthday, was nine years older and had a lifestyle that seemed worlds apart. By the time the Duke had served half his prison sentence in Sing Sing and New York was squaring itself for the prospect of Prohibition, Agnes was just an eighteen-year-old Hot Springs High School student celebrating her graduation. Among the school mementoes she proudly showed her parents was a graduation message scrawled in her scrapbook from Howard H. Russell, leader of the Anti-Saloon League, who campaigned for Prohibition.

Agnes's family was regarded socially as one of the best in Hot Springs. James Demby's job as postmaster was an elected position like that of sheriff. Under the iron administration of McLaughlin, it carried power and influence. "Nobody ever crossed a Demby," I was told. Young Agnes, bright and bubbling with life, was a "good catch" for any man of suitable standing, but she still enjoyed the freedom of remaining single. Despite pleas and marriage proposals, she preferred to cling to her independence. Marriage seemed dull by comparison, even marriage to the golf professional and the millionaire's son who wooed her over the years.

When Owney returned to New York, the carefree weeks in Arkansas were soon swamped beneath a wave of waiting trouble. Within a month of his arrival, Big Frenchy was kidnapped by Vincent Coll. By the time summer was drawing to a close, Maranzano, the ambitious Mafia boss, had died in a hail of steel-jacketed bullets. The treacherous currents of gangland were acquiring a dangerous undertow. Owney exchanged regular letters with Agnes but seldom touched on the full extent of the problems he was experiencing. He was shy and taciturn by nature, which made her anxious to know if his feelings were as strong as hers. Agnes had fallen for him heavily, and the feeling increased during the months of his absence. Owney, by force of habit, was reluctant to pour out his thoughts on paper. Their relationship, however, had clearly brought a softening in his outlook. His letters were warm and affectionate but became less frequent as his troubles grew. Agnes was at the gift store one morning when a telegram boy walked in with a Western Union message: "MY DEAREST DARLING. MISS YOU. HOPE TO SEE YOU SOON. LOVE, OWEN." It was one of many to wing its way to the Bible Belt at a time when sending love messages by wire was almost unheard of.

The authorities, encouraged by hardening political attitudes, began to harass Owney, holding him in custody on suspicion of minor offenses to flex their muscles. On some occasions, he was held for up to forty-eight hours until Joe Shalleck could lever him from their grasp.

"Haven't heard from my Darling for two days," Agnes wrote in her diary in June. "I felt that something was wrong, but got a wire tonight saying he had been to college for a couple of days."

By the following morning, she had received "a nice long letter" which lifted her spirits. Agnes, like Owney, was preoccupied with business and made an appointment to visit the landlord who owned her shop. Business had not recovered, despite the summer season, and many local merchants were very worried. Agnes persuaded him to reduce the rent by $25 for a period of four months.

"No business at all today," she wrote a few days later. "Joe Gould called me up tonite to tell me Owney would have to leave town and keep quiet for a few days." Gould had become their go-between, taking telephone messages from Agnes and passing them on to Owney. When the Duke's troubles worsened and nothing was heard from him, Joe kept Agnes informed as to what was happening. The strain began to affect her, and, when she unexpectedly fainted and injured herself, she decided to have a medical check-up. The doctor prescribed a tonic for low vitality and heart palpitations which eased her condition but did little to prevent her worrying almost constantly about Owney. Unable to cope, she closed up the shop for a few days to recuperate and collect her thoughts. By the middle of June, she was back behind the counter again, hoping for customers. A note in her diary read:

"Saturday: Came to the shop for the first time this morning since I fainted. My eye is still black and I feel bad. Business is punk. Haven't heard from Owney since a week today. I wish I was with him."

As the days dragged by, Owney's wires and letters became less frequent. By August, Agnes felt unable to take any more. She removed the envelope containing the Pullman ticket to New York from her drawer and set out to find him. Joe Gould made the arrangements and drove Agnes to Owney's apartment near 10th Avenue. She found him hobbling to greet her with an injured toe. It was a heady, heartwarming reunion in the city which her lover dominated. Ironically, his communications had slowed to a trickle because he was anxious for her not to visit New York.

With Coll on the rampage and the authorities taking a keen interest in his activities, he did not wish her to become a target. Owney arranged to have her chaperoned while he went about his business, asking Texas Guinan to take Agnes under her ample wing and show her the sights of the city. The Queen of the Nightclubs and the postmaster's daughter hit it off immediately. Arm in arm, they plunged into the whirlpool of New York nightlife, drinking late in speakeasies after Broadway shows and sleeping through the afternoon, ready to start all over again in the evening. Owney kept a low profile but tried to see her whenever he could. Agnes noted in her diary:

"August 22, 1931: Had a big time tonite at Woodmanston. It was raided at midnite but no liquor found.

"August 23: I knew something would happen as I was so nervous, I couldn't sleep, and on my way to the Napoleon Club, I saw Owney and jumped out of the cab and ran to him. Got him and we had dinner. I was so happy.

"August 26: Owney came to see me this afternoon. I was so thrilled to see him. He is so worried and looks bad. I wish I could get him away.

"August 27: Was at Texas Guinan's again last nite, and Rueben's later. Walter Winchell drove me home thru Central Park."

As the days slid by, Agnes managed to snatch meetings with Owney, but he was still anxious not to be seen too much around the city. Coll, by this time, had spread the word that he intended to follow Frenchy's kidnapping by abducting someone close to Madden. As the Duke distanced himself from Agnes, he ensured that she had company and the opportunity to enjoy herself. "Just got up at 4 p.m.," she wrote in her diary. "Was at Texas's place again last nite and had a marvelous time. Gardenias and all. Owen is still sick with a bad toe."

For an Arkansas girl, it was a dazzling kaleidoscope of the finest entertainment New York could offer. Owney bought her jewelry from
Tiffany's, gave her tickets to the latest Broadway shows, and ordered the
best of everything. The only thing lacking was his constant presence. He
continued to see her as much as possible, but his mind was preoccupied
in making plans. Coll's strutting threats were now the least of his problems. The investigations of Judge Seabury and Senator Hofstadter had
triggered an intense, official interest in organized crime, and the authorities began to look more closely at New York's laundry rackets.

Laundries, as steady, profitable local services, had attracted mob interest all over the country. The Purple Gang of Detroit was particularly
involved in them and thousands of honest companies were forced to pay
protection money. By 1929, New York's 372 laundries were each paying
around $100 a week to racketeers. Plus, investigators discovered that the
Brooklyn Neighborhood Laundry Owners' Association also paid
$30,000 in protection money to the police in 1930. Owney was not in-
volved in these practices since he had purchased his own laundry businesses as a cover to distribute bootleg liquor. However, the inquiry
threatened to drag him into the net. He was never called to testify, but
the publicity resulted in the action he had most feared. The State Parole
Board, attracted by the frequent appearance of his name in print, decided to reexamine his case.

Overnight, Agnes could no longer find him in his usual haunts. His
favorite table at the Cotton Club was empty. There was no reply from
his apartment and no one had seen him at Texas Guinan's clubs. Friends
seemed vague as to his whereabouts. Agnes experienced a rising anxiety
and confusion. That night, she went to bed early and wrote in her diary:

"I was told today that Owney had been shanghied by his friends and
put on a boat for Europe to keep him out of trouble, as conditions here in
New York are terrible. I feel so blue, but can't cry. I am so hurt and lonely."

The city began to acquire the empty feeling of the house back in
Hot Springs when her mother died. Without the assurance that Owney

was somewhere around, the places where she had had so much fun suddenly lost their appeal. New York's energy and excitement evaporated, and nothing could distract her thoughts from the knowledge that he had gone. Her diary entries told the story:

"September 2, 1931: I did some shopping today. Bought a suit with fur jacket and a black velvet evening dress. Spent $150 on myself.

"September 3: I might just as well go home as New York is a void to me without Owney. I'll have to readjust my life over again.

"September 4: Went out last nite for dinner. Saw the Vanities show this afternoon. I think I will leave for home tomorrow."

What Agnes did not realize, and had no way of knowing, was that Owney was not aboard a boat for Europe. Talk was plentiful in Manhattan clubs and speakeasies, and he had become a nightly topic of gossip. The Duke, they sensed, was on the ropes, but everyone had a feeling that, in his characteristically quiet way, he would bounce back. Agnes, excited and impressionable in the big city, was not yet ready to be allowed into his innermost plans. Owney realized that his disappearance would wound her, but he hoped the time would come when he could make it up to her.

As Agnes boarded the Pullman at Pennsylvania Station, surrounded by her luggage, Owney was halfway across New Mexico, chain-smoking Camels behind the long hood of the bulletproof Duesenberg, heading for California. He had driven alone along Route 66, sweeping through Joplin, Missouri, and Tulsa, Oklahoma, leaving a trail of dust at roadstops selling fishing tackle and turquoise jewelry as he burned up the long road west. Agnes left New York, dulled and depressed, delaying the inevitable return to Hot Springs as long as possible. She no longer had the heart for the house and the shop and the tedium of life alone again. At 7:30 that evening, the train pulled into Washington and, tired and worn out, she called on her sister, Kat. The following day was Labor Day, and Kat and Clay, her husband, insisted on taking Agnes to dinner and to a show. Eventually, she could no longer put off the inevitable and made the decision to return to Arkansas. In her diary, Agnes wrote:

"September 20, 1931: Will soon be home. I feel awfully blue going home without Mama there. I feel like I have no one to love or care for me.

"September 21: Papa had a date tonite and left me at home. My first nite home and I cried all evening."

Owney intended to stay away from the New York scene until the pressures on him died down. He traveled across to Honolulu and booked into a hotel. He passed the time alone on the beach and made sightseeing tours around the island, working out his options and revising his contingency plans. Back in Arkansas, Agnes took her diary to bed and wrote:

"No word from Owney. I might just as well forget him forever as he could not possibly care for me. I tried to fall in love with Joe."

Outwardly, things in Hot Springs had changed little, but since meeting Owney, Agnes knew that they would never be quite the same again. She went to the movies, worried about her father's friendship with a girl he had met, and prayed that business at the shop would pick up. The Depression tightened its grip on small-town America, and increasing numbers of merchants were forced into bankruptcy. As she sat in her empty shop, Agnes felt locked in a cruel twilight world between dream and reality.

"Business is absolutely dead," she wrote. "Life is very uninteresting. Am home alone tonite, reading my old love letters from Owen."

The Duke, too, was missing the company of close friends. Paradise Island made a fine hideaway but lacked any excitement. He decided to book a passage to California and look up George Raft. It was a visit which was to provide more action than he ever imagined. Raft, helped by money borrowed from Owney, had finally made it to Hollywood and appeared in several movies. When Owney arrived, he had been signed to make a movie called *Scarface* under producer Howard Hughes. It was his first gangster movie and was based on the life of Al Capone. George was to play Big Al's bodyguard with such authenticity and conviction that real gangsters began to call at the studios to ask if they could see the rushes. When the movie opened in Chicago, George had an unexpected visit at his hotel—a man in a pearl-grey fedora, with a message: "The Big Guy wants to see you."

With some trepidation, he went to the Lexington Hotel, Capone's downtown headquarters. To his relief, Al seemed amused by the movie. According to Yablonsky, they talked for a while, and, as Raft turned to go, Capone stopped him.

"Georgie," he said, "I see you tossing a coin all through the picture."

"Just a little theatrical trick," said George, wondering if he offended someone.

"A four-bit piece, yeah?"

"No, it was a nickel."

"That's worse. You tell them if any of my boys are tossing coins, they'll be twenty-dollar gold pieces."

It was only by chance that Raft had accepted the role. Owney had offered him a job between movies touring Florida with Primo Carnera to drum up business in the run-up to the title fight. He opted for the movie, and it became a turning point in his career.

His first film, in 1929, was *Queen of the Night Clubs* and starred Texas Guinan. This gave further evidence to Owney's influence in Hollywood. Within two years of Owney's visit, George was to be offered his first starring role, in *Night After Night*, a movie in which he passed over the opportunity of Texas as female lead, opting instead for their old friend Mae West. The young hoofer who had been overawed by the prospect of a part in *Sex* was to reverse roles and offer Mae her first Hollywood break.

Owney stayed at George's house where the actor, now in a position to repay his generosity, insisted on taking him out on the town. Their excursions around the fashionable, mob-owned nightclubs attracted the attention of newspaper gossip writers and the police. Within a few days, everyone knew that the Duke was in Los Angeles and, to his embarrassment, he was feted as a celebrity. The authorities were less pleased. Buron Fitts, the Los Angeles District Attorney, decided that Owney was not welcome and ordered his arrest. By the time a squad of officers had called at Raft's home, Owney had vanished.

George was summoned to the D.A.'s office to explain himself. "Mr. Raft said he certainly didn't hide Mr. Madden," wrote columnist Westbrook Pegler. "If a friend was a guest and he didn't know the friend was wanted, how could anyone say he hid him? Ridiculous on the face of it. George Raft, the actor selected from life by the movie industry to portray himself as a scowling, ominous gangster type for the idolatry of American youth, has steeped himself in his art."

As the hunt for Owney was stepped up, he was lying low with another friend who had moved into the area. Mae West hid him out in her newly acquired deluxe apartment for almost a week. Despite her joy at seeing him, she had to spend time doing the rounds of the studios, and Owney soon began to feel like a prisoner, cooped up all day in the apartment. He had no intention of allowing the minor business of a police hunt to interfere with his reunion with old friends and called George.

Raft immediately suggested that they go out for the evening. Unfortunately, the club they selected employed a doorman who doubled in the day as a part-time Los Angeles policeman. He recognized the Duke from an old photograph circulated at the precinct house and dropped a nickel in the pay phone. When Owney was arrested, he refused to identify himself for fear of being charged with parole violation. The officers guarding him reciprocated by making life uncomfortable. Late the following evening, when Raft visited him, he found that his old pal had been given nothing to eat. The actor asked the detectives questioning him if they would allow food to be sent in. When they refused, George persisted and eventually parted with $150 for two sandwiches to stave off Owney's hunger.

Mae, meanwhile, was helping in her own way. District Attorney Buron Fitts, by coincidence, was one of her long list of close acquaintances. She had met him when $12,000 worth of jewelry was snatched from her purse as she sat in a friend's car. Everyone dismissed it as a publicity stunt except for the husky D.A. who assigned two detectives to recover the stolen property. The Queen of Sex slipped into one of her favorite dresses and decided to intercede on Owney's behalf.

One of Mae's most memorable lines in *Night After Night* came when a hat-check girl remarked: "Goodness, what beautiful jewelry!" As she sashayed through the door of Buron Fitts's office, Mae knew better than anyone that "goodness" had nothing to do with it. There is no record of what took place in the intervening hour or so, but Mae, with her smoldering vowels and hip-swinging delivery, must have pleaded an appealing case.

"Bu-ron," she is said to have told him, "Owney's a good guy. Come on now, be big about it."

If Buron Fitts had not been convinced before Mae walked in, he had a remarkable change of heart during the course of their meeting. It was her own way of repaying her old flame, who had helped her out of Vaudeville into Broadway and then paved the way to Hollywood. Owney was released from custody and escorted to the city limits with a less-than-polite warning never to come back.

As Los Angeles journalist Florabel Muir recalled: "Like Raft, Mae West, the heartless Diamond Lil of stage and screen, owed much to Owney. It never mattered to the patron saint of sin on celluloid that the quiet, silent Madden was listed in the upper register of Public Enemies."

Owney decided to spend the next few weeks traveling around the country, looking up old connections. Word of his arrest, however, had already reached the State Parole Board in New York. The future, had he been able to read it, would have revealed a headlong stumble from one crisis to another.

Agnes, meanwhile, was studying her own signs and portents with great interest. Her diary entry read:

"Sunday, November 1st: Carmen spent the day with me, and Toots took us to White Sulphur Springs for dinner tonite. We had our fortunes told. I had a good one. I wished to hear from Owen and I was told I would get my wish real soon."

Her clairvoyant must have been uncannily gifted. The next morning a telegram arrived from Owney, who was in Dallas, Texas, saying he would telephone that evening.

"I was so happy I cried," Agnes recalled.

He talked to her for half an hour without explaining too much about what had happened. He preferred to save it for the following day when he promised to drive to Hot Springs for a two-week stay. Agnes booked him a room at the Majestic. She invited Toots and Carmen, who had taken her to the fortune teller, and the four of them played cards and celebrated Owney's return with pie and coffee. When they were alone, Owney explained how he had been unable to confide all his plans and told her how he had driven from California down to Mexico before reaching Texas. The next fortnight was an idyllic time for Agnes.

"Played golf this afternoon," she wrote. "I am enjoying my days with my darling. I love him so much. I know that he is all I can love."

The time flew by and Owney knew that he would have to return to New York and take up the long fight with the authorities to stay out of prison. With a heavy heart, he drove the Duesenberg out of Hot Springs, planning to call at Indianapolis to tie up some business before preparing himself for what lay ahead. Agnes went to a movie to try to take her mind off things but to little avail.

"It is raining," she wrote, "and I am so lonesome for my Darling. He called from Indianapolis and is very blue. He leaves for New York in the morning."

At 8:55 a.m., just before he climbed into his car for the long drive home, Owney stopped at a post office and sent her a Western Union wire, which read: "*Off now. Will hear from me in a few days. Love and my very heartiest for my darling. Owen.*"

It was a trying, dismal time for both of them. Agnes passed the days with friends and, when she was alone in the evenings, answered Owney's letters. His visit had cheered her considerably and helped to consolidate their relationship. At last, she felt she knew him better. At the end of

November, she cast her mind back over the month that had flown by and wrote in her diary:

"This has been the happiest month of the year for me. I was so thrilled to hear from Owen and to see him. I enjoyed every minute of the two weeks he spent with me. He is the only person in the world that I am completely happy with. All I want is to be with him forever and ever."

They spent Christmas and New Year's Eve apart. Agnes had dinner with some older members of the family. Owney watched the festivities at the Cotton Club and the Stork. The bells chimed in the new year of 1932 and each of them confessed a feeling of foreboding. Owney, the most peaceful of all the city's organized crime leaders, was certain to be the next candidate to go to Sing Sing. His Christmas telegram to Hot Springs was the last Agnes was to hear from him for almost two months.

Major William H. McMullen, a name Owney was to hear many more times, ordered his parole board staff to work over the Christmas period to find grounds for returning the Duke to prison. The Major was under pressure to produce a strong case but could find little to suggest that Owney had broken any laws. Two anomalies emerged in the course of his inquiry. Unlike other parole prisoners, Owney had not been asked to report to the Board, and there was a mystery and vagueness about his employment.

When officials interviewed Owney on his return from Hot Springs, he had told them that he was both in the cereal business and the laundry business. However, an audit of his income tax returns failed to show any connection with these two industries. The parole board may have been struggling, but the lead certainly whetted the appetite of the Treasury Department Intelligence Unit investigating his tax affairs.

When the report was finally published ten days later, the parole board admitted that it had failed to find any evidence against Owney. A search of the records revealed that he had reported for paroles on discharge from Sing Sing and was placed under the care of the Catholic Protectory Society, which was so impressed with his conduct that he was given permission to report by mail every three months instead of monthly in person. The authorities appeared to have lost the first round, but, in case he should disappear, they ordered him to report regularly again. Owney had served a minimum sentence in Sing Sing and somehow acquired the freedom to come and go as he pleased. His maximum sentence expired in 1935 and, in theory at least, officialdom had until then to get him back inside. There was, however, an unseemly sense of urgency about their efforts and, while the political tide was running, the full weight of the system was thrown into securing his conviction. Far from being over, Owney's war with them was only just beginning.

"On the afternoon of January 15, 1932," the *Herald Tribune* reported, "several well meaning ladies and gentlemen spoke in the assembly room of the Association of the Bar of the City of New York before the special Prison Survey Commission headed by Sam A. Lewisohn. They earnestly pleaded that the parole board be empowered to parole any felon serving his first term in prison after two years behind bars. And when they finished, the soft-spoken, scholarly jurist Joseph E. Corrigan of the Court of General Sessions reminded them that a first offender is generally a criminal whose cunning has warded off the whip of justice for years. 'And as for the parole board,' continued Judge Corrigan, 'there's Owney Madden, Public Enemy No. 2. The parole board let him loose, and everybody knows the night clubs he runs.'"

At the end of January, Owney telephoned Agnes to break the news of his minor victory, but she was not at home. To help keep their relationship alive, he urged friends to look her up when they visited Hot Springs. In a similar way to which Mae West was feted by the mob when she toured America, the gangs knew that Agnes was Owney's girl and dropped by to pay their respects. She was by now more secure in their relationship and, although worrying about him constantly, felt more in touch through the stream of visiting friends. Her diary from that time reads:

"February 1st, 1932: Had breakfast with the bunch and told them goodbye. Expected to be very lonesome, but one of Owney's friends arrived today, so maybe he will do.

"February 2nd: Owney's friend is an English Jew. He is Jackie Berg, the Welterweight Champion of the World. I went horseback riding with him this morning and he fell off.

"February 3rd: Rained all day. Jackie Berg is limping after falling from the horse, and everyone is kidding me about being rough on men. Am staying home tonite."

Jackie, fit and well and now residing in London's West End, remembers the incident well. He was training for a fight at the time and thought the Hot Springs baths would improve his condition. The rest of his stay was spent with Ruth Mix, daughter of Hollywood cowboy Tom Mix, who was also a friend of Agnes and perhaps a safer companion.

12.

Trouble in Mind

Owney was now facing attack on three sides. Deportation back to England, however, had been discarded by the government as an immediate goal. The law on deportation required jail sentences of at least a year each, on two separate convictions. Still, the authorities continued their efforts to remove Owney from the New York scene. The Treasury Department had examined his books upon his release from Sing Sing until 1931 and claimed that he owed $73,553 in "additional taxes and penalties." Admitting arrears and paying them off was no longer enough. The case of Waxey Gordon had proved that the government was out for blood, and it was highly unlikely, with Assistant District Attorney Dewey heading sixty lawyers bent on dismantling organized crime, that a prosecution could be avoided. The parole board stepped up its inquiries by paying a visit to the Hydrox Laundry in Brooklyn in an attempt to uncover the extent of his involvement there. And, Judge Seabury was now swinging his investigation in Owney's direction. He suspected that there had been some collusion in freeing him from parole restrictions in the first place and ordered a full inquiry. The outlook appeared bleak, but the authorities had overlooked Madden's long run of luck and cunning. The precautions he had taken over the years to keep a low profile and cover his tracks made him an elusive opponent. He was so elusive that it appeared some officials were not beyond resorting to "dirty tricks" to secure his imprisonment.

On February 9, 1932, Mad Dog Vincent Coll was machine-gunned to death in the telephone booth of the London Pharmacy. Three days later, the State Parole Board gathered in the somber conference room at Sing Sing and, after reading the evidence of its investigators, signed Owney's arrest warrant on charges of parole violation.

Warrants were issued at the same time for three of his associates who were said to be employed at the Hydrox Laundry—a convicted killer, Gustave Guillame, known as Little Frenchy; Jeremiah Sullivan, another paroled murderer who had the look of a pugilist; and Thomas Robinson, a burglar who went under the name of Terry Reilly. The warrants were rushed downstairs to a waiting car and driven at top speed to police headquarters where Commissioner Mulrooney was waiting to receive them. Under his orders, Acting Captain Patrick McVeigh dispatched a special squad of detectives to search for the wanted men.

Little Frenchy, described by the *New York Times* as "one of the city's toughest gangsters," previously had his sentence reduced by Governor Roosevelt for exemplary behavior. Sullivan's murder sentence had been shortened at the request of the prison governor, and Reilly had been released on parole for saving a guard's life during riots at Auburn prison.

The swiftness of the legal actions stemmed from a statement given to Judge Seabury's team by Israel Levy, a friend of Owney and, on paper at least, the proprietor of the Hydrox Laundry and Dry Cleaning Company. Issy, unaware of the complexities of the case, had promptly denied any connection with Owney when he was questioned. He was clearly unaware that the Duke had told parole officers that he was in the laundry business. "Levy, testifying under oath, made his denial more sweeping by asserting that Madden was not only not an employee, but that he had never been in any way connected with the Hydrox Laundry or its affiliated companies," the press reported.

The parole board, squirming slightly at Owney's confident statement that he was not officially obliged to report to it, issued a hasty statement to cover any blunder: "On behalf of the Board, it has been pointed out that the small staff of parole officers is too overworked to make a careful examination of all ex-convicts in its care." Behind the scenes, however, a frantic search for Madden's papers had taken place to see if he was telling the truth.

Levy's statement, for the moment, was enough to secure Owney's arrest on the grounds that he had lied to the board about his business connections. To ensure that no one had been overlooked, Issy Levy then was charged with contempt for failing to swiftly provide a full list of laundry employees.

The following day, the *New York Times* reported: "Owen (Owney) Madden, former convict and reputedly one of the city's biggest racketeers, was arrested late last night by detectives who had been searching for him for violation of his parole. He was arrested by Detectives Owens and Horan of the headquarters staff as he was entering his home at 440 West 34th Street.

"Madden told detectives he had been working as an investigator for a coal company. He will appear in the line-up this morning and then will be transferred to the Tombs to be sent back to Sing Sing later in the day, the police said. Under the law, there is no possibility of his obtaining bail, they said."

Owney was driven the short distance to the Tombs, the same crumbling jail where he was remanded to await trial for the slaying of Patsy Doyle eighteen years earlier. He was treated with great civility by the warders, just as he had been in the days of his youth, and was given a cell to himself.

In Hot Springs, Agnes read the newspaper report with anxiety. Joe Diamond had appeared, redoubling his efforts to win her affection, but her mind was elsewhere. On Valentine's Day, he covered the garden path at her house with candy and flowers, but Agnes was too preoccupied with Owney to be flattered by his attentions. Her diary at the time read:

"Monday, February 15th: Rained all day yesterday and today. Joe and I took a drive together. He is so sweet, but my mind is on Owen only. I wish I could fly to him and talk to him.

"Tuesday, February 16th: Spent a restless nite dreaming about Owney. He is being held in prison now. Rained all day again."

Diamond provided a shoulder to lean on and, as the end of his visit drew near, made one last bid to win Agnes. It was a turning point she might have considered seriously at one time, but she now knew beyond any doubt that there could only be one man in her life and noted this in her diary:

"Wednesday, February 17th: Joe left at noon today. Begged me to marry him, but though he is sweet I can't feel interested in him anymore to that extent. The only one I can think of now is O."

Terry Reilly was arrested about the same time as Owney near his home in Brooklyn. Sullivan and Little Frenchy walked into the offices of the State Parole Board in Center Street minutes after the building opened and gave themselves up. All four were searched and fingerprinted at headquarters before being questioned by Inspector Charles Stilson. All claimed to be in steady employment. The *Times* managed to have a reporter present:

"What is your business?" Madden was asked.

"I'm an investigator," was the answer.

"How long have you been an investigator?"

"Oh, a couple of weeks."

"Inspector Stilson then read Madden's criminal record. He had been arrested 140 times, but was convicted only once, for the killing of Doyle."

Once he was in the Tombs, the parole board wasted no time in trying to take Owney back to prison to complete his sentence. They were told, however, that no transport was available until the following morning. Reporters, anxious to know if he would be given special treatment, called Sing Sing. "He might be regarded around Broadway as the city's leading racketeer," said a spokesman, "but he will not receive any special consideration when he returns here."

Lawyer Joe Shalleck, meanwhile, had been busy obtaining a writ of habeas corpus to secure his release on bail. The authorities, nervous that

Shalleck was on the case, called a special meeting of all interested parties to forestall any surprise moves he might make. It came as no surprise to anyone that Shalleck had a card up his sleeve. The case was set for Monday and city desks prepared with relish for the legal contest. They all predicted a bleak outcome for Madden. "Sing Sing officials declared yesterday that out of all the numerous writs of habeas corpus obtained by paroled prisoners, not one has ever succeeded before the prisoner's maximum sentence expired," crowed the *Daily News*. Another headline put it more succinctly: OWNEY AND THREE ALLIES TRY TODAY TO BEAT PAROLE RAP. NO ONE EVER HAS. "The Al Capone of New York," as the *Daily News* was now calling him, spent a quiet Sunday in the Tombs, attending mass in the morning and reading the papers all afternoon. Owney sent out for his meals and had extra food brought in for prisoners who had to eat prison fare.

Monday morning, the press bench at the Supreme Court Building was packed when Judge Aaron J. Levy strode briskly in to hear the case. The white-haired justice, with a high, receding hairline like a bird of prey, perhaps was not entirely assigned to the hearing by coincidence. Back in 1913, he had served as the Democrat's leader in the assembly and was heavily backed by Tammany Hall. The case he was about to consider resulted in a judgment so controversial that the *Daily News* featured it in his obituary when he died in retirement in Florida at age 74. From the outset, the authorities knew that getting Owney back into Sing Sing was going to be more than a mere formality.

"Take a look at these men," said Assistant State Attorney General John T. Cahill, indicating the four prisoners as he paced the court. "See how they are dressed. The arrogance of these men is typical of their kind, and they should be made to fear and respect the law. Are the law enforcement agencies running this country, or are these men? The four should be returned to Sing Sing immediately. Only the State Parole Board has jurisdiction over these men at this time. The question as to their having the right to be at liberty is a matter for the parole board and not the Supreme Court..."

Justice Levy held up his hand to interrupt. "Is this speech intended for the newspapers?" he asked. "This seems to be an age of noise and hysteria. The court will deal with the matter in a thorough, legal, and just way."

Assistant State Attorney General Peter Brancato then rose to his feet to back his colleague's argument. If the court upheld the habeas corpus and bailed Madden, he said, "the parole board will be a joke." Therein, perhaps, lay the real thrust of his argument.

"Madden," he claimed, "violated his parole when he informed the parole board he was working, when as a matter of fact he was not, and has no legitimate employment."

Brancato added, with emphasis, that after the hearing he was going on to interrogate Israel Levy of the Hydrox Laundry on behalf of Judge Seabury's inquiries into the New York laundry industry.

Shalleck, immaculately dressed, was brief and to the point. He told the judge that the four men before him should be released on a simple point of law. "All of them were convicted before the present parole laws came into effect," he argued. Owney Madden had been a law-abiding citizen since his release from Sing Sing and was a victim of a newspaper campaign. Then, he drew a piece of folded paper from his pocket. Holding it aloft, Shalleck announced that it was a telegram, sent by his client to the parole board, asking for a chance to work, to be let alone, and be a law-abiding citizen.

"If he is the author of this telegram," Justice Levy observed, "then it sounds as though he may become a valuable member of society."

Encouraged, Shalleck swept his hand over Sullivan, Reilly, and Little Frenchy, who were flanking Owney. "These three," he thundered, "may be convicts, but they are heroes. Each one while in prison saved either property or the lives of keepers in prison riots."

Justice Levy listened attentively and decided it was time to recess for lunch. As the court cleared for the noon break, Shalleck handed the press copies of another telegram from someone called Moe Weinstock. In the telegram, Weinstock had offered Owney a job selling printing, stationery, and office supplies at $75 a week on a three-year contract—exactly the period, as it so happened, until the expiration of Owney's parole.

The judge returned refreshed from the break and evidently impressed with Shalleck's performance. "When Madden and his associates heard Justice Levy say he would not dismiss the writs, and it became evident to them that they would not have to make the trip to Sing Sing, grins spread over their features," the *New York Times* reported. All had been nervous and ill at ease during the arguments. The *Times* noted:

"Smiles were also evident on the faces of the ex-convicts' friends in the court room. As soon as Justice Levy fixed the amount of bail, representatives of a surety company began making out the necessary papers. They were so eager to get the four out of the custody of the detectives and guards from the Tombs, that the first batch of the bail forms were not properly filled in. Justice Levy rejected the papers, and it took more than an hour to fill in the new forms.

"It was not until after five o'clock in the afternoon that Madden and his friends walked out of Justice Levy's private chambers. The four did not go down the same elevators they used when brought under guard to Justice Levy's chambers, but left through the rear of the building, eluding photographers in the corridors."

Now free on a $10,000 bail, Owney went home to collect his thoughts. In Hot Springs, the strain was beginning to wear on Agnes, as she noted in her diary:

"Have been blue and nervous all day thinking about Mama and Owen. The papers say he is out on bail till February 24."

Depressed and deep in thought, she went to Greenwood Cemetery the next morning and laid flowers on her mother's grave. When she returned, a telegram was waiting from Owney, with a promise that he would call her that evening.

"His voice sounded so good," she wrote in her diary later. "I do so hope his trouble turns out alright. Will know in three weeks."

Reporters were ecstatic, not so much in finally being able to report on the reclusive king of New York's gangland at first hand, but to have the chance of snatching some pictures of him. As the courtroom battle unfolded, a front-page picture of Owney became a paramount priority. When he was arrested, someone tipped off the *Daily News*, which surrounded police headquarters with photographers. One of them managed a rare and lucky shot of the Duke being led by detectives through swinging doors, hands thrust deep in the pockets of a velvet-collared overcoat, with a grey fedora pulled low over one eye. Owney, in newspaper terms, was the only gangster who was the epitome of the gangster. Once forced into the open, he became a hot property.

OWNEY MADDEN MUGGED AT LAST, ran the *Daily News* headline. The *News* noted further: "That boss racketeer of Manhattan, Owen Madden, who has long ducked cameras and cops, was both photographed and arrested last night. Here's an exclusive picture of the racket boss as he left police headquarters."

In custody, the police photographer took a full-length picture of him, still in hat and overcoat, after he had been charged. (Owney was later presented with a free copy by the arresting officer for his family album). When it was pinned to his file, the authorities began to realize just how little information they actually had on him. The only other picture in existence was taken in 1915 as he entered Sing Sing. In the intervening years, no newspaper, federal agent, policeman, or Treasury Department investigator had managed to acquire a single photograph to positively identify him.

When J. Edgar Hoover discovered that even his elite band of agents had been outwitted, he became overtaken by a fanatical drive to pursue Madden and destroy him.

No one knew more than Owney the value of a Madden mug shot. The man who was notoriously camera-shy asked George Raft to take him to his studio portrait photographer in Hollywood, where he posed for a special picture for Agnes. He had it taken in his favorite cream-colored cloth cap, pulled jauntily over one eye. He presented it to her after his long drive from California to Hot Springs.

For the moment, Owney had more problems than he cared to handle. The Hofstadter Committee appointed Philip Wagner Lowry of its legal staff to discover whether political pressure had been applied to secure Owney's years of freedom. Even former governor Alfred E. Smith, the man who officially minimized his sentence, was hauled before Lowry for close interrogation. With Walter Winchell in hiding after his blunder over the Vincent Coll shooting, there was no one to dampen the enthusiasm of the press. Even Winchell could not have prevented the hysterical news coverage that followed. Owney was trapped for the first time in the searching beam of publicity and was, for once, powerless to do anything about it.

MADDEN'S INFLUENCE WITH POLITICIANS UNDER SEABURY FIRE ran the Page One headline in the *New York Times*. Piece by piece, the folklore and legends of the West Side were being fed right across the nation. "Madden's name has been linked repeatedly with racketeers and bootleggers, and once Federal Prohibition authorities charged that city policemen had interfered with a raid being made on a brewery in which he is said to have an interest," the *Times* revealed with cautious jubilation.

On March 2, 1932, Shalleck handed in a sixty-page brief to the Supreme Court, arguing that Owney had been fully discharged by the parole board and had never violated the agreed terms of his parole. Shalleck had toiled skillfully on the case. The brief contended that, since his release from Sing Sing in 1923 until 1932, "Madden received no communication or order or direction of any nature or description from the parole board." It added: "If the Board considered Madden still under its jurisdiction, it would not have permitted so many years to elapse without requiring Madden to submit periodic reports."

To back his argument, Shalleck had obtained affidavits from two former parole board officials. One of them was John Schildknecht, who had been supervisor of the Division of Protective Care.

"Schildknecht's affidavit," the *Times* reported, "said that in 1926 William McCabe, confidential agent of the Prison Department, informed Madden, in his presence, that Madden need not report any longer and that he might go wherever he pleased. He also declared that John P. Bramer, Director of the Division of Protective Care, formally recommended Madden's discharge." Somewhere along the line, the parole board had clearly made a serious error which, by fair means or foul, it would have to retrieve in order to put Owney back behind bars.

The defendant was not in court to hear Shalleck's eloquent brief. Something had occurred to make him drop everything and hurry away on urgent business. The nation's attention had been switched elsewhere in New York State to focus dramatically on a tragedy which eclipsed Owney's troubles and, in a curious way, helped him to escape from some of them.

On Thursday. March 1, 1932, Charles Lindbergh Jr., infant son of the record-breaking aviator who flew the Atlantic in 1927, caught a bad cold. The weather at the family retreat in Hopewell, New Jersey, had been wet and gale-lashed for days. The wind howled in the trees for hours, and Colonel Lindbergh and his wife, Anne, asked the baby's Scottish nurse, Betty Gow, to come look after him. She tucked baby Charles into his bed, secured the blankets with safety pins to prevent him kicking them off, and made her way down the wide staircase of the whitewashed country house.

Later that evening, around 10 p.m., Betty went up to check on the baby and found his bed empty. Twenty-month-old Charles was neither with his mother in the adjoining bedroom nor with his father downstairs in the study. Colonel Lindbergh and his wife hurried to the first floor nursery and stared at the empty bed where the pillow still bore the impression of their son's head. Their worst fears were realized.

"Anne," said Lindbergh in disbelief, "they've taken our baby."

When the first contingent of New Jersey police arrived at the secluded farmhouse, they found a ladder propped against the window and a chisel. On the radiator was a ransom note, and a small suitcase stood nearby. The note, misspelled and almost illegible, demanded $50,000 and promised that the child was in "gute care." Overnight, the case became a worldwide sensation. The shy Colonel Lindbergh's flying feat in his plane, *The Spirit of St. Louis*, had made him known to millions. Sadly, the investigation was to rapidly sink into a quagmire of forgotten clues, bribed witnesses, and disregarded testimony.

The State Police, the Bureau of Investigation (forerunner of the FBI), and the Treasury Department stumbled over each other for the next two months, conducting an inquiry which continued to yield secrets half a century later.

A state trooper, one of the first to arrive at the scene, searched the grounds for clues and, from footprints in the soft clay soil, concluded that the kidnap was the work of a gang of "at least two or more persons." Officers familiar with the burgeoning kidnap business immediately thought of the Purple Gang of Detroit, which had made kidnapping a specialty. Their record was grim and included the kidnapping of several youths. They had also shown evidence of callousness and cruelty to children. Two members of the gang were serving life imprisonment—Michigan had no death penalty—for the shooting of a fourteen-year-old boy who had shown too much curiosity in one of their breweries.

The gang's name had arisen from its reputation. Before the First World War, when they were all under sixteen, two shopkeepers in Hastings Street, a run-down area of Detroit, were raided by the gang. One of them turned to his neighbor, so the story goes, and said in disgust: "Those boys are tainted—off color." The other nodded his head in agreement: "Purple, that's what they are, purple," he replied.

It was known that the Purples had never attempted a kidnapping outside Michigan, but such was the hysteria generated by the Lindbergh case that names were flying around like autumn leaves. Someone remembered that Harry Fleisher, a senior member of the Purples, had fled Detroit a year earlier after a gang war and was thought to be hiding in New York. The hunt was on.

Federal agents were dispatched to search all of Fleisher's known hide-outs and, from the outset, the authorities made it clear that they meant business. One squad burst into an apartment armed with machine guns and tear gas but found nothing. As the trail revealed no clues, other gangsters were fleetingly named as suspects. Al Capone was mentioned, although he was in jail in Chicago. Back at Hopewell, the Lindberghs were in touch with the kidnappers through a series of personal ads placed in the *American* newspaper. More ransom notes were received, and marked Treasury notes were prepared for an exchange. Colonel Lindbergh, a wealthy man in addition to being a national hero, worked closely with Colonel Norman Schwarzkopf, New Jersey's police chief, but made it known that he was prepared to explore any avenue to secure the safe return of baby Charles.

In the first few days of the kidnapping, when it became clear that Fleisher was a suspect, Colonel Lindbergh opened his own communication channels with the underworld. His first contact was through a lawyer named Robert Thayer, who was known to patronize New York speakeasies. Thayer had a client—a small-time hoodlum named Mickey Rosner—who agreed to make inquiries in the underworld for a fee of $2,500 and a promise that he would not be followed by federal agents. Rosner called in two other minor characters, Salvatore Spitale and Irving Bitz, but it was clear that none of them could make any headway without the authority of Owney Madden. New York gang leaders were becoming harassed by police looking for Fleisher, and something had to be quickly done to draw away unwanted attention. Lindbergh and a lean attorney friend, Colonel Henry Breckinridge, had no doubt that Madden was the man best able to help, and he was officially appointed to the inquiry.

If baby Charles was a victim of a gangland snatch, they believed, then Owney Madden would be able to track down those responsible. By the time Elmer Irey, head of the Treasury Department's Intelligence Unit, had been called in to trace some marked notes which had been left for the kidnappers outside a cemetery, Madden was already on the case. Irey was astonished to find himself working on the same team with the man who was next on his hit-list for tax evasion.

Once organized crime had been suspected of involvement in the kidnapping—a fact, incidentally, which Owney considered highly unlikely—the Duke felt a responsibility to his fellow members of the Atlantic City Convention. Anything which might further outrage public opinion was most undesirable, and Owney made every effort to assure himself—and the Lindberghs—that none of the mobs were responsible. If it was the work of criminals, then there was every likelihood that they were lone operators. Finding Fleisher became imperative, and Owney enlisted help from gang leaders from all over the United States. To calm public fears, Shalleck stepped into the limelight three days after the kidnapping to clear the air. "The important mob leaders," he told assembled reporters, "are doing their very best to bring about the return of the baby." And, as one reporter wryly commented, "it's only fair to suppose that Joe knew what he was talking about."

Owney worked as discreetly as possible to help the investigation, yet there was one man who would have reveled in all the publicity. Al Capone, languishing in jail on tax evasion charges, had already sent a message saying, "I know how Mrs. Capone and I would feel if our son were kidnapped." He offered to find Fleisher, if they would let him out, and summoned editor Arthur Brisbane to his cell. "I can do as much as anybody alive in getting that baby back," Capone told him, "and I'll protect the government by bail of any size while I'm doing it. I've heard all the rumors about my connection with the case, but the fact is, I never dreamed the Lindbergh kid would be snatched and I had absolutely nothing to do with it. I think I can prove that if I get loose for a while.

"I'm pretty positive a mob did it. Nobody else would get away with that job at a spot surrounded by bridges, and tough in every way. If I'm right about it being a mob, anyone knows that I ought to be able to turn up something in the case. Well, I'm willing. Let's get going."

The biggest catch in organized crime naturally got no further than his cell door. Capone made appeals through his lawyers, but Chicago federal judges and police officials refused even to consider his generous offer. As far as Lindbergh was concerned, Owney was the underworld connection he had been hoping for. The police, meanwhile, appeared to be steering the case in a completely different direction.

A week after the kidnapping, Colonel Lindbergh was an exhausted, desperate man, prepared to clutch at any straws whipped up by the gale of attention the crime had generated. Letters and offers from every aspect of the lunatic fringe poured into the besieged family home, and few went ignored. On March 6, Police Chief Schwarzkopf and Colonel Breckinridge arranged to meet a spiritualist medium, Mary Cerrita. She claimed to have received a message from "the other side" prophesying that the baby's body would be found on the Heights above Hopewell. Owney had been asked by Lindbergh to follow up the lead. Exactly what happened during his meeting with Mary Magdalene, as she was known, and her live-in lover is not recorded, but the spirits suddenly declined to send any more messages and she did not contact the Lindberghs again.

Owney had a great fondness for children. The Lindbergh case was close to his heart, but it would have taken much more than a deep sympathy with the family's terrible plight for him to risk his eternal dread of newspaper exposure. With an evasiveness drawn from the streets of Hell's Kitchen, he drove in his enormous bulletproof Duesenberg three times to Hopewell for meetings with the investigating team. On each occasion, he deftly managed to avoid the regiment of newsmen camped at the end of the drive. His motives for helping Lindbergh were never questioned but, with the authorities squeezing him from every side, a display of public-spiritedness would not have been detrimental to his position.

Fleisher of the Purple Gang surfaced voluntarily a month after the baby's disappearance and managed to clear his name, but Owney's efforts had not gone unnoticed by Colonel Lindbergh. He expressed his deep gratitude for the Duke's contribution and, perhaps by some strange coincidence, the Treasury Department Intelligence Unit decided not to pursue Owney and the outstanding question of $75,553 in unpaid taxes.

Life after the brief interlude of Hopewell was equally demanding. With the tax problem "overlooked," Owney and Shalleck applied themselves to the daunting task of fighting growing pressure to put him back in Sing Sing. On March 5, Assistant Attorneys General Cahill and Brancato filed their own brief with the Supreme Court in reply to Shalleck.

"It is a matter of common belief that Madden is a racketeer of no little importance in the illicit traffic of beer. It is common gossip, indeed, that Madden supplies New York City with a large percentage of that commodity, and that he has introduced his racketeering activities even in legitimate businesses, such as prize fighting and other sports."

One of the ironies of Prohibition was that while New Yorkers, including police, attorneys, and the judiciary, freely availed themselves of Owney's beer in Owney's clubs, still he was considered "fair game" and his bootlegging activities were used against him.

While Justice Levy was weighing the arguments of the two opposing briefs, Governor Roosevelt was anguishing over his prospects for the presidential nomination. Sensing that Owney was boxed into a corner, he took the opportunity to curry support from the law-and-order lobby by offering prosecutors Cahill and Brancato correspondence from his personal file to strengthen their case. It was the letter Owney had written to him in 1929, asking for a pardon on the grounds that he had not broken the law since his release from prison. In it, Madden mentioned that, at the time of writing, he was employed by the Hydrox Laundry.

It was good news for Cahill and Brancato, who immediately sent a copy to the state supreme court with an explanatory note claiming that it "showed the deceitful nature of Madden."

"I note," Shalleck replied, "that the parole board did not dare to say anywhere in their brief of affidavits that Madden did not receive his discharge. They are careful to say only that there is nothing in the record to show that such a discharge was given."

Once Shalleck had the merest shred of a case between his teeth, he seized it with terrier-like tenacity. This was one angle, the board realized, that would not simply go away.

By the end of the month, Shalleck had unearthed more evidence to bolster his theory. It came in the form of an affidavit from Anna Brady, a stenographer at the Catholic Protectory Society, to which Owney was paroled after Sing Sing.

"Miss Brady said that on the Madden folder in the society's files, she had found the word 'closed' in her own handwriting," the *Times* reported. "This word was written on the folders of those conditionally discharged, and conformed to her independent recollection of the discharge."

The board, now in some consternation, issued a statement saying that Shalleck's claims were nothing but "hearsay, conjecture, and in some instances untruth." There was no record of Owney's discharge from parole, they added. Judge Aaron J. Levy announced that he would give his verdict in five days' time.

In Hot Springs, Agnes caught up with the news: "My darling called last nite about 11:30 and talked till 12," she wrote. "I was thrilled to hear his voice. He is having so much trouble."

Agnes missed him badly and worried about the infrequency of his telegrams and letters. The country girl was, however, widening her circle of acquaintances as Owney's friends loyally called to pay their respects. Her social life had, at one time, revolved around bridge parties with local ladies and dinner and dancing with passing tourists or salesmen. Now she played golf with Joe Adonis, of whom it was said: "Cross Joey A and you cross the national combination." She went horseback riding with Meyer Lansky, destined to become the mastermind of organized crime in America, and accepted cozy dinner invitations from Albert Anastasia, the "Lord High Executioner of Murder Inc." Albert's solution to any problem, they said, was homicide—but, like all her new friends, they were never less than perfect gentlemen.

Their jovial, unsophisticated company took her mind off things, but Agnes still spent most of her time alone, worrying about what was happening in New York.

"Didn't sleep a wink all nite," she wrote in her diary on April 2nd. "I was so upset over Owen not calling. Sent a long telegram today but still got no answer, so I am going to the Belvedere to make whoopee with the crowd."

Judge Levy, meanwhile, was issuing his verdict. Owney, Little Frenchy, Sullivan, and Reilly were all set free by the sympathetic judge, who just swept aside the issue of whether any of them were employed. The onus, he said, was on the parole board to produce evidence from their own records that the Duke was not discharged from parole. Levy also addressed the references to the "common gossip" and "common belief" that Madden was a racketeer. If this were true, he noted, there should be ample evidence for a prosecution.

"If Madden committed all the misdeeds of which he is accused," Judge Levy adjudicated, "he should have been apprehended long ago. His arrest on flimsy and highly technical grounds, with the purpose of returning him summarily to the state prison, is an attempt to convict him under color of law for wrongs which cannot be brought home to him by competent evidence."

There was an uproar at the decision, which reverberated from the corridors of the parole board to Governor Roosevelt's office. With the Democratic Convention only two months away, Roosevelt had to do something to win public support for his nomination amidst New York's quagmire of corruption. He chose to launch an unprecedented attack on Judge Levy's ruling, knowing that he was certain, at least, of solid newspaper backing. Any story producing a headline which could be linked to Owney Madden was good copy, and F.D.R. threw his weight behind the aggrieved parole board.

Heartened, the board announced that Madden's liberty put the whole of the parole system at risk and lodged an immediate appeal.

Shalleck, noting the depth of official indignation, warned Owney that worse perhaps was still to come.

Roosevelt was walking a particularly dangerous tightrope because the next target of the authorities was New York's Mayor Jimmy Walker. Having attacked Owney, it would be difficult for him to remain silent about the man whose influence could make or break his presidential nomination.

New Yorkers regarded it as inevitable that Jimmy Walker would sooner or later fall foul of the Hofstadter Committee's zealous inquiries. Many of them would have genuinely preferred it later than sooner. Jimmy's beaming smile and happy-go-lucky lifestyle captured a much-needed spirit in the city during the days of the Depression. Despite the excesses of his administration, few historians have left him without a fond word.

"He reminded the city of a time that was colorful, sometimes charming, and even elegant, although corrupt," wrote Carl Sifakis.

"Walker represented the 'good old days,' It was hard to hate a man who had taken a ton of money and had now rather obviously run through it. Jimmy Walker simply was Jimmy Walker."

When Walker appeared before Judge Seabury at the Hofstadter hearings, he had to run a gauntlet of hundreds of cheering New Yorkers. They lined the court building steps, shouting, "Good luck, Jimmy" and "Atta' boy, Jimmy" as he waved back in greeting. Inside, the welcome was much less cordial. The mayor was asked to explain how a million dollars—$700,000 of it in cash—had passed through his bank account on an annual salary of $40,000, which was supposed to cover all his expenses. There was, of course, no acceptable answer—especially to the question of the $26,000 oil deal in partnership with a taxi-cab operator and the $246,000 profit on a joint stock account with Brooklyn publisher Paul Block.

To F.D.R.'s acute discomfort, however, Seabury dropped the whole issue in his lap by announcing publicly that he had sent transcripts to the Governor for his observations.

Walter Lippmann, in his column for the *Herald-Tribune*, put it: "The Governor seems to be mostly deeply irritated at the fact that the Seabury investigation has been producing testimony which compels him to choose between condoning corruption and striking it. He has displayed a singular petulance toward everybody who has had any part in putting him in a position where he might have to make a decisive choice between breaking with Tammany or surrendering to it."

For Owney, Frank Costello, Jimmy Walker, and others, Roosevelt's next move was bound to have a marked influence on their future. He was in a position to give the growing move for city reform all the powerful backing of his office. The role of crusader against crime would undoubtedly enhance his image—only the restraining hand of ambition rested heavily on his shoulder. There were now only days to go before the Democratic National Convention in Chicago. Roosevelt, tortured by indecision, finally responded by passing on Seabury's charges to Walker himself. By placing the ball squarely in the Mayor's court, he believed he could play for time. It was a mistake, however, to underestimate Jimmy's agility.

On June 23, 1932, Walker thanked the Governor for his package and promised that he would answer all the allegations. Unfortunately, he added, he was leaving for Chicago and could not give them any consideration until after the convention. Clearly, the price of a ticket to the White House would have to be certain private assurances for Jimmy and all his pals.

America's crime bosses had become more organized and inclined toward mutual cooperation since the Atlantic City gang convention. The old marriage of politics and crime was dissolving, as events in New York were proving.

A new era was about to emerge, and its importance was underlined by the strength in which they gathered for the Democrats' convention in Chicago. As the delegates went about debating party policy, the real business of selecting the next president of the United States was being discussed in the rooms and corridors of the elegant Drake Hotel.

Mob leaders and Tammany Hall bosses shared accommodations side by side as the delicate process of selection and negotiation got underway. Unknown to the politicians, the gangsters were covering all their options. Costello, sharing a room with Jimmy Hines, was overtly supporting Roosevelt. Lucky Luciano, the grey-haired Sicilian, and Tammany district leader Albert Marinelli appeared to be backing his rival, the amiable Al Smith. Meyer Lansky, always the shadowy background figure, tested the support of powerful provincial figures such as Huey Long of Louisiana and Boston's James Curley.

The combination's immediate goal was to offer the prospect of nomination to the candidate who would call off the pressure on Mayor Walker, Owney, and other New York characters. In the long run, they sensed that the power of Tammany Hall was finished and that a new power structure would have to be forged, if possible, directly between the mob and the White House itself. It was an ambitious project, but the underworld barons had never considered that thinking big was a drawback.

Longy Zwillman, crime boss of New Jersey, was allotted the task of putting the deal to the Roosevelt camp. His biographer, Mark A. Stuart, gives the only detailed account of what took place. Longy met one of Roosevelt's senior aides in the crowded basement restaurant of the Drake Hotel. At first, the aide, whose name was never revealed, pushed the gang leader to give financial support for F.D.R.'s campaign.

"If your man is nominated," said Longy, quietly.

"What help are you prepared to offer?" was the next question.

"We offer nomination, all wrapped up," shot back Longy. He was tired of indirect discussion.

"That sure, are you?"

"Yes," said Longy, speaking softly. "We have the votes to put your man over the two-thirds majority he needs for the nomination."

"I don't buy that," said the F.D.R. aide.

Longy smiled. "Then why," he asked silkily, "are we meeting?"

The aide stared. In front of him, he saw a supremely confident young man, someone who could pass muster as a member of his own patrician club on 5th Avenue. The aide had been prepared to encounter a wiseguy gangster with a Lower East Side accent. This fellow was unexpectedly quite different. The aide decided to drop all pretense.

"What's your price?"

"Your man has to call off Judge Seabury."

"That's impossible. The scandal would ruin my candidate before he even got started on the campaign trail."

"Your man is smarter than that. We don't expect him to fire the judge. There are other ways to accomplish what we need. I'm sure your man is wise enough to know how to get the nomination for president without compromising himself."

A long pause. The Roosevelt aide pursed his lips, sensing he was out of his depth.

"I'll have to get back to you," he said.

Roosevelt gave his answer by calling a press conference in his hotel suite to talk about crime. He told the assembled newsmen that he backed Judge Seabury's efforts, but that cases such as those of Walker, Hines, and others should be dealt with by the courts.

About the same time, a similar proposition was being put to Al Smith. The contender shook his head regretfully. He was not prepared to run the risk of a head-on collision with Seabury. Anyway, he added, the only person who could do that was the Governor of New York. Meyer Lansky returned from his discussions with the word that Huey Long, Curley, and others were prepared to back Roosevelt. The choice was all but made. All that remained was to inform Al Smith, out of courtesy, that he would not deliver the news. Smith took it well, considering that his hopes were dashed. He had known Luciano for years and, before he left, offered some heartfelt advice.

The Sicilian, in his autobiography *The Last Testament of Lucky Luciano*, recalled Al Smith looking him squarely in the face: "Charlie," he said, "Frank Roosevelt will break his word to you. This is the biggest mistake you ever made in your entire life, by trusting him. He'll kill you."

"When I walked out of Smith's suite," Luciano added, "my knees were shaking. My bones told me that we'd walked into a trap—that Smith was right."

Owney was noticeably absent from Chicago. His presence possibly would have alerted reporters to what was happening behind the scenes at a time when secrecy and discretion were of paramount importance.

Over the years, he confided to friends that he had little trust in politicians and used them only when they could help serve his purposes. Perhaps Owney saw Roosevelt's weaknesses more clearly than his associates. What is certain is that he distrusted him. On July 1, 1932, when the delegates were waving placards and balloons celebrating the election of their new candidate, Roosevelt, Owney shared none of the euphoria. He was busy drawing up his own plans for a future independent of Roosevelt's New Deal.

Agnes spent the weeks leading up to the Democratic Convention in solitude. Owney's gangster friends had all departed to prepare themselves for the trip to Chicago. Many had bought lavishly at her gift shop before they caught the train, but business was now back in the doldrums. There was no one to keep her company and, more importantly, no word from Owney. Agnes guessed that pressing business was occupying his time.

"Dotty and I went swimming," she wrote in her diary. "I read in the New York papers where Owney was taking up flying and has ordered a plane."

The reports were correct. Owney was spending time each day squeezed behind the controls of a flimsy trainer aircraft, grappling with the complexities of learning to fly, apparently in a desperate bid to obtain a license. If the worst happened, he was determined to have his escape route planned.

"I see in the New York papers that they are trying to reverse Owney's decision and make him go back to jail," Agnes wrote on June 14.

Most of her information these days seemed to be gleaned from newspaper reports. The following evening, she added, depressingly:

"I am still worrying about O. I know he has forgotten me, but I still love him, the Sonofabitch."

It was now early July. The Chicago Democratic circus was over, and the private fears of Lucky Luciano were being realized. Roosevelt, euphoric at the backing of his party, lost no time in proving to the nation that he had muscle. With the White House now close within his reach, he set about plucking the deepest thorns from his side. Before anyone had time to take stock of the changed political scene, Owney was put behind bars and Jimmy Walker was forced to resign.

Just twenty-four hours after Roosevelt's nomination, five judges of the Appellate Division of the Supreme Court backed the parole board's appeal and ordered Madden's arrest. Unable to prove that the Duke was still on parole, the board took an abrasive stand and demanded that he should provide his certificate of discharge, which was given to all prisoners freed from restrictions. Owney had never been issued a certificate, and his defense finally collapsed.

Events now moved at tornado speed. As soon as the detention order was signed, detectives and parole board officers sped to Owney's apartment off Broadway. The suite was empty and, to all appearances, the bird had flown. A bulletin was flashed around Manhattan with strict orders to pick him up on sight as one of New York police department's widest manhunts gathered momentum. Newspapers lost no time joining the pack. The headline in the *New York Times* ran: CANADA AND MEXICO HUNT FOR MADDEN: They Think He May Have Fled in Plane.

A strange silence descended over Broadway. Owney was not to be found in any of his clubs and apartments. There was none of the usual loose talk in any of his favorite haunts. Everyone the authorities interviewed shook their heads or gave a non-committal shrug of the shoulders. The Duke was on the run and no one was prepared to help them find him. Owney may have been crushed by the political and judicial machine, but his friends in the speakeasies and underworld hang-outs stood shoulder to shoulder in support. Sullivan, Reilly, and Little Frenchy had also disappeared, giving rise to wild speculation among their pursuers.

"Police detectives and agents of the State Parole Board think they may have crossed the Northern or Southern border in a plane," the *Times* reported. "Since Supreme Court Justice Aaron J. Levy sustained a writ of habeas corpus last April, freeing him from the custody of the parole board, Madden has been taking flying lessons. The lessons were started soon after the State Attorney General announced that he would appeal against Judge Levy's decision."

No one, it seemed, paused for a moment in the midst of the hysteria to assess the caliber of the man they were desperately hunting for. It occurred to none of the investigators assigned to the case, in the great triangle stretching from New York to Canada and Mexico, that Owney's recent behavior had been completely out of character. Why had the man who so hated the press publicized his flying lessons to all the New York newspapers? It seemed like he was announcing his intention to everyone to flee, although the old fox had never been so slipshod in his entire career. A watch was concentrated on border crossings in the hope that his aircraft might be traced leaving the country.

As the manhunt fired the imagination of New Yorkers, their small, quiet hero was still in his own backyard. What the authorities had also failed to realize was that Madden was talking to them through his friends. After a few days, his tight-lipped associates began making comments to detectives, which were ignored in the frantic scramble to track him down. The *Times* gave a hint of what was happening:

"Friends of Madden expressed the opinion that he and the others would surrender to the police shortly. They asserted that the four had been confident that the decision releasing them from the custody of the parole board would have been sustained by the Appellate Division and that the unexpected reversal did not give them any opportunity to arrange their business and financial matters. It was said that once these matters were arranged, the four would give themselves up."

Owney was indeed making arrangements to have his large empire run in his absence, but he was also spending his last days of freedom in precious seclusion with Agnes. She had received a telephone call in Hot Springs ordering her to pack immediately and catch a train to New York. There, she was met by Owney's friends and driven in a curtained limousine to his safe house. It was a private, moving time for the postmaster's daughter and the Duke of the underworld. Agnes held the brief interlude as a deeply treasured memory. Pages relating to Owney's missing week were torn from her diary long ago, and, when interviewed years later, she gave a shy smile and declined to say much about it.

Late in the afternoon of July 7, 1932, Owney held Agnes close and kissed her goodbye before climbing into a waiting car with curtains drawn tightly round its windows. It glided away through Manhattan's bustling streets at an unhurried pace in the direction of Sing Sing. "Madden," said the newspapers, "drove up to the prison gates with two other men in an expensive closed automobile bearing New York license plates. He shook hands with the occupants before alighting. As he walked toward the gates, the machine turned and disappeared in the direction of New York City."

It was a warm, pleasant evening, and Owney, in a lightweight, double-breasted suit and straw hat, walked with a slight stoop down the short concrete roadway toward the tall prison gates. His old bullet wounds had been troubling him during his week of hiding, making it difficult for him to stand upright. The only man ever to give himself up at Sing Sing rapped on the steel doors and saw the cover on a small grille open. The guard was a new man, to whom the lean, pale face meant nothing.

"What do you want?" asked the uniformed head and shoulders, suspiciously.

"The name's Owney Madden. I believe the warden has a cell waiting for me."

The guard smiled skeptically, believing it was some kind of joke.

"Beat it, pal," he told the well-dressed prankster. "Get the hell out of here."

It was only by chance, the *Times* reported, that Owney was not faced with a long walk back to Manhattan. "Although Madden's description had been broadcast by the police, he was not recognized by Ernest Crocker, the guard at the front gate, who refused to let him in. Then, through the bars, Madden saw Clement Ferling, secretary to Warden Lewis E. Lawes, approach.

"Hello!" the Duke shouted. "Mr. Ferling. It's Owney. Open the gates."

Ferling, who remembered him from his first sentence and subsequent visits to receive treatment from Dr. Sweet, ordered the guard to open up. Warden Lawes greeted Owney sympathetically and offered him some supper, but his unexpected prisoner politely declined, saying he had already eaten. In the years since 1923, they had met several times, and Lawes was particularly grateful for the kindnesses Owney had shown to his wife.

The gates clanged shut with an ominous echo, which signaled the capture of the Duke of the West Side. Ambitious men in the Attorney General's office, the parole board, and the police department exchanged handshakes. Roosevelt was happy. Seabury was satisfied, and Assistant D.A. Thomas Dewey was delighted. None of them, however, accounted for the determination of Joe Shalleck, Agnes Demby, and Frank Costello.

13.

Enter the G-Men

Among the handful of personal effects in Owney's suit pockets when he changed into the drab prison uniform were a "considerable" amount of money and a doctor's prescription for a stomach disorder. Dr. Charles Sweet, the prison surgeon who had twice operated on him during his years of freedom, gave him a thorough medical examination and pronounced his general health to be "not too good." In addition to his ulcerated bullet wounds which were causing intestinal problems, Owney had severe bronchial trouble, exacerbated by his chain-smoking through the stressful days of his appeal.

After being photographed, fingerprinted, and passed through a system with which he was now familiar, he was questioned by Sing Sing's principal keeper, John Sheehy. According to stories leaked to the press, Owney told him that he had been in New York attending to personal matters since the news that he had lost his appeal. Asked why he had given himself up at Sing Sing instead of at the parole board in New York, Owney replied: "I did not care for the publicity that would result." He denied any knowledge of the whereabouts of Jerry Sullivan, Terry Reilly, and Little Frenchy. Depriving the board of its moment of public glory was a typical Madden move. He resented being hunted and would give himself up only in his own time and at the place of his choosing.

When reporters telephoned the prison for a quote about his disappearance, they were told: "He figured that he didn't get a good break in court."

"Does he expect a good break in Sing Sing?" they asked.

"He expects a break no better or no worse than anybody else," said the spokesman protectively.

Warden Lewis Lawes also defended Owney by stating: "I am glad to have him back with me again. Not that I wish any man to be in prison, but he will help us here. He is a good influence upon the men."

The parole board, however, thought otherwise. Hours after Owney's admission, officials were talking of transferring him upstate. "He is now regarded as the type of criminal who would be better off in a prison other than Sing Sing, where he would not mix with first offenders. For the next few weeks, Madden will receive none of the prison privileges."

Owney did not take well to returning behind bars. Other prisoners treated him as a celebrity, but he retreated into the privacy of his cell and soon became known as "Owney the Hermit." He was, at times, according to Stanley Walker who knew him, "enveloped in bitterness and melancholy."

Agnes stayed for a short time in New York with Texas Guinan after Owney gave himself up. For a while, she somehow felt closer to him being around his old haunts than back in Arkansas. There was a finality about his imprisonment and also a possibility that Agnes did not want him to surrender.

"If only Owney had listened to me, he would have been so much better off," she wrote after returning to Hot Springs, adding, "I might have had more trouble and worry, though."

For long periods, there was no word at all from New York. Obtaining news from Sing Sing proved more difficult than Agnes had imagined, and she turned her mind to problems facing her at home. Business was bad again and her father, James, had remarried. Agnes did not get along well with Ruth, his new, young bride, and there was tension in the house. When the landlord of her shop demanded a rent increase to $100 per month, she at first tried to fight it, then realized that the shop's closure was inevitable. Her sales at this time during the Depression averaged only three dollars a day, and survival became increasingly difficult. Dismantling the little store, which had given her so many happy memories, was an emotional experience, as she relates in her diary:

"Wednesday: Started taking down electrical fixtures today, and my name sign. I sure hate to give up my little shop that Mama and I had so much fun planning and decorating."

Agnes put her remaining stock in a friend's shop in the arcade beneath the Arlington Hotel and spent the next few days moving the coffee-shop furniture with the help of an aunt. It was hard work and, as with Owney's imprisonment, there was a feeling that it was the end of an era. She noted:

"Saturday: I opened my shop on the 11th and closed on the 11th. Today I moved out completely and left the empty building tonite. No more 'Agnes's Shop.' I am dead tired."

The time was still too early for either of them to realize that a new era was beginning for Agnes and Owney. For the moment, separation brought worsening health for both of them. While her father and his new wife were away, Agnes settled into an austere routine, cleaning and scrubbing the house each morning before calling at the doctor's for a daily medical check on her condition and retiring early to bed at night. With her spirits at a low ebb, she had become prey to a bewildering variety of illnesses, mostly painful and debilitating. Enduring them and the treatment she was prescribed became almost a form of imprisonment in itself.

In Sing Sing, Owney's stomach condition worsened and, for a time, Warden Lawes and Dr. Sweet thought he might die.

Indeed, some considered it a miracle he had managed to survive so long after the Arbor Dance Hall shooting. Only his toughness—the strength which Mae West found so attractive—kept him alive. When Dr. Sweet felt cause for concern, he issued a statement: "Madden is dangerously ill," he announced. "Enemies used their guns on him at times and caused a serious intestinal condition. The ailment has recurred from time to time. He has just been operated on. He is in a serious condition."

As the weeks went by, Owney rallied and finally pulled through. When he emerged shakily from the hospital wing, Warden Lawes encouraged him to take an interest in horticulture. Owney hoed the prison flower beds and puttered around the greenhouses, visibly improving with some gentle exercise. After a bleak winter of illness and depression, he began to revive with the coming of spring. By Easter, Sing Sing was able to announce with pride: "The lilies on the chapel's altar for Easter Services have been grown by Convict Owen ('Owney') Madden, famed Manhattan beer baron."

As Owney attended Mass that Easter, Agnes was staying in Panama, recuperating with her sister, Kat, who had had a baby, and husband, Clay, who had taken a post at a hospital near Panama City. Agnes had been confined to bed, and her father suggested that the trip might help her convalesce. At first, she was reluctant to go, but when a ticket arrived from her sister, she made the effort. She felt weak and looked forward to her first boat trip with a little apprehension. On the train down to New Orleans she made friends with a girl heading the same way, and they shared a hotel room together.

Agnes boarded the white SS *Cefalu*, which left New Orleans at lunchtime and reached the mouth of the Mississippi Delta by sunset. She survived the choppy water of the Gulf of Mexico and the trip to Havana where the ship anchored overnight.

When the ship docked in Panama, Kat was on the quayside in Cristobal to meet her. Agnes took to the new baby instantly—"he has blond curls and is as smart as a whip," she wrote in her diary—and was soon drawn into a languid, tropical world of bridge on lantern-lit verandahs and elegant dinner parties.

By the time Agnes sailed back for New Orleans, her health had improved, but her nerves were still affected by problems at home and the separation from Owney. The Duke was also making a good recovery.

Warden Lawes, who had a great affection for him, turned a blind eye to the rule book and allowed Owney to walk out of the prison accompanying the guard whose duty it was to post the letters. The arrangement suited Owney well as it gave him the opportunity to by-pass the prison censor and post his own mail directly. The infrequency of his letters to Agnes lay in the fact that he did not enjoy having them intercepted and read.

"You know it is difficult for me to write to you when I am in college," he said in one letter to Agnes. "I have to go a few miles from here in order to mail my letter. It is tough for me to keep in contact, but hopefully it will not be for much longer..."

Unlike many convicts of lesser stature, Owney could have wielded immense power in prison. Instead, he preferred to lead a quiet life. His second stay in Sing Sing was bringing about a further mellowing of his character. Flowers and reading were now his only preoccupations. Owney managed to turn Sing Sing from an enforced confinement into a place of sanctuary where he could recuperate and rearrange his affairs.

News was brought to him during his imprisonment that his sister, Mary, had died in New York City. The Maddens were a closely knit family. Owney's mother often kept house for him. He saw his elder brother, Marty, regularly and had visited Mary and her husband as frequently as he could. Owney generated a loyalty and affection among New Yorkers which was demonstrated when he was released for a day, in the company of a guard, to attend her funeral. Word spread quickly that he might make an appearance at St. Michael's Roman Catholic Church on West 34th Street.

When he stepped from the car just before 9 a.m., wearing an overcoat and dark suit, three thousand friends, neighbors, and associates surged forward to welcome him. Sing Sing, alarmed by the response, was worried about being criticized for assigning a lone guard to the visit. The prison issued a hurried statement: "Convict Madden has been a model prisoner ever since he surrendered as a parole violator last July. Furthermore, his appeal is now being placed before the Court of Appeals and it was felt he would not risk his case for temporary freedom."

While the prison authorities made little secret of their fondness for their star convict, the parole board still remained very embittered toward Owney. Each month, it met at Sing Sing to consider the pleas of prisoners seeking release on parole. When Owney's turn came, there were eighty-two similar applications to be heard by the chairman, Dr. Joseph Moore, and his panel.

"When the Board met in the prison shortly before 9 a.m., Madden was tenth in the line of prisoners waiting to go into the hearing room," the *Times* reported. "A few minutes later he was removed from his place near the head of the line and put at the end. His case was not reached until about 5 p.m., and the board gave it less than ten minutes."

Owney argued that, since his release from Sing Sing in 1923, he had at no time broken the law and had no convictions. When the board adjourned without giving him an answer, word swept the prison grapevine, according to the *Times*, that "Owney is out of luck." The report added that "Madden was exceedingly glum when informed he would have to wait 'for some time' to find out what the board had decided in his case."

Joe Shalleck was fighting for his release through the courts, backed by what newspapers rumored as "considerable political pressure." The extent of this pressure was to emerge more clearly later. For the moment, the Board won another round when the appeals court ruled that they had the right to return Owney to Sing Sing "without red tape or court proceedings." Jerry Sullivan had avoided capture by signing up for two months as a crewman on a rum boat but was arrested outside the Waldorf Astoria as soon as he came ashore. Reilly and Little Frenchy remained on the run.

In November of 1932, the Board finally announced its verdict—Madden would have to serve a year in prison for parole violation. The term would run from the date he surrendered. "His release," a spokesman added ominously, "will depend upon his conduct in prison and whether or not he has developed plans for the future which will satisfy the board that he will lead a law-abiding life." The sword hanging over Owney meant that, even on release, he could still be arrested to serve the remaining two years and four months of his original prison sentence. The slaying of Patsy Doyle, for which the evidence suggested he was innocent and possibly framed, continued to haunt him.

Agnes heard from Owney by letter or from friends, but the news was infrequent. Her health remained poor, but her initial despair had dissolved into a deeper longing for them to be together again. Both of them realized that it was now a matter of sitting it out until July of 1933. Owney, as Warden Lawes had stated, was a model prisoner and bulletins confirming his good conduct were issued from Sing Sing:

"OSSINING, NY–Owen Madden, New York racketeer, has been put to work in the prison greenhouses near the Hudson River dock, where the late Charles E. Chapin toiled until his death last year. Madden, who suffers from a bronchial ailment, was transferred from light work with the yard company to this job."

At home in Hot Springs, Agnes relived the memories of their times together in New York, listening to Ellington and the big bands and snatching private moments together.

"Think I'll read my old love letters from Owney again tonite," she wrote. "The radio is playing 'Star Dust.' That always makes me think of him. Wonder if he does of me..."

The program she tuned into is not recorded, but it may possibly have been the weekly, networked broadcast from the Cotton Club, which attracted huge audiences across America. As the songs floated from the radio through the old, white wooden house, Agnes jotted down the lyrics of one of the song hits of 1932–"You're My Everything"–in the back of her diary.

As the end of his year approached, Owney convinced the parole board that he had secured a job as a $50 a week checker with the Champion Coal Company. The board appeared to have undergone an astounding change of heart, even to the point of sympathizing with his poor health. "His condition," said a spokesman, "offers a fertile field for tuberculosis." He even suggested that a change of climate might help. It was the first small indication that something had happened toward the end of his sentence. Whatever it was, the parole board's warmth and cooperation toward Owney became almost embarrassing. It was hard to imagine what could have brought about this fundamental change of attitude. Maybe Frank Costello and Jimmy Hines knew the answer.

On July 1, 1933, Owney stepped into the sunlight of Ossining and walked a few paces to a waiting green limousine. Several people were glimpsed inside before the door slammed and it sped away toward the distant skyline of Manhattan.

"Owney Madden, reputed Broadway racketeer, walked out of Sing Sing prison today with $48.40 in his pockets," Washington's *Sunday Star* reported. "All but $20 of this amount he had earned taking care of the flowers in the prison greenhouses at eight cents a day. The remainder came from the prison rehabilitation fund." There was no mention of the "considerable" sum in his pockets when he surrendered a year earlier.

Officially, the terms of his parole meant that he was unable to leave the state of New York and had to report in regularly. Owney had other plans, however, and embarked on travels which first reunited him with Agnes in Hot Springs and took in a wide area of the United States. Curiously, the parole board, after pursuing him mercilessly for parole violation, adopted a more lenient and protective attitude. A year was to elapse before rumor and gossip surrounded the officials once so determined to remove him from the underworld map.

In the meantime, he was back with Agnes, and their romance flourished more strongly than ever. Hot Springs became both a haven and a springboard from which to consolidate his secret plans. Owney, at first, traveled between Arkansas and Manhattan so that his absence from the scene would not be too apparent. A physician's certificate recommended that the climate in the south was conducive to his recovery. As he made brief business trips here and there, his presence did not go entirely unnoticed, and the parole board came under pressure to explain why he appeared to have such unlimited freedom.

In September of 1933, just three months after his release from Sing Sing, Owney visited San Francisco while buying interests in West Coast race tracks. Someone in the police department recognized him and set the alarm bells ringing, just as they had in Los Angeles.

Madden meant trouble, and Police Chief Quinn began to get nervous. A meticulous man, he decided to double-check his identity before arresting him. On September 9, he telegrammed J. Edgar Hoover's Bureau of Investigation in Washington. The message read: AIR MAIL IMMEDIATELY FINGERPRINTS AND PHOTOS OF OWNEY MADDEN RECENTLY RELEASED SING SING. Beneath the message, Western Union had printed the slogan: "The quickest, surest way to send money is by telegraph or cable."

Nothing went unnoticed by the bullet-headed, heavy-jowled Hoover. He sat long into the night in his executive office, overlooked by the grim death mask of John Dillinger, hanging like a trophy on the wall, checking reports and cables from his agents scattered across America. Hoover sat behind a desk built like a mausoleum and attacked his mound of papers with a heavy pencil. Everything was subject to his scrutiny, and little escaped those unerring, puffy eyes. The bureau can only just bring itself to smile about the operative whose typing strayed sloppily into the margin. Hoover contemptuously scribbled: "Watch borders." Within hours, dozens of fearful agents had deployed themselves across the Mexican frontier.

Senior aides were familiar with the sound of Hoover's adenoidal breathing, which rose and fell like an old percolator as he examined their work. The bureau was his pride, and he bitterly resented any criticism of the elite image he expected his men to live up to. When Hoover saw that no one had been able to supply Chief Quinn's request, he was consumed with annoyance. He detested incompetence and resented being made to look a fool by Owney Madden. The bureau, in 1933, was sandwiched in an uncomfortable role somewhere between the police force and the government and was an easy target for jealous rivalry. If the chief of San Francisco police decided to start sniping, then everyone would have to duck for cover.

Hoover immediately telephoned his Bay City division and ordered Vetterli, the special agent in charge, to drop everything and smooth things over at the police headquarters. Vetterli squirmed through an embarrassing meeting which ended with Quinn handing him a photograph of Owney and suggesting that the bureau keep it in its files for future reference. Vetterli tried to breeze over his discomfort in his report to Hoover:

"While at San Francisco Police Headquarters today, making contacts, we had a very splendid visit for approximately three-quarters of an hour. Police Chief Quinn advised that he was very anxious to secure a photograph of Madden because, if he was in San Francisco, he wanted to incarcerate him immediately in jail as a vagrant.

"He suggested the advisability of the division keeping photographs of all known gangs and gangsters in Washington. I informed him of the work we are doing at the present time, and he is well satisfied with it, but he could not quite understand why no photograph of Madden was in the files of the division. He turned over to the writer a copy of a photograph of Owen Madden, and I suggest the same should be placed in the files of the division."

Hoover read Vetterli's masterpiece of understatement and heavily underscored the name Owen with a note in the margin that he was known as "Owney." The dictatorial director was known to nurse wounds until an opportunity arose to get even. Owney, driving up and down the hilly streets of San Francisco, had no idea that he had suddenly achieved promotion to the top of Hoover's unofficial retribution list.

Unable to take any effective action, the director descended in anger on Tolson, the agent in charge of the records department, and demanded an explanation. The best Tolson could manage at short notice was to plead a heavy workload. That very week, he explained, eighty-four records had been photocopied in response to inquiries and another 300 were backed up in the pipeline. One of the unit's technical staff was working through the night to clear accumulated work. Even at this rate, Tolson added, it would be another three months before the department was functioning normally.

It was perhaps not the best approach to adopt with a director who worked so hard and long that he often slept in his office, but it was honest enough to dampen Hoover's anger. The chief issued a memo which barely concealed his annoyance:

"I am still at a loss to understand why the identification unit did not recognize the case of Owen Madden. The reputation of Owney Madden, as he is more often referred to, is almost as well known as that of Al Capone and I would think that at least someone in the identification unit should familiarize himself with the current press. If this had been done the unit should have immediately recognized the request of Chief of Police Quinn when he asked for a photograph of Owney Madden.

"I recognize the fact that it is impossible for anyone to be familiar with all of the gangsters and hoodlums in the country, from either working in this division or reading the newspapers, but it would be possible to recognize those who have outstanding records over a long period of years. Among these Owney Madden ranks as the first in the East, and particularly in New York City."

Owney managed to slip through Quinn's fingers because of the bureau's incompetence and returned again to Hot Springs. Agnes was happier than she had ever been. Her tough, quiet lover was at last within her reach, and soon newspapers were picking up rumors of the unusual romance. The tabloids, ready for any excuse to revive the Madden saga, were hysterical:

"Broadway gets laugh on Madden," ran a headline in the *Daily Mirror* in November of 1933. "Reports that romance has bloomed in the life of Owney Madden, big-shot racketeer, reverberated from Times Square to Columbus Circle yesterday in gales of laughter."

"Owney—married? 'Naw.'" That was the comment of his intimates when informed that Madden "had succumbed to the charms of Miss Agnes Demby, daughter of the postmaster down in Hot Springs, Arkansas."

Besides, they wouldn't admit that he was in Hot Springs. Terms of his parole forbid him to leave the state, they explained, and by doing so he would be electing himself to another term in Sing Sing.

As in the case of the flying lessons, reporters were so enraptured with the story that none of them paused to wonder how they happened across it so easily. Owney's romance with Agnes was to play a crucial role in his future plans. The nature of them began to unfold on December 5, 1933, the day on which Prohibition was repealed. Eight months after becoming president, Roosevelt signed Proclamation 2065, officially declaring America wet again. The announcement was made before a battery of newsreel crews and on live radio by acting Secretary of State, William Phillips. He solemnly read a statement repealing the Volstead Act as millions gathered around their radio receivers. When he concluded, amidst applause, and walked away from the forest of microphones, none of the jubilant millions heard his assistant hiss: "Sir, you forgot to sign the document."

In speakeasies all over New York, patrons raised glasses of Madden's No. 1 in salute as the celebrations began. "Prohibition effigies are hanged from a flagpole at Broadway and 51st street," Henry Lee reported, "electrocuted in Harlem, drowned in the pool of the old Park Central Hotel, and even shot by the firing squad of an American Legion Post in Freeport, Long Island... Drugstores and soft drink stands get more beer than coffee orders (even for breakfast). Brewers have to borrow milk trucks to make deliveries... There are cheers as a horse-drawn brewer's van lumbers to the Empire State Building and drops off a case... Outside the Rivoli Theater, lines are waiting to see that pioneer monster film *King Kong*, but beer still gets top billing every place else in town. At busy 7th Avenue and Broadway, a black Packard limousine snarls mid-afternoon traffic as the livened chauffeur stops to buy two containers for madam and himself. The cop on post nearby smiles indulgently..."

Had America been spiritually cleansed by its thirteen years of enforced abstention? The figures speak for themselves—beer consumption in 1919 was officially recorded as 27,593,437 barrels. By 1934, the first full year after repeal, it had risen to 32,266,039 barrels. "The American," as Mark Palmer remarked, "is an individualist and a rebel," a fact which the Anti-saloon League sadly failed to appreciate. Also, it could not have foreseen that this "big thirst" soon would help elevate crime to a level more organized and sophisticated than ever before.

The Madden residence on West Grand Avenue in Hot Springs.

Madden in the backyard with his terrier, Sissy. Courtesy of the Garland County Historical Society, Hot Springs, Arkansas.

Madden drives friends around Lake Hamilton in Hot Springs. The boat was a gift from his friend George Raft. Courtesy of the Garland County Historical Society, Hot Springs, Arkansas.

Agnes Madden entertains in Hot Springs during a visit from Frank Costello (left), known as the "Prime Minister of the underworld," and New Jersey gang boss, Willie Moretti.

Madden clowns around with a fake gun at the Happy Hollow tourist attraction in Hot Springs. From left are Harry Cook, Eddie Mead, Madden, and Bill Farnsworth.

Sitting on the running board of his Packard Victoria, Madden visits with former Gopher gang member John McArdle (left) and Mike Best. McArdle served time for his part in the killing of Little Patsy Doyle.

Mr. and Mrs. Madden at their home in Hot Springs.

14.

Symphony in Blue

Owney was one of a handful of immigrants who lived through the distinct phases of the dark side of America's history. He rose from the ranks of an unsophisticated street gang to become one of the administrative geniuses of bootlegging and now stood on the threshold of a new era. With each step he had grown in stature, maturity, political experience, and cunning. His equals regarded him as a man of wisdom and integrity. It cannot be doubted that Owney was a self-made man, but he was also created by forces which ironically now sought to destroy him.

The repeal of Prohibition was a turning point for New York's gangs. Mayor Walker had resigned and slipped away for an extended holiday to Europe. After a brief interlude, he was succeeded by Fiorella LaGuardia, hailed by many as New York's greatest mayor. On his first day in office, the tough Italian known as "Little Flower" galvanized his police force and declared war on the gangsters. To prove he meant business, the slot machines Frank Costello had invested in after Prohibition were rounded up for photographers. LaGuardia publically smashed them with a sledgehammer and dumped them in the East River. Life in New York would never be the same again.

Owney, like Frank, opted for what Costello's lawyer referred to as "victimless crime" and turned his attention to gambling. The wisdom of the remark could be debated, but the popularity of gambling had never been greater. Casinos and racetrack betting were mostly outlawed across America, but the older statesmen of the Atlantic City convention saw them as a way to spread their wings. "It's a big country out there," Meyer Lansky said. "There's no need to fight each other for a piece of the action."

Hot Springs, as a law unto itself, was an attractive proposition. Who better to take over the town and develop it in the way the grand strategists envisaged? Bubbles was quiet and orderly with gambling, which attracted high-rollers and little attention. Lansky made no secret of his distaste and distrust for the young bloods who had maneuvered their way into the rackets. The new era of expansion required men of experience who knew the value of old-fashioned trust and loyalty.

Hot Springs began to play an important role in Owney's plans but, before he could operate with the freedom he required, it was clear that some kind of deal would have to be struck with the authorities. The small print of the final agreement will never be known but it was a deal of enormous proportions, negotiated in great secrecy. Those who knew of the bargaining that went on still decline to speak of it. "It was a deal," said Q. Byrum Hurst, "that was many, many months in the making, and it involved some of the greatest people in this country." If Owney were to leave New York, it could not be left to chance that he would go unmolested. Agreements would have to be struck at the highest level, backed by copper-bottomed assurances. To secure such guarantees for a man of Owney's stature would involve a large amount of money and the cooperation of several influential figures. Where and when the talking took place cannot be stated with accuracy, but the conditions which emerged became clearer as time went by. Owney could not be seen to benefit from what occurred and, in turn, would also have to present no further threat to the authority of those in power.

Negotiations were complex and delicate. The eventual outcome would be that Owney's parole would be transferred from New York to Hot Springs, where he would remain in exile for the rest of his life. If he left Arkansas, he could expect the full force of the law to he applied to put him back behind bars. If he lived out his days with discretion, he would be free to do whatever he pleased. The bargain ran against everything the American way of life stood for.

Some of his friends still maintain that it was a travesty of his constitutional rights as an individual, but they are old and wise enough to know that morality and noble sentiment have little place in politics. Abdication must have been a difficult choice for the King of Manhattan. The pressure and publicity, however, had taken their toll, and he had no wish to live out his life continually pursued by his enemies. After much soul-searching, he realized that he had little option.

For a while, Owney remained under the jurisdiction of the parole board in New York while residing in Hot Springs. It was, as the board said, a climate conducive to recovery. When the right time came, he would be paroled to the care of postmaster James Demby. His romance with Agnes, and talk of marriage, provided evidence of his intentions to settle there permanently. While exile appeared to be the lesser of two evils, the quiet years Owney imagined lay before him were little more than a dream. After he was misled by Roosevelt, other agencies were embarking on a drive to hunt him relentlessly until the day he died.

Someone—the name most frequently mentioned is Frank Costello—continued to administer his business interests in New York in exchange for a percentage of the enterprise he intended to develop in Hot Springs. He also undertook to protect Owney's businesses in his absence and ensure the smooth transition of his affairs. At least, that was the theory. Unstoppable prosecutors, who had no part in the deal, were still determined to put him back in prison. In their zeal and enthusiasm, they unwittingly pushed some of those involved in Owney's exile to the verge of ruin and exposure.

In 1934, as New York's campaign against corruption rolled on, the Champion Coal Company came under scrutiny. The firm, which supposedly employed Owney for $50 a week, was found to be short-weighting the city to the tune of hundreds of thousands of dollars a year. Like the laundries, the breweries, and the numbers game, it appeared to be another of New York's teeming rackets, and the D.A.'s office was determined to discover who controlled it.

The man who could help their inquiries was thought to be living in Hot Springs. It was potentially disastrous news. Owney still had another year of his parole to run and could be imprisoned for many years if he was implicated.

The parties involved in the Madden deal will probably never be fully known and neither will the exact sum of money that changed hands. But the events of the Coal Grand Jury hearing cast an interesting light over all those concerned. In July of 1934, New York Assistant District Attorney Maurice Wahl, charged with investigating the coal rackets, was puzzled to find all his attempts to get Madden to testify blocked by the parole board. The curious about-face attitude attracted the attention of reporters who recalled the board's vehement efforts to prosecute him only a year or two earlier.

New York's *Evening Journal* ran this headline in one edition: "Owney a big shot racketeer? Not to boys on parole board."

"All Madden wants to do is get away from it all," the *Journal* noted. "No more rackets. And he wants to marry the Demby girl."

"'Yes, but about Mrs. Madden...'

"Parole Commissioner Bernard J. Fagin waved his hand impatiently. 'They haven't been together for twenty years. But we're not talking about her—we're talking about him.'

"And then the commissioner went on to talk about Owney. He said plenty, too. And what he said, mostly, was that this Owney-the-racketeer stuff was a big pipe dream. They might talk of Owney the Big Shot with a finger in this and a fist in that, but where's the evidence? The parole board couldn't find it. The parole board, in fact, has Owney pretty well sized up. Here's the verdict:

"Madden's not a killer. He's not a racketeer. He's just an overrated guy. He's supposed to have owned a brewery. He's supposed to have run a racetrack and racing sheets. That's what he's supposed to have done.

"Then the commissioner added, reflectively: 'But how he could is beyond me. He's no mental giant. I checked all his supposed activities, but I couldn't find any Madden link in them.'

"The reporter looked surprised and the commissioner said sharply: 'I know everyone thinks there's sugar being passed around. You can say that none of it has showed up around here. Why, it would be suicide to take money from racketeers. You'd always have to take orders from them.'

"The commissioner smiled. 'You know,' he said, 'I've had many a headache out of this Madden case. I approved of his going to Hot Springs because he was ill. Also, I was happy to have him out of New York so that if anyone was knocked off I wouldn't have to go out and find him for the police.'

"Commissioner Fagin, who has been criticized because of the 'protective' actions of his men, said he regretted that, though the cry was to send Madden back to jail, no one had yet come forward with any proof that he has violated his parole.

"'I sent him away two years ago,' said Fagin, 'because he lied about his employment by a laundry company. But at that time, I begged Police Commissioner Mulrooney, Inspector John Sullivan, and Captain Patrick McVeigh to point out what Madden was doing that violated his parole.'

"'I even had government agents in here asking them for any proof that Madden was connected with any parole violation. But no one could give us any help. The government tried without success to prove he operated a brewery. When Vincent Coll, Charles Entratta, and some pal of Legs Diamond were killed, everyone charged a Madden link, but the police couldn't find it if it was there.'"

On July 17th of 1934, Owney and Agnes made the long drive from Arkansas to New York City. On the journey, which took them through small towns along monotonously straight roads, he was nervous, apprehensive, and smoked a lot. But, for the first time, there was someone in whom he could confide his fears. Neither of them knew whether the future held further separations, but Agnes was determined to stand by him throughout the grand jury hearing. She had a stubborn loyalty which he appreciated.

The D.A.'s office had already made it clear that they intended to give him a rough ride on the witness stand. Even before the car reached the outskirts of New Jersey, Assistant District Attorney Maurice Wahl was telling reporters: "If he does not show up on time, the parole board will have a lot of explaining to do."

Wahl was irked by their protective attitude toward Madden, which aroused his suspicions that something was being concealed. Champion Coal was registered under the name of a Mr. E. A. Thompson, and Wahl wanted to know the exact nature of Owney's relationship with him and the company.

A heat wave hung low over the city as Owney ran briskly up the wide steps of the Criminal Courts building. Waiting reporters dabbed their brows with handkerchiefs, and the shirts of the photographers who swept forward to meet him were limp with the humidity. Owney looked cool—"exceedingly dapper," they said—in a grey and blue sports suit, blue tie, straw hat, black-and-white shoes, and rolled-down socks. He put on a relaxed smile and good-naturedly posed for a brief picture before ducking into the Grand Jury anteroom. The crowd of newsmen surged after him, jostling for pictures as he was met by parole board commissioner Bernard Fagin. The heavy-featured man with the beak-like nose was also suffering visibly from the heat. His pale hat was pushed back on his head, and the knot in his striped tie was shoved out of shape from constantly running his fingers around his collar.

Fagin was immediately wary of the wave of newspapermen and shooed them away when they tried to move him closer to Owney for a photograph. When they begged for his cooperation, Fagin flatly refused. The Duke drifted away from the melee, leaving the parole commissioner to fend off all the photographers.

According to the *New York American*, "Fagin refused to pose with Madden, recalling that a woman sheriff in Indiana and a prosecutor had been criticized for posing with Dillinger. He expected that he might have to send Madden back to Sing Sing.

"Fagin also said he understood Madden and Miss Agnes Demby, daughter of the postmaster of Hot Springs, where Madden had been recovering from his bullet-impaired health, would marry if possible. That, he intimated, depended on whether Mrs. Madden obtained a divorce."

Even as he spoke, Dorothy, Owney's first wife, had checked into a hotel in Reno to file papers for a "quickie" divorce. The offer of an attractive settlement in cash and property persuaded her to go through with the proceedings. Wedding plans, Owney and Agnes agreed, would bring them closer together and perhaps even help his case.

Owney was met in the anteroom by his brother-in-law, John Marrin, who had been married to his sister, Mary. Marrin, a tough West Side Democratic district leader, wanted to be there to give his support. As they sat side by side on a row of polished benches, Owney felt increasingly uncomfortable in the suffocating heat. He took off his coat and repeatedly wiped his face with a blue-bordered handkerchief. The oppressive humidity made him restless and played on his nerves. In the previous three days, he had lost twelve pounds in weight with the worry of his court appearance. As he wiped his neck, the photographers broke away from Fagin and surrounded him in an exploding wall of plate cameras.

Owney rested his elbow on his raised knee and tried to cover his brow with the back of his hand. From the corner of his eye, he caught sight of Assistant District Attorney Harold Hastings and called him over.

"Get these people away from me," he demanded. "Get them out of here." Hastings waved the photographers toward the exit with outstretched hands, like a shepherd steering his flock. One cameraman dodged past him protesting: "Hey, Owney, how about one more shot?"

Owney threw him a mean look and warned in an even voice: "I'll give you a shot if you don't stop pestering me. Get out of here."

As the photographer scuttled away, visibly shaken, the Duke turned to John Marrin and said: "If they don't leave me alone, I'll sock somebody."

Two parole board officers, William Corcoran and Jack Doyle, hurried over to offer assistance. Doyle asked if he could get Owney a cold drink or open a window. "Corcoran," said the New York World Telegram, "even offered to have a reporter for the Sun put out of the anteroom, but the reporter avoided a controversy by voluntarily leaving the room. It was too hot to argue.

"Madden and Marrin are two great pigeon fanciers, but were too preoccupied, or too hot, to notice the criminal court pigeons which had alighted on a nearby window ledge."

After the wait of almost two hours, Owney's spirits began to drop. Just before he was due to appear, Assistant D.A.s Wahl and Hastings appeared from the grand jury room and asked him to sign a waiver of immunity before he testified. Grand jury witnesses could enjoy freedom from possible prosecution to encourage them to speak frankly. Owney, clearly not to be afforded the privilege, refused to sign. After a huddled discussion, he offered to put his name to what he described as a "limited waiver."

"There's no such thing as a limited waiver," Wahl growled. "You'll have to sign the regular form or face the consequences."

Owney reluctantly agreed, but when they began to ask questions about his past life, he refused to answer. Then, he and Fagin, flanked by the assistant D.A.s, walked in to face the grand jury. The inquiry into coal rackets centered on allegations that some New York coal companies under contract to the city had given short weight, while others had supplied lower grades of fuel than the quality specified. The D.A.'s original interest in Owney's suspected ownership of Champion Coal had widened. "Public officials," reported the New York American, "now want to know if that was a legitimate job or one designed to get Madden out of Sing Sing, and if his health really was impaired when he went to bask in the Arkansas sun, a privilege not usually accorded to paroled men."

Owney testified for an hour under Wahl's questioning and returned to his bench looking strained. Fagin, who had taken the stand after him, was ordered to return to court with Madden's record and two other members of the parole board whom the grand jury wanted to question.

"Madden," the *Sun* reporter wrote, "was a wilted symphony in blue when he emerged from the grand jury room. Mr. Hastings said he complained about the heat and the humidity." He had not been an obstructive witness, Hastings added, but it was clear that the grand jury was now little wiser about his activities. Wahl looked peeved as he followed Hastings from the courtroom. He was annoyed by the protective attitude of the parole board toward him.

Corcoran fussed around him when photographers closed in for more pictures. Owney posed briefly—an indication that he was perhaps not unhappy with his courtroom performance—but the parole officer ordered them away. His attitude so annoyed the district attorney, watching from a distance, that he stepped forward and told Corcoran bluntly:

"I don't know what your interest is, but I don't like it. And my assistant, Mr. Wahl, who has charge of the investigation, doesn't like it either."

Wahl joined his superior and told him: "Corcoran is acting as a bodyguard for Madden and I object to it."

Commissioner Fagin took the heat out of the situation by asking reporters if they had any questions. They had plenty. In particular, they wanted to know the whereabouts of the lovely Agnes?

"I am sure," Fagin replied expansively, "that Agnes Demby, in whom Madden is said to be interested, did not return to New York with him. She may be in the city, but I doubt it."

"Let's ask Owney," someone shouted.

But the Duke had quietly melted away into the cool shadows of the court anteroom and disappeared into the city he knew so well. The press turned back to Fagin with a barrage of questions which he did his best to field:

"Commissioner Fagin admitted it was he who had approved Madden's request for permission to leave New York State," the *World Telegram* reported. "He also said the board, and not the district attorney, was defraying Madden's expenses to and from Hot Springs. He placed the blame for the current criticism of the parole board on the 'officiousness' of William Corcoran, the parole supervisor who has Madden's case in charge. He said Corcoran had gone out of his way to make complaints about reporters who sought to interview Madden.

"'Madden's parole has a year to run,' Commissioner Fagin said. 'I can send him back to prison any time I want to, but I shall not do it unless I have evidence that he has lapsed back into criminal ways. Madden means no more to the parole board than does any one of the 5,000 persons under its jurisdiction.'"

Wahl and the district attorney remained in the background, taking everything in. Their suspicions were aroused, and the board, rather than Owney's involvement with the Champion Coal Company, attracted their interest. Within a year, Fagin and other members of the panel were to weather a grand jury investigation into the whole New York parole system. Nothing was to emerge from the inquiry, but more hearings were to follow closely on its heels.

Crime writer Hank Messick added an important footnote to underworld history when an unnamed source told him of a secret meeting which took place in New York's Waldorf Astoria Hotel early in 1934. Most of the 132 representatives who attended the Atlantic City Convention took part in the gathering behind the locked doors of a conference suite. Leading crime bosses addressed the meeting, which had been called to discuss further strategy in the era of Roosevelt's New Deal. A few noticeable faces were absent—Waxey Gordon and Al Capone were in jail for tax evasion, and Dutch Schultz, the next target of youthful prosecutor Thomas Dewey and Internal Revenue chief Elmer Key, was in hiding.

There were several problems that needed to be resolved. The Lindbergh case had attracted unwelcome attention to organized crime, but Owney's efforts had fortunately offset public disquiet. Mayor LaGuardia had waged war on Costello's slot machines and, exactly one minute after taking office, ordered the arrest of Lucky Luciano.

The assembled leaders, groomed and besuited, voted to take note of the administrative system Roosevelt had introduced to put the country back on its feet and form its own regional councils. There would be no overall leader, and the aim of the new organization—the National Crime Syndicate—would be to spread its interests across America in a spirit of mutual cooperation.

As Longy Zwillman, the man who tried to buy Roosevelt in Chicago, put it: "We just can't afford to have people bumping off anybody they please or kidnapping big shots. We've got to have control and cooperation. It isn't like it used to be when it was every man for himself. We've got to learn to act like businessmen."

One of the final acts before the long meeting broke up was to divide up the territory and interests of Dutch Schultz, who was facing an inevitable jail sentence for tax evasion. When the National Crime Syndicate settled down to the business of slicing up his empire, Owney was awarded Miami's lucrative Tropical Park racetrack "for services rendered." Lansky, as chairman, had the task of deciding who should be allocated virgin regions around the country. Owney, whom he admired and trusted, was assigned complete control of Hot Springs.

Schultz, meanwhile, through the hard efforts of his lawyers, managed to remain at liberty and was less than happy when he learned what had happened. After mulling over the problem, he visited Lansky and offered him a deal. If the syndicate would kill Dewey, he was prepared to step down and relinquish any claim to his empire. If they did not, he argued, then he would shoot the bastard himself. The crime bosses talked it over and, by a majority, decided that, while Dewey was dangerous, it would cause more damage to the syndicate to assassinate him. The prosecutor was ambitious and already had his sights set on the governorship of New York. Soon, with luck, he would have the D.A.'s office and move higher up. One day, he might even prove to be of use to them. The biggest nuisance by far was Schultz, who seemed intent on going through with his insane plan. "The Dutchman," as Messick put it, "was sentenced to death for reasons of policy as well as greed. Schultz was an old-timer, a Mustache Pete in his own right. To knock him off would produce no heat—just the reverse."

Schultz "got his," as the newspapers phrased it, in the Palace Chophouse in Newark. Several hours passed before he lapsed into a coma and died in Newark City Hospital. In his last period of consciousness, he rambled, mostly incoherently and occasionally poetically, as a police stenographer took down every word at his bedside. Before the end, among the jumbled phrases tumbling from his dying lips, he murmured: "... they are Englishmen, and they are a type. I don't know who is best, they or us."

Dutch belonged to the old New York from which Owney was happy to be free. It was the city of Patsy Doyle, Vincent Coll, Legs Diamond, and all the countless others whose greed and ruthlessness had posed a constant threat to the quiet way in which he preferred to operate. It was a world without sentiment. Such feelings were reserved for wives, lovers, family, and close friends. Compassion, affection, and concern were interpreted as indications of weakness and the brutal were always ready to prey upon the meek.

Life in Hot Springs with Agnes was more soothing to Owney's nerves and his health. With the ordeal of the Coal Grand Jury behind him, Owney adjusted to life in the small mountain town where a month seldom went by without old acquaintances dropping in.

He was discreet in his contact with old underworld faces. Hot Springs was under the watchful eye of the Little Rock division of the Bureau of Investigation, and it was not worth jeopardizing his freedom with less than a year of his parole left to run. Owney spent the early months of 1935 in New York, arranging the transition of his affairs. He still found it difficult to shake loose from the interest shown by the press in everything he did. Newspapers were hungry for the slightest excuse to write a story about him. On June 6, the Associated Press filed this story from New York:

"The parole period of Owen Vincent Madden, pigeon fancier and horticulturist, ends June 15 at midnight, after which he will be free to come and go as he pleases.

"According to reliable reports," the New York Herald-Tribune said, "Mr. Madden's first action as a private citizen will be to go to Hot Springs, Ark., to rejoin Miss Agnes Demby, whom it has been said he will marry. Miss Demby is not in Hot Springs, and her father said last night that he knew nothing of the New York report and did not care to discuss it.

"Miss Demby said recently: 'Anyone who knows Owney could not help but love him. It's a shame about his troubles, isn't it?'"

Agnes, as might be expected, was with her man, enjoying the familiar sights and sounds of the city again and gleaning, with her interest in business, a little knowledge of how the affairs were run. Her bedtime reading was the Wall Street Journal, and she had an instinctive feel for the ebb and flow of the market. Owney preferred that she know nothing of his dealings but, as time went by, Agnes was to capably handle some of his interests.

When the long-awaited day finally arrived for the end of Owney's parole, newspapers across America recorded the event with mixed feelings, a factor which depended largely on individual reporters' experiences of Owney. The Chicago Tribune, for instance, ran the story through its syndication service with a tone of fond familiarity. With a headline that declared "unlimited liberty to Madden," the paper wrote:

"A benevolent parole board, gulping down a sizable throat lump, blew its nose loudly and gave up its kindly jurisdiction over Owen ("Owney the Killer") Madden at midnight tonight, and Broadway, over its dawn beers, was wondering whether the ex-hellion of Hell's Kitchen would resume his romance with a pretty Arkansas postmaster's daughter.

"The wise money was laid on the affirmative side, largely because Joseph P. Folkoff, supervising parole officer, in a public statement laid sympathetic stress on Madden's ill health which, Folkoff said, prevents him from working. The reasoning ran apparently as follows: (a) Hot Springs, Ark., is a swell spot for a sick guy (b) Madden is a sick guy (c) Agnes Demby, the gal, lives in Hot Springs (d) therefore Madden will very likely land in Hot Springs and give Agnes a buzz..."

The unanswered question was, of course, how had Owney managed to change the whole stance of the parole board from unmitigated aggression to kindly solicitude?

Jimmy Hines is known to have applied considerable political pressure to keep Owney out of Sing Sing, in addition to letters of petition from well-known New York celebrities and politicians. But, once in motion, the full weight of the prosecuting machine was difficult to stop. Hines's most influential associate at this time was Owney's close friend, Frank Costello, a man who believed with evangelical conviction in the power of the bribe over the bullet. It was obviously too risky for Owney himself to make the approach. Such matters, in any case, were traditionally done indirectly. His accounts were open to inspection and the disappearance of a large sum would not have gone unnoticed. The hand of Frank "everyone-gets-their-share" Costello is almost certain to have interposed. There was much more at stake than Owney's welfare. For example, the development plans of the National Crime Syndicate depended heavily on his liberty. Newspapers had no inkling of the underworld's reorganization, but reporters were wise enough to suspect that someone was behind the parole board's sudden display of humanitarianism.

Their opportunity to investigate further came when board members were subpoenaed to testify at a grand jury into vice, policy, and bail bond rackets in 1939. The *New York World Telegram* sent a reporter up to Auburn to lean a little on Major Frank Hanscom, a member of the board. On the basis of nothing more than intuition, the newsman managed to pry loose much more information than he bargained for.

"Was someone bribed in the Owney Madden case?" the reporter asked, expecting a denial.

"There was never a definite or tentative offer of a bribe made," Major Hanscom replied. "There was merely a bribe suggestion. If a bribe offer had been made, we should have had the person who made it arrested."

There is a possibility that Hanscom imagined the newspaperman knew more than he did and figured that a half-admission would clear the air. The reporter, however, was unexpectedly tenacious.

"Who made the suggestion?" he asked.

"A group of people."

"Was one of them a well-known politician?"

"I didn't say that," snapped Hanscom defensively, straying into deeper water than he had intended.

"Was it Jimmy Hines?" the reporter inquired.

"Hines's name," the major replied huffily, "is taboo to the parole board. The mere mention of his name makes it doubly hard on a prisoner. It adds years to his sentence. Hines knows where he stands with us."

The major was conveniently overlooking the fact that, far from making life hard for prisoners, the intervention of Jimmy Hines ensured that it would be an exceedingly comfortable one. The reporter appeared to ignore the remark anyway.

"Well," he asked, "who made the offer?"

"Madden has a lot of friends."

"How did the bribe offer come to you?" The World Telegram man clearly sensed he was onto something.

"It came by a circuitous route—from some big shot, I should judge," Hanscom answered vaguely.

"Was it a specific offer of one million dollars?"

Hanscom refused to be drawn in.

"My answer is the fact that Madden went back to prison. I did say that not even for a million dollars would the board be influenced."

Other members of the panel were quick to close ranks.

"Dr. J. W. Moore, chairman, who was at Auburn attending a meeting, denied that he knew anything of the overtures that had been made," the World Telegram added. "Joseph Canavan, former secretary to Governor Lehman, who succeeded Mr. Fagin as a member of the board, said the whole matter was 'just a lot of hooey.' Police Commissioner Lewis J. Valentine was asked whether any evidence linking Hines with rackets in the city had been uncovered. 'No,' the commissioner replied. 'If there had been any evidence, the proper action would have been taken.'"

It was a remarkable statement, considering that, at the time, Hines was known to be virtually in partnership with Costello, Madden, and others.

Owney adjusted himself to exile from New York and, once free from parole restrictions, turned his mind to thoughts of marriage. The day for which Agnes had waited long and patiently was set for November 26th, 1939. It was one of those bright, crisp mornings when the brooding outline of the Ouachita Mountains stood in sharp relief against an azure sky. Owney had taken great pains to keep the arrangements secret from the press, but news of their intentions somehow managed to leak out. New York newspapers, sharply divided between outrage at his manipulation of the parole board and barely concealed affection for Manhattan's most colorful character, pursued the story energetically.

Mrs. Madden recalled the incident with a smile years later when I spoke to her in the cool, high-ceilinged dining room of her home on West Grand. "Owen and I didn't want all that publicity," she said. "Even Paramount newsreels pestered us to come and take pictures."

They were married in great secrecy at a beautiful resort at Mount Ida, twelve miles northwest of Hot Springs and overlooked by the Pine Ridge Hills. Agnes's father, James, acted as witness in a short ceremony conducted by the Reverend Kincaid, an elderly local minister. There was no immediate honeymoon, and the contented couple drove home to celebrate over a quiet dinner together. Owney was forty-three years old, and Agnes was thirty-four. Together, they were to make a formidable partnership.

15.

Bubbles

In Arkansas's olden days, the Natchez, Quapaw, and Osage Indians traveled on foot across the mountains to the sacred Valley of Vapors and its hot springs. The warriors returned with a story. In a cave hidden deep under a mountain lay the home of an evil spirit. When it was restless, it turned and shook in its lair, sending smoke issuing out from the cracks in the rock face. The Indians prayed that the Great Spirit would help them overcome the entity, which took the form of a dragon. The Great Spirit obliged and destroyed the monster, which struggled so fiercely in its death throes that hot water began to gush from the mountainside. From that day on, it became a special place. No warfare was permitted in this area, as it was considered neutral ground. All life was held safe in the valley.

By 1936, thanks to the good offices of Mayor Leo P. McLaughlin, the situation had changed very little. For someone pursued by the federal authorities, it was still the safest place to be. Hot Springs's head man was a shrewd, intelligent lawyer who loved money, horses, and women, probably in that order. His great weakness was power. Like a snake hypnotized by a mongoose, McLaughlin was fascinated by it. Owney Madden exuded power. Like the Duke, the mayor was of Irish descent, and they soon struck up a friendly business relationship. McLaughlin knew the Dembys well—he himself had appointed James as postmaster and was a family guest at his birthday parties. Owney was accepted into the closed ranks of McLaughlin's machine known as the Little Combination. However, the mayor suspected that Madden was a respected member of a much bigger one.

For many years, it was thought that Al Capone, who first began to visit Hot Springs in the 1920s, came to strike deals with small bootleggers who operated in the hills surrounding the town. Capone's best-kept secret was that his Hot Springs bootlegging connections were on a scale far bigger than anyone ever imagined. The ring, led by a local electrician named Bill Stevens, worked in underground chambers and catacombs excavated beneath buildings, with a large bottling plant concealed in a warehouse on Park Avenue. The tip of Stevens's iceberg was finally uncovered in 1930 by a teetotaling sheriff, Garland Van Sickle, who raided Stevens's neat little cottage on Watt Street. How the eccentric Van Sickle ever gained office in McLaughlin's easy-going administration remains a mystery. Because he tended to overlook illegal gambling, however, Van Sickle was only considered a minor problem for McLaughlin.

Excavations beneath the house had taken a year and cost an inestimable sum. At first, Van Sickle and his deputies found nothing unusual until three separate entrances leading below ground were discovered. "What did they find?" asked the *Hot Springs Sentinel Record*. "Why, they found a—shh. Let us whisper—a still. Yes sir, and a big still and a good one, too. Why, Mr. and Mrs. So and So live out that way—(gasps of astonishment over the grapefruit and coffee). To be perfectly explicit, these officers found a distilling plant, of a large size and good quality."

The piece rambled on for more than two columns in wonderful, down-home prose, revealing what greeted the good sheriff when he opened the trap door. Stevens had a room containing a boiler, which was part of a 300-gallon still of sophisticated design. It also featured an electric pump to remove waste. Next door, there was a storage room with twenty-one oak kegs ready for delivery.

It took the sheriff and his men three hours to dismantle the still, and there was no sign of Bill Stevens. The liquor from this and similar underground operations was shipped to Chicago, it was said, in rail tankers bearing the brand name of "Mountain Valley Water," which was bottled in Hot Springs.

The subterranean liquor and moonshine from hillbilly stills sustained Hot Springs throughout the years of Prohibition, and there was a lot left over for Chicago. Some of the powerful men who ran them were part of the mysterious Little Combination. Members included politicians, silent backers from the oilfields of Arkansas, Texas, and Oklahoma, and gamblers and restaurateurs from a wide variety of ethnic backgrounds—Native Americans, Irish, Greeks, two Italians, a Syrian, some Lebanese, and several Jews. A person's origin was not important against the main objective of sustaining the powerful machine they had created. It ran on all cylinders, with only a few misfires, from 1900 to the late 1950s. It made Hot Springs one of the wealthiest and most influential resorts in America. The year before Owney died, government records show that the gross annual profit of Las Vegas was $240 million. Hot Springs, by comparison, grossed $200 million for the same period. These, of course, were only the declared figures. What vast fortunes were skimmed off and secreted away is open to speculation.

With hindsight, it is reasonable to suppose that only an immense bootleg operation would have attracted Capone in the first place. Bubbles became his favorite resort, and others of his kind were soon to follow. One advantage of having Owney living in the town, the Little Combination discovered, was that they had a resident guarantee against any trouble. The spa continually attracted the attention of gangs from all over the country, and Owney's presence provided a vital buffer against any outside intervention.

In return, he was made "one of the family" and given the freedom to make unlimited investments. Information about newcomers or news of intended visitors was relayed directly to the Duke to see if he wanted them in town. Over the years, many were turned back at gunpoint by sheriff's officers including, ironically, Big Al himself. When Capone was released from jail for tax evasion in 1939 he planned to travel straight to Hot Springs to unwind and take the waters. Capone, however, forgot that times had changed and Owney was now running the town. Under the delightful heading, "Raspberry says Al Capone not welcome here," Police Commissioner Welden Raspberry issued a warning through the local press:

"The erstwhile Public Enemy No. I, about to be released from federal prison, it has been rumored, would immediately visit Hot Springs for a course of baths, and had already engaged a suite of rooms at one of the leading hotels.

"'Al Capone, his gang, and his so-called friends are not welcome in Hot Springs,' said Raspberry. 'If and when Al Capone steps foot into Hot Springs, he had better call off all engagements, for his first stop will be a cell at the city jail.'"

Bubbles was no longer a place to drop in and catch up with underworld news if your face did not fit. Owney wanted his operation to run smoothly without interference or attracting attention, although he was not averse to helping old friends in trouble.

By 1936, the newlyweds were settled down to their new life together and had sacrificed old habits. Agnes drastically curbed her previously hectic social life and was rarely seen in her old haunts, preferring to stay at home sewing and cooking. Owney had to give up his independent ways and adjust to small-town life.

Some years before his death, Owney took tea in the Arlington Hotel with a man and his wife who were newly arrived holiday visitors.

"Where do you live in Hot Springs, Mr. Madden?" the woman asked. "Not far from here," Owney replied. "On West Grand."

"West Grand? We passed that. Why, it's right in the heart of the city."

Owney gave her a gentle smile and said: "Madam, this has never been a city. It will always be a town."

From time to time, he missed New York with a deep yearning, but as the years of exile slipped by, it bothered him less. In his early years in Hot Springs, Owney would drive down to the Diamond Jo railroad station to pick up the morning paper from New York. Perhaps after rolling off the city presses earlier that same day, it carried with it some of the crackle of Manhattan. Owney, so the story goes, would sit on the station bench watching the train toil around the ridge, steam-blasting the scrub pine and clanging like the bell of hell to announce its business—a living embodiment of all the thrust and clamor of the city that still tugged at his heart.

Marriage was not without its ups and downs. Agnes had a fiery temper and Owney was stubborn. "Agnes was her own woman," Roger Rucker, her former bodyguard, recalled in one interview. "She had spirit. She told me that Frank Costello and the boys came for dinner one evening, here at the house. Owney asked her to make something special, something they'd like. Agnes thought maybe pasta, because they were all Italian. They all came around and sat down at the dinner table. The maid brought in the pasta in a big bowl. She and Agnes had worked all day getting things ready. Frank takes one look at it and says to everyone: "Hey. What say we all eat out tonight?" Agnes just picked up that bowl and threw it all over him."

Roger laughed, continuing on to another story: "You know, I heard that Frank used to tease him a lot over golf. They'd be out on the green with Agnes, and Frank would say, 'Hey, Owney. How come you play for $100 a hole when we're together and only fifty cents when Agnes is around?' That kind of thing..."

Agnes apparently thought her Scorpio horoscope so apt that she cut it from a magazine and kept it. The horoscope read: "Your husband should realize that you face great opportunities and great dangers. He must be careful not to let the force of your impulsive nature lead you into indiscretion and excess. Your husband's problem is simplified by the fact that you are a one-man woman."

The latter was certainly true. Agnes became immensely protective of Owney, turning away any casual callers and newsmen, and ensuring that his business in Hot Springs remained private and unseen. Owney bought percentages in illegal gambling, hotels, and entertainment—including the prestigious Southern and Belvedere Clubs—and increased his stock whenever opportunities arose.

Being affiliated with the National Crime Syndicate meant, by the terms of its constitution, that he was working for himself but could draw upon the protection and cooperation of one of the strongest, wealthiest organizations in all of America.

"Owney was the single most powerful man in Hot Springs," one of his old associates said. "He always remained in the background because he didn't need to be important. But, he was important and everyone who mattered knew it."

His attorney, Q. Byrum Hurst, echoed the sentiment: "Owney never carried protection," he said. "He didn't need protection. If anything, the sheriff, the chief of police, and all the authorities maybe thought they needed protecting from him."

From reading the newspapers, Owney must have felt some relief at having left the New York scene. Dewey, "that arrogant young man with the ridiculous mustache," as someone described him, was continuing to establish his name as a crusader against organized crime. His prime target, in a wide-ranging investigation into the prostitution rackets, was Lucky Luciano, or Charlie Lucky, as he was called. The police rounded up dozens of prostitutes and took them to rented offices and hotel rooms where they were quizzed in secret about their connections. Questioners from the D.A.'s office repeatedly injected Charlie Lucky's name into the conversations to try to find any kind of link with him. Girls and madams who showed signs of recognizing the nickname then were held on a $10,000 bail as material witnesses.

The secrecy of the operation was essential. Dewey did not want Charlie Lucky to get advance warning that he was the main figure in the inquiries. With luck, it would appear no more than a concerted drive to round up hookers. Each day more attorneys were assigned to the case to pressure the girls. "Those being questioned soon realized that if they could talk about Charlie Lucky, somehow ring him in, all would go well with them," according to Luciano's biographers, Martin Gosch and Richard Hammer. "Not only would charges against them be dropped, not only would they be granted immunity from prosecution if they testified at a trial, but once Luciano was safely in jail they might find living a lot easier. And the same message made its way into the prisons around the state where there might be other potential witnesses. The choice between jail for silence and freedom for testimony stirred forgotten memories."

While Dewey's forces were closing in, Owney had to travel to the West Coast on some racetrack business. It was his first attempt to venture from Hot Springs since his exile and he planned to slip out quietly, hoping not to attract any attention. Agnes went with him, and they intended to make the trip a belated honeymoon and visit old friends in Hollywood. There was a happy holiday atmosphere as they set off, and they vowed to make up for all the time they had been forced to spend apart previously. By any standards, it became a honeymoon to remember. The loving couple had hardly arrived in Los Angeles when word reached the police that Owney was in town. That evening there was a loud rapping on the door of Owney and Agnes's holiday apartment. The Duke opened it to find the unsmiling face of Detective Captain Jack Chriss of the LAPD and two of his men.

In the words of the *Los Angeles Herald-Express*: "Madden's honeymoon was interrupted by the official hint that the ex-beer runner and racketeer was not considered a desirable resident of California, even if he was there for a romantic occasion." The *Herald-Express* related the conversation:

"'I've got a message from someone who'd like to see you, Owney,' said Chriss, taking off his hat.

"'Who's that, boys?' asked the Duke, who already had a good idea of who it was.

"'I believe you recall him—Buron Fitts, the D.A. He wants you in his office at 9:30 tomorrow morning. And if I were you,' added Chriss, dropping the geniality, 'I wouldn't be late. Would you like to do that?'

"Owney shook his head. 'No, I wouldn't. I'm afraid it's too inconvenient. If he's so keen to talk to me, get him on the telephone—right now.'

"Chriss thought for a moment. He did not relish calling the D.A. at home but it was preferable to Madden failing to turn up the next day. Owney sat relaxed on the sofa and lit a cigarette, waiting for his reply.

"Chriss shrugged. 'Why not,' he said, picking up the phone. He dialed a number, spoke for a few moments close to the mouthpiece, and held the receiver to Owney.

"'I believe you want to see me tomorrow,' the Duke said. 'Is it a social call or business?'

"It was sufficient to trigger Fitts's annoyance. 'You were rousted out of this city last time you were here, Madden, and you are about to be rousted out again.'

"Owney explained that he was on his honeymoon and would like to see more of the races at Santa Anita. Fitts barely concealed his anger and ordered Owney to be in his office the following morning.

"'That's not possible,' said the Duke. 'The last thing I want is to run a gauntlet of newspaper photographers and reporters hanging around your office. It's not on.'

"Fitts delivered an ultimatum—either Owney reported to his office, on time, or he left town immediately.

"The Duke hung up. 'Agnes,' he said. 'Pack the cases.'"

Chriss and his detectives waited until they were ready and escorted their car to the city limits. Owney had just received the first lesson in "the deal"—his unusual parole arrangement—and now knew that law enforcement officials around the country were allied in an effort to enforce it and make sure he stayed in Hot Springs.

Agnes was learning quickly what it was like to be married to someone living under such a strange life sentence. She found it hard to accept that the quiet, romantic man who bought her flowers was treated like a dangerous criminal. Agnes's attitude toward the outside world began to harden. How could she trust the authorities, the newspapers, and the openly curious when they threatened to persecute the man she loved? Just three months into her marriage, fun-loving Agnes became a very private woman.

Soon after their return to the comparative sanity of Hot Springs, Lucky Luciano experienced grave problems in New York. Dewey had assembled a mass—more accurately a mess—of evidence against him, much of it hearsay and fabrication. The prosecutor decided to gamble on his chances in the courts and ordered Luciano to be pulled in. Two detectives were dispatched to his apartment in the opulent Waldorf Towers to arrest him. Lucky paid the concierge a regular retainer of two hundred dollars a week to tip him off whenever anyone asked for him downstairs. As an added precaution, he registered his name in the list of residents as "Mr. Ross." When the worried doorman buzzed to tell him that two detectives were on their way up, Lucky decided to cut and run. With nothing more than the clothes he was wearing and $4,000 in his pocket, he inched open his door and, checking that the corridor was clear, ran for the freight elevator. The police missed him by minutes. By the time they appeared, breathless, in the lobby, Charlie was gunning his big car out of New York.

On the spur of the moment, he decided to drive to Philadelphia where he borrowed money from crime boss Nig Rosen, who was also friends with Owney. Nig provided a Cadillac while Charlie hurriedly bought himself a new suit of clothes and a toothbrush. Before saying goodbye, he telephoned friends in New York who told him that a big hunt was now under way. His only consolation was that, from the places detectives were looking, Dewey had little idea where he was. Luciano, unused to being tracked like a fugitive, needed time to collect his thoughts and make his plans in safety. There was only one place where sanctuary was guaranteed. He drove Rosen's car to Cleveland, parked it out of sight, and then jumped on the first available train to Hot Springs.

Charlie found more than he had ever hoped for when he arrived. Owney had not only established himself with influence, but appeared to have total control over the city police and judiciary. On April 1,

Luciano opened the New York papers in his hotel room and read that Dewey's grand jury on vice and prostitution had indicted him on no less than ninety charges. Dewey explained why he needed to parade a succession of pimps and prostitutes as witnesses to nail the man he wanted: "Today, crime is syndicated and organized. A new type of criminal exists who leaves to his hirelings and front men the actual offenses and rarely commits an overt act himself. The only way in which the major criminal can be punished is by related but separate crimes on his behalf."

Shortly after his arrival in Hot Springs, Charlie needed some air and took a stroll along Bath House Row, which was bustling with some well-dressed visitors. He was in the company of the spa's chief of detectives, Dutch Akers. As they walked the tree-lined promenade in the spring sunshine, a familiar face ambled toward them. It was a sure sign to Lucky that this was not to be his day.

"Hi, Charlie, fancy seeing you here." It was John Brennan, a detective from the Bronx.

Brennan had arrived in Arkansas the previous day to locate a murder suspect and knew that Manhattan was being combed for the man Dewey described as "Public Enemy Number One in New York." The detective, who had been friendly with Lucky for years, advised him to give himself up and travel back East with him by train. Lucky was highly suspicious, not of Brennan, but of Dewey's attempts to prosecute him on what he regarded as flimsy evidence.

"Why don't you keep out of it, Jack? Go back as though you haven't seen me," Charlie suggested.

Brennan explained that, if word got out that he had seen Luciano, he would lose his job. To cover himself, he would have to tell the authorities that they had met.

A few days later, Hot Springs police chief Joe Wakelin received a telegram from New York asking him to arrest Luciano and arrange his immediate transportation back to New York under guard. Since Luciano now was being protected by Owney Madden, it was not a request that

Wakelin was anxious to fill. When Wakelin called Owney and told him the news, the Duke drove to Charlie's hotel to explain the situation.

"Owney said not to worry about a thing," Luciano wrote in his autobiography. "It was all set. I'd go down to the courthouse and be released that afternoon. And, as far as extradition was concerned, I could fight it in Arkansas and win. I mean, with our connections in that state, I figured there was no reason at all to worry."

Owney's clubs, the Belvedere and the Southern, put up a $5,000 bail when Lucky appeared before Sam Garratt, the local justice. He was released immediately.

When the news was wired back to New York, Dewey expressed his astonishment. "I can't understand how any judge could release this man on such bail," he said. "Luciano is regarded as the most important racketeer in New York, if not the country. The case involves one of the largest rackets and one of the most loathsome types of crime."

The stocky, confident young prosecutor commanded the respect of the authorities in New York but had little grasp of the subtleties of the Hot Springs political machine. The cocky little spa city had never jumped to anyone's tune, least of all to that of an upstart D.A. from New York. Dewey began to apply tremendous pressure on McLaughlin and Chief Wakelin, who declined even to reply to his communications. He then took his case higher. He called Arkansas Governor Marion Futrell and the State Attorney General, Carl Bailey. However, they knew that the internal affairs of Hot Springs had never been entirely within their jurisdiction.

Dewey, baffled by the apparent lack of action, warned the governor that he would ensure that he was portrayed by newspapers across the nation as a man who harbored known criminals. Futrell panicked at the prospect and personally ordered Chief Wakelin to arrest Luciano at his hotel and hold him in custody until further orders. Reluctantly, law officers asked Charlie if he would mind spending a short time in jail, promising him that he could have visitors and the use of the telephones. Charlie agreed and took a girlfriend along to keep him company. Owney advised him to sit tight while he pulled a few strings, but even Madden's strong influence failed to move the governor from the daunting prospect of bad publicity.

One of New York's top criminal lawyers, Moses Polakoff, flew down to Hot Springs to organize Lucky's case. He suggested that his client should draft a reply to Dewey's charges and call a press conference to put his own views across. Local reporters were ushered into the cell while Luciano protested his innocence. With Polakoff at his side, attempts to extradite him could be further delayed. The lawyer and Dewey exchanged telegrams for days, with neither side prepared to lose an inch of ground. According to Gosch and Hammer, it was an impasse: "There was no hurry to hold extradition proceedings and the mood of Hot Springs was such that, even if they were held there, the New York request might be denied."

Bailey, threatened with a similar fate to that of Futrell, ordered Hot Springs law enforcement officers—a dubious term under the circumstances—to transfer their prisoner to Little Rock, the state capital. The police chief and chief of detectives appeared to be stricken with a sudden case of terminal deafness when Bailey insisted that a decision could no longer be delayed. Under Owney's instructions, the Hot Springs police refused to hand the prisoner over. A few hours later, five carloads of armed Arkansas state police swept into town and surrounded the jailhouse. Inside, their senior officer found Dutch Akers and his men guarding Charlie's cell with a small arsenal of weapons. The message from Little Rock was short and simple—Akers either handed over the prisoner or they would blow the jail apart and drag him out. There is no record of Akers's call to Owney but, as the Duke had so far directed operations, it is fair to assume that he issued the final command. Hot Springs police stood aside while Lucky, dressed in a new suit, was handcuffed and led away.

Despite a personal offer of $50,000 from Owney if he turned Luciano loose, Bailey decided not to risk his reputation. Fearing reprisals, he ordered all entrances to the Little Rock courthouse to be guarded by state troopers armed with machine guns while the extradition hearing took place. To absolve himself in the eyes of New York, Bailey told the judge: "Every time a major criminal of this country wants asylum, he heads for Hot Springs. We must show that Arkansas cannot be made an asylum for them."

Luciano, listening to the speech in handcuffs, later recalled in his autobiography: "When I heard that crap coming out of Bailey's mouth, I couldn't believe my ears. The truth of the matter is, Bailey was always working with us in Arkansas and we never had a problem with him before. Everyone who was there thought he should have been able to handle the pressure from New York a lot better than that."

The case opened on May 11 in New York and ended with Charlie Lucky being sentenced to thirty-to-fifty years in prison, a punishment which stunned the underworld. In the course of cross-questioning and lengthy arguments over points of law, Lucky was asked how he could explain carrying two pistols, a scatter gun, and forty-five rounds of ammunition in his automobile without permits.

"To shoot birds with," he replied.

"What kind of birds, Mr. Luciano?" Dewey asked.

"Peasants," said Charlie.

Hot Springs Police Chief Joe Wakelin and Dutch Akers, who enforced Hot Springs's version of law and order, were tied closely to the Little Combination but also ran their own lucrative sidelines.

Wakelin sold and exchanged firearms with visiting gangsters and had a unique business arrangement with Mayor McLaughlin. Each month, all the whorehouses in town would empty, and the girls, dressed in a variety of exotic hats and gowns, made their way in a procession up Central Avenue to the courthouse. To stay in business, each in turn would step up and plead guilty to prostitution and receive a nominal fine to be distributed between the mayor and police chief and a small percentage for court officials.

Anybody who was anybody paid somebody in Hot Springs. Police officers collected commissions from the madams, and those higher up the ladder in the gambling business sent cash in envelopes by special messenger to nameless recipients. The system maintained itself on an endless flow of protection money. Bubbles was a mutual preservation society centered on the sole aim of continually fueling the political machine. As long as it ran smoothly, business could continue uninterrupted. It was rare that anyone complained or felt cheated, and McLaughlin, in turn, had his own way of handling elections to ensure that he had no opposition. Owney, of course, had seen it all before on a far grander scale and was an old hand at using politicians to his own advantage. In terms of statewide power, he towered above McLaughlin, though few actually realized it. The influence of Frank Costello and Meyer Lansky in the south ensured Owney's standing in Arkansas, and his own reputation made him worthy of the respect he was afforded.

If it is possible to graduate such things on a scale of importance—and in Arkansas it was—then the license plate fixed on Owney's black Cadillac convertible may offer a clue to his status.

During my visit to Hot Springs, Roger Rucker handed me the blue and white tin rectangle, which Agnes had kept for old times' sake, and explained: "Mr. Madden's number was 9-506. He wanted 506 because it was the number of his house. But it's the nine that's important. He was awarded that specially. After the governor and his family and some senior officials, Mr. Madden was Number Nine in Arkansas." He spun it around in his fingers. "Take it from me, that's pretty important."

By April of 1936, Owney was firmly established as a controlling figure in the spa's power structure. Lucky Luciano was settling down to the prospect of a long residency in Dannemora, a bleak island prison fortress near the Canadian border, known to the underworld as "Siberia." His conviction was a feather in Thomas Dewey's cap, but J. Edgar Hoover—the man who should have been at the center of the arrest—had played no part in the drama. Many senators were unhappy with the enormous amounts of money demanded to run his organization. And, despite the image he had carefully built around his government agents—the so-called

G-men—their results were disappointing. The final slap to Hoover's bull-dog jowls came from one of his chief critics, Tennessee Senator Kenneth McKellar. Hoover was humiliated by McKellar at a Senate committee hearing when the senator turned the meeting around and put both Hoover's own competence and the FBI's record on trial. The jibe, which caught some headlines, was that Hoover had never, ever personally made an arrest. Above all else, this stung the pride of the boss of the G-men, and he resolved to put the record straight.

Alvin "Creepy" Karpis, nicknamed for his pale, horror-movie looks, had waged a running feud with Hoover for more than a year. When the FBI director announced, for instance, that train robbery was officially a crime of the past, Karpis held up a train in Garrettsville, Ohio. Hoover, in short, could not think of a better target, particularly since Karpis was living under Owney's protection in Hot Springs. He had moved into a simple, white frame house in leafy, respectable Palm Street, with his lover, Grace Goldstein. Grace ran the Hatterie Hotel, regarded as the most celebrated brothel between New Orleans and Chicago, on Central Avenue next to the notorious White Front Cigar Store. Owney probably knew that Karpis was using Bubbles as a base to rob banks all over America by chartering flights out of Hot Springs but did not ask too many questions.

Someone must have tipped off Creepy because he managed to es-cape from Grace Goldstein's house and take off across the fields before the G-Men's arrival. He was finally cornered in New Orleans and per-sonally "arrested" by Hoover in a blaze of publicity. The FBI and Hoover were finally vindicated. At least, that was how the story remained until Karpis wrote his autobiography and gave his own version. Hoover, he claimed, hid safely around a comer until Alvin was held at gunpoint. When the coast was clear, Hoover was said to have stepped out and or-dered: "Put the handcuffs on him." There followed a moment of silence and embarrassment. The agents had to admit that they had forgotten to bring any along with them.

That summer, for the highlight of Arkansas's centennial, President Roosevelt visited Hot Springs. A huge crowd waited to meet the president's special train as it drew into the Missouri Pacific Depot. Outside the Arlington Hotel, the U.S. Marine Corps Band played "Stars and Stripes Forever" while 250 children presented a pageant entitled "Arkansas Through The Years." Before leaving for lunch, Roosevelt smiled and waved to two children dressed as Miss Liberty and Uncle Sam. Notable among those absent from the celebrations were the town's two most influential citizens, Mr. and Mrs. Owney Madden.

Karpis made coast-to-coast headlines, but the real business of national crime was being discussed at a secret conference hosted by Owney and attended by Frank Costello, Meyer Lansky, Dandy Phil Kastel, who ran the New Orleans operation, and a delegation from Louisiana. They met at the Arlington Hotel, of which Owney was said to have been a secret shareholder, to plan the expansion of gambling in the south. During a recess, some of the boys, who had a raw, thigh-slapping sense of humor, found an old woman on the street outside—Bubbles's answer to a "bag lady"—and paid her to deliver a message. Owney, who had a reputation for being shy and nervous, was deep in conversation when she burst in with a toothless grin, shouting: "Where's my sweetheart, Owney Madden?"

The group decided to step up the number of slot machines in New Orleans and "persuade" a proliferation of small independent operations to fall in line with their syndicate. When it came to the question of running Hot Springs, Costello and Lansky met Owney privately for a heart-to-heart talk.

Owney already had made tremendous inroads into controlling the town within a very short time, but Lansky felt that the spa still needed something to attract more of the right type of gamblers. There was room for more slot machines, too, Costello noted. It was a situation in which the new National Crime Syndicate was ideally suited to help. Owney felt that the resort should grow but that people who lived there should feel that they were benefitting, too. In the long term, which was the way he liked to plan, it would be bad for business if only the Little Combination—those seen to have the power—prospered. Lansky and Costello could see the logic of this. They were always in favor of sidestepping trouble and working as much as possible within the scope of the law. They, too, liked big profits but not at the expense of endangering the whole enterprise. Another aspect of the system was that taxes—subsidized by gambling profits—would be kept at a reasonable level so that residents would be inclined to put their "X" in the right box at election time.

One of the first requisites, they all agreed, was a huge injection of cash to provide a pay-off fund for politicians from the state capital down to the local level. This would ensure that gambling flourished uninterrupted. The figures involved have never been revealed but sources indicate that these "overheads" far exceeded those Owney was used to paying, even in the heyday of Prohibition. Someone in Hot Springs told me that the payoffs ran as much as $20,000 a day during the peak season. Given the scale of Owney's enterprises, it does not seem like a wildly unreasonable amount. Owney's generosity, and from time to time, that of Frank Costello, gave the town many public amenities, few of which have ever been recognized.

One of the ironies of the running conflict between the church and gambling interests was that if money was needed for a particular project, the church members had no compunction about asking Hot Springs's madams and casino owners for a generous hand-out. Today, these allegations would be greeted with horror, but in the past there was often little distinction between the politics of some churches and the politics of man. Maxine Jones, who once ran the most opulent whorehouse in Hot Springs, recalled many an occasion when she handed over cash in "the name of the Lord."

"The church people didn't fail to call on me for donations. I never turned them down. They'd drive right up to my place of business and come in and collect the money. Once, a deputy in the sheriff's department, who was also a part-time preacher, told me: 'Maxine, we need a cross for the top of our church and we don't have enough money.'

"I said, 'Well, how much money do you need?'

"'About $200 more would put the cross up there that I have picked out,' he answered.

"When I gave him the money, he says: 'You just don't know how much I appreciate this. When I get up to preach, I'll tell the congregation that you donated the money to the church.'

"I don't know if he did or not, since I didn't hear his sermon, but their knowing wasn't really important to me."

The Hot Springs Conference constructed a well-oiled machine which ran until Owney's death. Maxine explained how things worked in the 1950s. "There was a lot of money changing hands and a lot of people getting their share of it. Some of the money went to the governor, via a little black bag. Hubert Hankins was the one responsible for delivering it in a special plane that flew to Little Rock. The rest of the money was put on a train and shipped back east to underworld figures there. There was a special carrier for that money, too."

Costello and Lansky provided the capital to extend Owney's flagship, the Southern Club, Hot Springs's grandest gambling house, located opposite the Arlington Hotel. The Southern had a colorful history. It was built just after the 1893 Chicago World's Fair by a consortium from the east that regarded it as their "southern club." In the 1890s, Frank James, brother of outlaw Jesse James, retired to Hot Springs and opened a concession in Happy Hollow amusement park. He loved to sit outside the Southern Club with his friends and tell stories about the old days, just as Owney sat at his table in the Southern Grillroom throughout the 1930s, 1940s, and 1950s recalling times past. When the Duke arrived in Bubbles, the club was owned by a group headed by Sam Watts, a wildcat oilman, and his partner, Bill Jacobs, a charismatic business genius who bore a strong resemblance to actor Sidney Greenstreet. Watts and Jacobs also owned the Club Belvedere.

By 1939, money from the National Crime Syndicate had financed a quarter of a million dollars worth of improvements at the Southern. Jacobs bought out Watts's stock, and both men died soon afterward of natural causes. The shareholders, partners, and silent partners of such enterprises formed layer upon layer in a complex system of ownership. It was complicated because that was the way they intended it. Often, those seen to have control exercised little power, and Owney's influence behind the clicking dice and tumbling roulette balls was virtually untraceable. The FBI tried many times to uncover the full extent of his business interests but always failed in its efforts.

Hot Springs historian Mark Palmer is a no-nonsense kind of guy, descended from the Cherokee tribe, outlaws, and staunch Baptists. He was raised on tales of Hot Springs's lawlessness. One half of his family opened up the gambling, while the other half fought to close it down. They tried to keep liquor and gambling out of Hot Springs because they wanted to make people more productive. He told this to me on my visit to Hot Springs in the 1980s as he sat in the driver's seat of his car outside what was left of the Southern Club.

"It all backfired because the American people are extreme individualists," Palmer explained. "That's why the thirteen colonies rebelled against England, you know, King George III in 1776. George Washington had trouble with the hillbillies, too, in the Whisky Rebellion. No establishment, no nobility can do anything with the American people the minute they find out that someone is trying to protect them from themselves. Laws can be passed against whisky, beer, gambling, dope, even tobacco. They can levy heavy taxes to discourage Americans from doing anything that might be bad for their health. And you know what? They will do it ever the more, just for spite. That's the nature of Americans—personal rebellion. People will cheat at just about everything. They vote "dry" and drink "wet." Vote against gambling, then sneak out and gamble.

"Anyway," he flipped his cigarette butt through the open window, "the Mafia knows this. That's their great foundation of power in

America. Al Capone knew it. Frank Costello knew it. And Owney Madden knew it, too."

Hot Springs began to make the news after Owney's arrival as a succession of famous friends dropped in to see him. George Raft sent him a polished, wooden Chris-Craft speedboat on a trailer for his birthday and later came to see him. Owney took him to watch the Hot Springs Bathers, the local baseball team to which he had made numerous gifts of money for equipment. At the railroad station, photographers jostled to try and get pictures of Madden and Raft.

"The movie celebrity was greeted by Owen Madden, a friend of many years, as he stepped off a Missouri Pacific train from Chicago," the *Hot Springs New Era* reported. "His first question was, 'How's the boat?' He was referring to a high-powered craft which he sent Madden several months ago. It was only a short time until Raft and Madden and two of the film celebrity's friends who accompanied him here were on their way to Lake Hamilton for a spin in the craft."

George, enjoying all the attention, gave a brief interview as Owney stood in the background. The *New Era* reported:

"Movie topics were shunted aside as he said, 'Let's talk about Hot Springs. If what my friend, Madden, tells me about Hot Springs is true, this is the place I should come to take off a few pounds. I'd say he was one of your best boosters.'

"The movie star came here to fulfill a promise to Madden to visit Hot Springs and take a course of the world-famous mineral baths. 'There's a lot of hard work ahead for me,' Raft said, 'and now that I have the opportunity to enjoy a little vacation, I'm going to make the best of it.'"

Soon afterward, another movie star, Wallace Beery, arrived in town. He had piloted his own aircraft from Los Angeles. One newspaper wrote:

"The noted film character, who looks so natural off screen that you expect him to start rubbing his hand over his face at any time, attracted wide attention as he strolled up Central Avenue. A small crowd was congregated about him almost constantly as he sat in the lobby of the Arlington Hotel later in the day."

Owney may have been in exile, but he was certainly back in business. Word spread and friends who had patronized the Cotton Club called in to pay their respects at equally glittering establishments in Hot Springs. Red Buttons and Joe DiMaggio were frequent guests, and Duke Ellington and his orchestra flew in to play at the National Baptist, an African-American hotel. Even years later, it was still remembered as a night when segregation was swept away and blacks and whites danced side by side. In his own club, the Duke recreated a Broadway atmosphere with big-name singers and bands, good food, and excellent service. Many remarked that the impressive staircase of the Southern Club, which also had an escalator to speed gamblers upstairs, bore a strong resemblance to that of the Cotton Club.

Every bar in Hot Springs was packed to the doors on a Saturday night. Every hotel, whorehouse, and gambling joint would be full. In the afternoons at Oaklawn, race-goers would congregate around Owney wherever he walked.

"They just wanted to look at him, touch him, hold his hand," his attorney, Q. Byrum Hurst, wistfully recalled. "There would be thirty, maybe thirty-five people trying to get into my little box to be near him. Those FBI men, who were supposed to be following him, had to control the crowds."

Apart from the glitterati, the majority of Hot Springs's visitors were middle-aged. They came for the invigorating baths and the opportunity to have a go at the gaming tables. It was a trouble-free trade and kept any problems with drugs and prostitution at a minimum to avoid adverse publicity. In fact, the U.S. Senate's investigation of organized crime—the Kefauver Hearings—completely overlooked Hot Springs in 1950. It was odd that Senator Estes Kefauver forgot about Hot Springs. The love of his life was stolen by a rival from Hot Springs, Herbert Coates, who later married her. Coates, a tough character, had shot dead the chief of police on

Central Avenue in 1925 after a difference of opinion and was acquitted by a jury after only an hour's deliberation. To anyone who visited the spa, however, Hot Springs always appeared to be a tranquil and charming place.

Owney's friends knew they could still seek refuge there, and the system ran smoothly for all concerned. Only the FBI had any real suspicion of what really went on behind the town's effervescent facade. Hoover turned his attention to Madden and requested regular reports on his movements from FBI men based at nearby Little Rock. Agents embarked on an undercover operation, building up a network of local informants who monitored all Owney's activities from behind lace curtains. Their identities are still protected by the bureau but, for what little information they fed back, Owney could have briefed them himself:

"Madden has been in Hot Springs continuously for the past several months, residing with his wife. (The informant) has no knowledge of Madden's sources of revenue, insomuch as Madden spends most of his time either hanging around the White Front Cigar Store at 310 Central Avenue or playing golf at courses in the vicinity of Hot Springs.

"Madden appears partial to Buick automobiles, buying a new car every few months. The personal car of Mrs. Madden is a Packard convertible coupe. It appears to be a 1938 model, four-passenger, in black, with a tan canvas top."

Hoover, aware of Owney's cunning, wrote to Little Rock asking exactly how much importance they were giving to the case. The reply avoided the issue and pointed out that "Madden bears the reputation of living entirely within the law in the city of Hot Springs and there has been no allegation of any kind, or rumor, that he is presently engaged in the rackets in any manner. (Informant) stated that Madden is the first individual to contribute to the various charities and usually makes substantial contributions to same."

Owney liked to foster the impression that he had retired, and many casual visitors went away convinced that he had after meeting him. When they went so far as to confirm their belief in print, so much the better. Joe E. Lewis, a nightclub comedian whose throat was slashed by the Capone mob in the 1920s, visited Owney, who drove him back to the railroad depot at the end of his stay. An article on Lewis later noted:

"Joe looked out of the coach and waved, dejectedly. The forlorn little man, who once had had everything except peace, now had nothing but peace. He remained in the shadows and leaned against the ancient depot, out of habit. No one would ever get behind him again, if he could help it. But it was only an illusion of his pride. No one wanted to get behind him. Owney the Killer was dead. The only thing he could kill was time."

Owney was so delighted with such pieces that he made a hobby of collecting them to smile over. Many of his former associates lacked the self-discipline to maintain such a low profile. They would have bridled with indignation at any public suggestion that they were a spent force. Accordingly, many of them died before their time. In contrast, Owney felt no necessity at all to prove how big he was.

Lewis also mentioned that the Duke felt nostalgia for New York which, from time to time, was true. In Hot Springs, he dictated the action on his own terms, but there were occasions when he missed the glitter of the big fight nights. In May of 1940, he risked for a second time breaking the terms of his "parole" deal. He slipped away from Hot Springs to watch Buddy Baer fight Nathan Mann at Madison Square Garden. A reunion with the boys was too tempting to miss. Trainer Bill Duffy obtained tickets for Owney, Marty Krompier, a former lieutenant of Dutch Schultz, Jerry Sullivan, on parole for life after attempting to duck Sing Sing, and Tom O'Neil, described as "a forty-year-old hoodlum of no outstanding attainments whose record began in 1916 with a charge of homicide."

Mingling with the large crowd on the way out of the fight, Owney was arrested by waiting detectives. To prove that there was no prejudice, all of his friends were arrested, too. They were handcuffed and taken to West 47th Street police station, where the Duke was asked to identify himself.

"I'm just a mineral water salesman from the Mid-West," he protested to a chorus of wide smirks.

There was no doubt who he was, but the matter was clearly too important to be dealt with locally. "They were detained for a while, but not booked," The New York Times reported. "Then they were whisked away in an automobile to an undisclosed place for questioning."

Owney was interrogated long and hard by anonymous officials, who seemed determined to teach him that "the deal"—his parole—could never he broken. The Times, sensing that something important was happening, asked chief of detectives Conrad Rothengast why the men had been arrested and on what charges. No one appeared capable of giving a satisfactory answer. Rothengast made a vague excuse that Madden, Duffy, O'Neil, and Sullivan had been picked up "in connection with a case I am investigating."

"What about the other guy, Krompier, then?" reporters asked.

"Oh, I have a policy of taking him into custody any time I see him around," said the captain.

He walked away, refusing to say anything more about the incident, leaving puzzled newsmen wondering if they had a story or not. Legally, Owney had done nothing to break the law, but the secret terms of his exile made it necessary for action of some kind to be taken. He had tested the authorities and would have to be shown that it could not happen again. He spent a night in the cells, and next morning, despite having pockets stuffed with money, was charged with vagrancy. All five appeared before Magistrate Thomas A. Aurello in West Side Court at 10 a.m. It was obvious that the evidence was flimsy, and Magistrate Aurello ruled that there were no grounds for keeping them in custody on a charge that they were "vagrants with no visible means of support."

As he dismissed them from the stand, Aurello turned to Owney and wagged his finger: "You better keep moving. New York isn't the New York it was any more."

In order to save face, the police announced that they had "established a pattern of association which might prove useful in the future."

With that, they escorted Owney to the station and remained there until his train going west had pulled safely out of sight.

Back home, the FBI inquiries were plodding on. "Madden," Little Rock informed Washington, "does not have any occupation in Hot Springs or vicinity. He is quite a fisherman and has several boats, including some speed boats. (Informant 'A') states that Madden does not drink and does not gamble, and is apparently living a legitimate life, and all he asks is to be left alone. (Informant 'B') states that, in his opinion, Madden has plenty of money and interests, but these interests are not in his own name."

The second informant's loose speculation was enough to convince Hoover that Operation Madden should be stepped up.

16.

The Quiet American

It was a troublesome time for the Duke. In a small place like Hot Springs, it was easy for him to know that the FBI was showing a close interest in his affairs. He began to adopt a daily routine of such an intensely boring nature that even the most determined agent would find it difficult to maintain any interest. In Florida, the authorities were making inquiries into racetrack ownership and, sooner or later, the strands of the web would lead to him. Tropical Park, near Coral Gables, for instance, had been bought by the Atlas Finance Company of Montreal and remodeled to the tune of $800,000. Atlas was owned by Canadians who had operated the northern end of the old bootleg chain centered on the isle of St. Pierre. They were former partners of Owney, Frank Costello, and Big Bill Dwyer.

Dwyer, who had been released from prison in the early 1930s, was appointed managing director of the track. By 1936, in the wake of the formation of the National Crime Syndicate, ownership of Tropical Park changed to an odd assortment of solid citizens. Among the notables were a certain Agnes and James Demby of Hot Springs, Herman Stark, who once fronted the Cotton Club, Bill O'Brien, the brother-in-law of Owney's elder brother, Marty, and Jane Fox, Frenchy DeMange's wife. The name Madden did not appear anywhere on the list of directors, but any good investigator could have figured out that he was involved.

In these early years of the 1940s, America was at war, sharpening Owney's awareness of his British citizenship. In 1941, FBI agents, acting on Hoover's orders, went to Hot Springs City Hall and asked if Owney was legally registered as an alien. News of the inquiry did not bother him unduly. He had carried his British passport from boyhood through far worse troubles. Applying for naturalization would, in itself, have attracted so much attention that his request would almost certainly have been opposed and possibly even result in deportation.

Back in New York, Thomas Dewey was now running for governor, and Lucky Luciano was helping the war effort from his prison cell. He was running a network of longshoremen to report on foreign agents to U.S. Naval Intelligence. Talk everywhere was about the war effort. Owney, who was not in a position to do anything for either Britain or America, followed events closely through the newspapers and radio reports. Agnes's uncle, Wilfred Demby, was the lawyer representing three racetracks in which they had interests. Whenever they met, he urged Owney to take out U.S. citizenship, but the Duke would only smile and say, "I'll get around to it sometime." Wilfred Demby pushed and persisted until Owney began to think seriously about his position.

To obtain naturalization in the right way—which meant attracting as little publicity as possible—would be an expensive and delicate process. Negotiations were as complex as those involved in his exile to Hot Springs, but, at least, would be confined mainly to Arkansas. Owney is said to have paid a quarter of a million dollars to secure U.S. citizenship in a deal which included payoffs to at least one senator and members of the judiciary. The hearing took place on March 16, 1942, before an elderly federal judge in circumstances which the *Police Gazette* described as "cloudy." Judge John E. Miller heard Owney's attorney, Hurst, outline his client's donations to charity and gifts to the community. Hot Springs had benefitted immensely from his presence, he said. It was an undeniable statement of fact, as anyone in the spa city would testify. Agnes followed with an equally eloquent testimony: "We are fighting a world war to do away with intolerance and persecution," she pleaded. "I believe Mr. Madden is entitled to some consideration." The judge weighed up all the evidence and signed the papers.

"Some people kind of resented that," Hurst recalled later. "But Owney had such a genuine reputation for goodness, kindness, and citizenship that there was nothing they could do."

The first indication of a backlash came on an anonymous postcard that was pushed through Owney's front door. The message, scrawled in thick pencil, read: "Friend Owen—The preachers had a meeting and they are going to prove you lied when you got your papers before Judge Miller. They know you are a partner in the Southern gaming house. One of our partners is giving them dope on you. They want to get rid of you. I am telling you as a friend."

Owney was not particularly worried because he knew he had a watertight case. Ten years later and with the encouragement of the FBI, certain officials in the Naturalization Department were still trying to reverse the decision.

"The judge said later that he had acted 'on the recommendation of the Naturalization Bureau,'" the *Police Gazette* reported. "'I knew nothing of Madden's past,' the judge declared. Owney himself insisted that he had told the Naturalization Bureau 'everything.'

"'I omitted nothing,' he said.

"Judge Miller said he did not 'intend to get excited about the case at all.' Neither did anyone else in authority. The Miller decision stood."

Many of Owney's "acts of kindness" could not be reported at the hearing, but everyone in Hot Springs knew about them. "In the early 1940s," one resident told me, "a group of kids from Hot Springs High School went to New York for a band competition. These kids didn't have much money, but one of them knew that Owen Madden was kind of important back east. He walked into a high-class night club—maybe it was the Cotton Club, I can't remember—and he told the host that he had a group of friends outside on the recommendation of Mr. Madden.

Oh, boy! All the kids were shown in and given dinner and the best of service—no charge. Yes, sir!"

It was likely that the band member was carrying a note from Owney, written on a sheet from his personalized memo pad. He often handed this same note out to fond acquaintances. It usually read: "To whom it may concern: (name) is a good friend. Sincerely, Owen Madden." The message also was followed by a telephone number. Occasionally, he might write the message inside the flap of one of his books of matches, which bore his name in silver against a dark green background—his personal colors.

Someone else recalled another story which gives a measure of the man:

"There was this local businessman who used to beat his wife," he said. "Owen knew the couple and one night, the guy beat her so bad that she was put in St. Joseph's Hospital. Owen heard about it—he heard about most things—and went to see her there and then. The light was out and the blinds were drawn when he entered the room. Mr. Madden asked her how she was and she told him she was fine. He turned on the overhead light to look at her bruises.

"'This won't happen again,' he told her, and left.

"Next day, when her husband was out on a job site, a car drew up. Two hard-looking men got out and went over to the building where the man was up a ladder. 'Hey, buddy. Come down—we gotta talk,' they shouted.

"Well, he did, because they didn't look like any ordinary guys. Anyway, they told him:

"'We got a message for you, pal. Lay one more finger on your wife and you're gonna disappear. Never be seen no more. Got it?'

"He got it okay. He left town and stayed away for several years. When they got a divorce, he even signed everything over to his wife."

There are countless similar tales, mostly about Owney's generosity with money. At the Southern Grill, on the first floor of the Southern Club, Owney had his own reserved table. If anyone sat there in his absence, particularly if they looked poor or were a young married couple, then everything was on the house.

Seclusion in Hot Springs meant that he could move more freely out of the spotlight of publicity, but the media still maintained a keen interest in his activities.

Owney was deluged with offers from Hollywood studios to film his life story. He never answered their correspondence but filed it all away for amusement. Box Bixler, an executive with Paramount Pictures, wrote him: "Get in touch with me and I will show you how to get $100,000 for your biography in a full-length picture featuring the 'Owen Madden Story.'" Even his comedian friend, Joe E. Lewis, tried to get Owney's permission to portray him in a film, "in return for the standard $10 fee," as he jokingly put it. After running from publicity all his life, a movie was the last proposition he would have seriously considered. The world may have conveniently thought him retired, but the Duke was as active as he had ever been.

In 1944, Agnes and Owney had their house remodeled and enlarged. Decorators and builders worked for weeks on designs they had drawn up together to retain the old-world character of the frame house. The result was so in keeping with the original that it was impossible to imagine that the entire edifice was not built a hundred years previously.

Agnes, much to Owney's exasperation, would insist on painting the white boardwork herself, secured only by a rope from the roof tied around her slim waist.

"Jesus, Mary, and Joseph, woman," Owney would shout up at her. "Get a man in to do that kind of work. It's too dangerous."

Agnes would ignore him, humming as she painted. The owner of a local hardware store recalled her walking in one day for an 80-cent can of white paint and offering him a $1,000 bill.

Owney had idiosyncrasies left over from his bachelor life which Agnes found difficult to adjust to. "Agnes was always very thrifty," Roger Rucker recalled. "But Mr. Madden just loved flank steak. He could eat it for breakfast, lunch, and dinner. He was sitting in the living room eating a sandwich one night. He opened it and asked Emma Lee, the maid, what was on it. When she told him it was beef tongue, he just went through the ceiling.

"'I bring all this money in here and you're feeding me beef tongue,' he told Agnes.

"Mrs. Madden was quite a good cook. She could fix anything and make it taste good. Agnes told me she once worked hard to prepare a nice Thanksgiving table. There were all kinds of different dishes laid out, with turkey and dressing, and a big party had come to dinner. When Mr. Madden sat down, she heard him say quietly to Emma Lee: 'Gosh, I'd give anything for a big flank steak.' Agnes was furious. She wound up destroying the whole table and everyone had to eat out."

When the house renovation was finished, Agnes returned to her two great hobbies—her chickens and puttering among the flowers in the garden. Owney, always a great pigeon man, looked after his loft. The nervous clucking of the chickens irritated him, and he complained about them incessantly.

"The neighbors always complained about them, too," said Rucker, "but she never took any notice.

"Once, Agnes left to go to a flower show in New York and, as soon as she had gone, Mr. Madden got rid of all the chickens. To make up for it, he planted tulips right along the front of the house for 122 feet. It was his way of saying, 'I'm sorry for getting rid of the chickens when you went to the flower show, but here are some beautiful tulips instead.'

"The first thing Agnes asked when she walked in was: 'Where are my chickens?'

"'Got rid of them,' Mr. Madden said, and asked her if she liked the tulips.

"Agnes stormed outside, took a spade, and pitched every one of them onto the parkway out there."

When mounting pressure in Florida forced Owney to abandon his racetrack interests, Agnes personally handled the sale, from the negotiations to instructing the attorneys. The authorities, suspicious of

Owney's connection and past record, issued an ultimatum that unless he sold his Hialeah track, all licenses for racing there would be withdrawn. Agnes found a buyer, and the sale is said to have brought in $2.3 million. The check from the sale was the largest deposit ever made in the Arkansas Trust Company Bank in Hot Springs.

The end of the Second World War saw a turning point in the turbulent history of Hot Springs. Many of the young men who had been called up to fight for democracy returned to find the old place still the same under the rigid control of Mayor McLaughlin. To one small group, the administration bore a disturbing resemblance to a similar regime they had been away fighting against. Their leader, Sid McMath, a tough, square-jawed amateur boxer who had grown up in poverty and worked his way through law school, organized what became known as the GI Revolt. Among the handful was young veteran Q. Byrum Hurst, who later became Owney's attorney. The group met in 1946 at Hammond's Oyster Bar on Central Avenue and plotted the overthrow of the man everyone thought had previously been impossible to unseat.

The voting system was one of the main reasons McLaughlin had been able to remain so long in power. At every election, the mayor was wearing his customary red carnation and acting as though he didn't have a worry in the world. He liked to drive around town in an open carriage, which was pulled by his favorite horses, Scotch and Soda. Sooner or later during the day, two trains would pull into the Missouri Pacific railroad station and disgorge thousands of black workers and poor whites from homesteads and lumber camps from the outlying areas of Prescott, Hope, and Malvern. As each one alighted, election workers handed out poll tax receipts—which were necessary for voting— with a dollar pinned to them, and the message "Vote McLaughlin." The police, fire department, civic workers, and their families all had the same instruction.

According to Arkansas law at the time, representatives of the mayor could buy blocks of poll tax receipts by proxy for voters. The law also said that the slips had to be handed to their rightful owners within five days, but this tended to be overlooked.

The Record, published by the Garland County Historical Society, carried an interview with someone who dared to speak out:

"Opposition came when a local businessman criticized McLaughlin for using city fire trucks to campaign for Governor Carl Bailey, who was running for a third term as governor. A fire downtown destroyed a cleaners, a funeral home, and a garage before the trucks could be located. The businessman made the statement that 'no one should use city property to campaign for anyone.'

"The next morning, Leo called the man and said: 'I am in politics, and you are in the automobile business. I am going to break you and run you out of Hot Springs.'

"'That was the beginning of a political battle,' the businessman said. 'He told the gamblers not to buy any more cars from me. Two men had the guts to go ahead anyway, but that was the extent of my new car business. Up until that time, McLaughlin and I were friends.'"

When the mayor decided to name the local airfield after himself, the GIs thought he had gone too far. Even the local paper carried a cartoon of him announcing: "We must honor the memory of our boys who made the supreme sacrifice. I therefore designate this airport as the Leo P. McLaughlin Field." The homecoming veterans, hungry for reform, ran a tough campaign, labeling McLaughlin "Der Fuehrer of Hot Springs."

Their opening move to smash the political machine was to field candidates for two key posts—circuit judge and prosecuting attorney. If these could be secured, then McLaughlin would have less chance of escaping justice. It was a no-holds-barred election with the odds stacked against them. As Spider Rowland, the *Arkansas Gazette*'s columnist, put it: "Mayor McLaughlin is slicker than a bucketful of greased eels. The GIs can expect a double injection of major league trouble. In fact, they're going to run into more difficulties than a guy trying to light a wet cigar in a revolving door."

The GIs took their case before Judge John E. Miller, the justice who gave Owney his citizenship, and brought in an FBI handwriting expert from Kansas to prove that signatures authorizing the purchase of proxy votes were forged. The judge ruled in their favor and ordered an honest election. It was the last thing the McLaughlin machine wanted.

"A few days following Judge Miller's ruling, gunmen held up two GI campaign workers who were conducting a house-to-house check on poll tax purchases," wrote McMath's biographer, Jim Lester. "They stole all the evidence the workers had collected, including further affidavits by citizens who had denied that they had authorized the McLaughlin organization to obtain their poll tax receipts. On another occasion, Q. Byrum Hurst, the GI candidate for county judge, received a series of phone messages threatening his infant daughter. Finally, on election day, after the McLaughlin-dominated County Democratic Committee attempted to override Judge Miller's ruling, the veterans toured the county like a combat patrol, their automobiles loaded with guns. They also stationed poll watchers with cameras at several places and even started rumors that the FBI was gathering evidence of a voting fraud."

By January of 1947, McLaughlin stood down as mayor, and the new regime closed down most of Hot Springs's casinos.

To Owney, watching from the wings, it was as though his final years in New York were being re-enacted. Oddly enough, Mayor McLaughlin had been widely known as "The Jimmy Walker of the Southwest," and there were also distinct parallels between McMath and Dewey. Once elected prosecutor, the GI leader soon had his sights on running for governor, an ambition which, like Dewey, he managed to achieve at an early age. As a great student of form, Owney nimbly changed sides as the campaign gained momentum and backed the veterans. In the cleanup that followed the election, most of his business interests were left untouched.

In summing up McLaughlin and the election, McMath later recalled: "He could have been a great man and they would have built a monument to him when the boys came back, had he said: 'Boys,

I've had enough: y'all want it. I'll help you.' But he didn't do that. He was too greedy."

A grand jury hearing inspected the books of all the gambling houses in Hot Springs and estimated the annual profit to be $30 million. This was a conservative figure since the usual practice at the end of each evening's business was to skim off at least ten percent of the take. The total income tax declared on the sum was $1.6 million, while the McLaughlin machine imposed fines of only $31,000 for gambling. "We find several individual gamblers have incomes in excess of $100,000, one being $176,000," the grand jury added. "Circumstantial evidence indicates that there was a pay-off by gamblers to law enforcement officials of the city and county."

As the GIs pursued their new careers as judges and administrators and contemplated running for higher offices, life in Hot Springs quietly returned to normal.

One result of the shakeup was that many small gambling houses, which were no more than shacks or roadhouses, closed down, concentrating business on the big establishments which drew patrons from all over the country. Spurred by the spa's success story, the National Crime Syndicate went to work in the Nevada desert, laying the foundations for a new venture which many thought would never work. The site they had chosen was an undeveloped wasteland called Las Vegas.

Hoover stepped up his surveillance of Owney, ordering his men to concentrate on any hint of illicit business interests. Agents, acting on tips from informants, were instructed to find out if he was involved in a fur company, a jewelry store, and an auction house, all without success. The Duke was making heavy profits from the gambling interests, but most of his personal share steadily disappeared in the direction of anyone who seemed in need. One FBI report, based on the inspired guesswork of informants, stated that he kept $300,000 in cash in a vault beneath his house. Owney gave money not only to local charities, needy residents, and civic projects, but also to friends who lived out of town. His daily mail was enormous and often contained letters from old associates asking for hand-outs. Many were characters he had not heard from in years. In times of trouble, however, they were quick to remember his legendary generosity.

One poignant appeal came from Nils T. Granlund, former impresa-rio of Texas Guinan's clubs, who had moved out to Hollywood. He had landed what was considered a plum job as master of ceremonies at the Florentine Gardens for $60,000 a year until his contract was canceled. Granlund withdrew to New York to write his life story in a hotel room at the Great Northern while clinging to the hope that friends would buy the Florentine Gardens and reestablish him.

"Right now I need $300 desperately," he wrote. "I hate to ask this, Owney, but you have always been a good friend and a grand guy. It will mean more to me than I can ever tell you right now, and I can have it back to you within a month." Owney, as always, reached for his Arkansas Trust Company check book and sent the money by return mail. Many conveniently forgot to repay him. Others returned the money with thanks when their situation improved and never contacted him again. He seldom appeared to mind. As long as people had a genuine problem, he gave money away. Most of the donations were made without consult-ing Agnes—he had no intention of changing his ways.

Hot Springs historian Mark Palmer once mused on the generosity of those he called "gamblers and sportsmen fellows": "Secretly, a lot of them were like little boys that never grew up. Mean on the outside, soft on the inside. They got ashamed of themselves and hated some of the people they had to deal with. They fell in love with beautiful, dizzy women that they could feel sorry for and dreamt of redeeming their lives, but they couldn't because of their own bad reputation. So, they gave their money away to kids, servants, and poor people as a sort of secret way of trying to redeem themselves with God. You know, Owen Madden wasn't like that. He was a kind guy who really cared. I guess Shakespeare got it right about Owen: 'The evil that men do lives after them; the good is oft interred with their bones.'"

Much of Owney's time was occupied with friends from the underworld who enjoyed walking unrecognized in Hot Springs. There was an amusing incident when the talkative wife of New York columnist Leonard Lyons took a vacation in Bubbles and, desperate for a golf partner, approached three men setting off for the first hole at the country club. When she asked if she might tag along they smiled and said they had no objection. The lady, a blonde sociology student, happily chattered non-stop around the course, unaware that her partners were Owney Madden, Frank "the Enforcer" Nitti of Chicago, and Big Frenchy DeMange. Her husband was horrified when she later told him the story.

Twelve years later, back in Hot Springs, she bumped into Owney in the Arlington Hotel drugstore. After confirming his identity with the barber, Mrs. Lyons cornered him. Her husband reported the encounter in his column:

"The retired gang lord was wearing the white linen cap he always wears, which stamps him as unmistakably as the eight-inch waxed moustache of Salvador Dali.

"'How do you know me?'" he asked, suspiciously, forgetting about the cap.

"She told him he hadn't changed since their golf match twelve years ago with 'Mr. Fox.'

"'Oh, you mean DeMange-Fox,' he said, and my wife nodded.

"Madden said that he hadn't played golf in twenty months because of his ill health. He said that when he was younger he had been shot up so much that now he's beginning to feel it.

"'It hurts only where they took out the bullets,' said Owney. The bullets that are still lodged in his body don't bother him at all.

"My wife asked him if there were some lesson to be learned from his life, which might be helpful to the boys of America.

"'The only way I can help boys is financially,' said Madden. 'I've always done that.'

"He became suspicious and asked her why she was asking such questions.

"'We read biographies of famous men,' she said, 'and learn from them what to do, or not to do.'

"'From the famous, yes,' Madden said, 'but not from the infamous.'"

Owney remained far from forgotten, especially by an unfortunate racegoer named Coley Madden (no relation), who was banned from attending racetracks all over America because officials thought he was the Duke. He brought a court action against the Aqueduct Racetrack in an attempt to clear his name, but Queens County Jockey Club, unconvinced that he was not New York's most famous racketeer, defended it. Coley won the first round, but the racetrack appealed to the Supreme Court and retained the right to keep him out. The unfortunate Mr. Madden still had some money left from past winnings and hired an attorney to take his case right up to the Court of Appeals. Weighing the implications, Judge Stanley H. Fuld upheld the Jockey Club's decision. Coley, the only American citizen to experience what life was like for Owney Madden, subsequently gave up his interest in horse racing.

From an underworld point of view, the McLaughlin years had provided illegal gambling with an unrivaled stability, just as the Jimmy Walker regime had propped up Prohibition in New York. Each election which followed the downfall of McLaughlin made gambling a major issue and it was by no means a certainty which side would win.

Casinos were closed and reopened several times between the mid-1940s and late 1950s, interrupting the flow of cash which Owney administered on behalf of his silent partners, Lansky and Costello. The uncertainty was reflected in the national climate as 1950 approached and the U.S. Senate began to turn its attention toward organized crime. Frank Costello, by this time, has amassed a $200 million industry in slot machines and oil, mainly in the south. Florida had become the favorite playground and investment area of the mob, but when they wanted peace and anonymity to discuss important issues, Owney still played host in Hot Springs.

It was by no coincidence that in 1950, trains and planes carrying the most powerful men in America began to converge on the mountain spa for a meeting to analyze the significance of Washington's all-out investigation into organized crime. The Senate Special Committee to Investigate Crime in Interstate Commerce, led by Senator Estes Kefauver of Tennessee, was to become the most famous inquiry into organized crime in American history. It was helped by the fact that the hearings were televised daily to an audience of millions. More than 600 witnesses—from major criminals to petty thieves and public servants—paraded before the five-man committee. The Kefauver Hearings also became responsible for introducing a well-worn phrase into the American vocabulary—"taking the Fifth." During the testimony, major racketeers invoked the Fifth Amendment to the U. S. Constitution and declined to testify on the grounds that their evidence might incriminate them. It was a heaven-sent loophole, even if some had problems phrasing it correctly. Frank Erikson, for instance, who was employed by Frank Costello, took the Fifth because it "might intend to criminate" him.

It was wonderful television. After Costello objected to the presence of TV cameras in the hearing room, an agreement was reached. After that, viewers sat on the edge of their seats for a week, watching only Costello's hands. Virginia Hill, a beauty who worked for many big crime figures, floored New York reporter Marjorie Farnsworth with an extremely professional right to the jaw, telling the press on camera: "You goddam bastards. I hope an atom bomb falls on all of you."

By the end of 1951, the mob retreated to lick its wounds. Agnes's old golf partner, Joe Adonis, was deported. Her dinner party guest, Willie Moretti, was assassinated by those who feared his nerve had gone. And Uncle Frank, the man she once dumped pasta on, found his activities somewhat curtailed. Her husband, however, had been completely overlooked, save for oblique references to his past.

The committee called Frank Wiener, former chairman of the Pennsylvania State Athletic Commission, to give evidence on the fight rackets. Members were particularly interested in the details of one of Primo Carnera's fights. Wiener told the committee:

"I knew that racketeers were back there because they threatened me when I suspected Carnera and said he would never fight in Philadelphia again. Fellows like Duffy and Owney Madden and those fellows from New York who were managers of Carnera did everything they could to me to try to make me reinstate him. I told them he would never be reinstated as long as I was on the commission, and he never was."

It was all history and the committee duly made a note. What they were obsessively interested in, however, was the part Owney and Hot Springs played in the affairs of the National Crime Syndicate. Evidence was produced of telephone calls made by crime bosses to Owney, and witnesses were probed about their associations with him.

Harry Stromberg of Miami Beach, better known as racketeer Nig Rosen, was vague about Owney despite attempts to quiz him about Costello's trips to Hot Springs. There was a moment when Nig wondered if the committee was fishing to uncover information about the secret meeting in Bubbles. To his relief, they apparently were unaware of it:

COUNSEL: Did you see Owney Madden there?

MR. STROMBERG: Yes. He lives there.

COUNSEL : Did you talk to him?

MR. STROMBERG: Oh, sure.

COUNSEL : Did you ever have dinner...

MR. STROMBERG: Pardon me for interrupting. When you asked me about a meeting, an arranged meeting to meet in Hot Springs? Is that what you mean?

COUNSEL : No, no. Sit and talk with people there.

MR. STROMBERG: You see everybody on the street. The whole town is four blocks square.

COUNSEL : Who did you see? Could you tell us some of your friends you meet there?

MR. STROMBERG: I don't remember. You see so many people when you just go about your business.

The Kefauver Committee based many questions on reports filed by its own special agent, Vivian Lynn, a tall, striking woman who resembled the movie star Lauren Bacall. Lynn, who strolled around Hot Springs in heels and smoking cigarettes, turned heads wherever she went, including Frank Costello's. She had piercing blue eyes, an attractive gap in her front teeth, three decks of pearls, and a pill-box hat with a veil perched on her dark curls. The press could not keep away.

"This resort town has been having some interesting visitors lately," the Arkansas Gazette reported. "One is a suave, portly, well-dressed New Yorker named Frank Costello, who is currently relaxing in one of the three suites reserved in his name at the Jack Tar Courts. Another is a trim, blue-eyed native of Little Rock named Vivian Lynn, who turned a good many heads and lifted Costello's eyebrows when she went strolling on Central Avenue last week.

"Costello's presence in Hot Springs alone would have justified Mrs. Lynn's trip from Washington. But, as it happens, the resort has been honored in recent months by visits from several other citizens who have been prominent in the news made by the Kefauver Committee. So many, in fact, that Senator Kefauver himself tonight referred to the Arkansas city as the nation's 'No. 2' gathering spot for men with Costello's general reputation. Florida, says Kefauver, has an edge on Arkansas in this respect. 'Actually, we've had our eye on Hot Springs for a good long time now,' he said.

"'Back in April and May, Joe Adonis put up at the Arlington. In the same period, Harry Stromberg of Philadelphia, who is known professionally as Nig Rosen, was also in and out of town. And at approximately the same time, Art Samish, gambling boss of the West Coast, turned up in Hot Springs. More recently, Gus Gargotta, whose brother wound up as a front-page corpse in a Kansas City Democratic precinct club not long ago, has been in town.'"

The crime figures converging on Bubbles discussed the ramifications of the Kefauver hearings and then turned to local business. Like Owney, they were concerned with the unpredictable political climate surrounding gambling. Owney formed the view that, in order to safeguard his own interests and those of the syndicate, it might be advisable for him to be seen to "retire" while setting up an alternative enterprise. Most people, in any case, thought he already had.

As the hearings continued, Owney was one of the few organized crime figures who did not make the trip to testify in Washington. Nate Gross observed in his syndicated column:

"I met Owney Madden in Hot Springs, where he is a permanent resident. When things got lonesome at night in the Arlington Hotel, I'd cross the street to the Southern Grill and wait for Owney. Slight of build and aging, he wears a cap. We'd sit in the restaurant window, watching passers-by and talking. Mostly, I listened to stories of his days at Sing Sing and how Franklin D. Roosevelt, then governor, made things so uncomfortable for him in and out of jail that he left Gotham. Sometimes he indicated he had made a mistake. He should have stayed, even if F.D.R. pushed. Other times, he seemed contented in his small town. Some of the boys who used to stop by to say hello haven't been in Hot Springs this year. They were too busy testifying, or refraining from testifying, at the Kefauver Hearing. I am sure Owney Madden wouldn't trade places with any of them. He knows that investigation is a trouble that always threatens a racket. He, himself, has peace of mind. Owney retired from rackets years ago."

In the mid-1950s, on the verge of another election which threatened to shut down gambling, Owney made arrangements to "retire." They were carried out in an atmosphere of local political pressure against the Southern Club. Nationally, Hoover had made remarks about the "lawlessness" of Hot Springs—probably out of frustration at his inability to prove anything against Owney. Then, Walter Winchell, that familiar old voice from the past and now a confidante of Hoover, began attacking gambling in Bubbles in his Sunday radio broadcasts. Owney was furious at Winchell's remarks, which were deliberately made to draw attention to him.

There followed a complex series of Madden maneuvers, so intricately constructed that, to this day, no one is entirely sure what they concealed. On January 18, 1956, the *Hot Springs New Era* reported that Jimmy Phillips, one of the Southern Club partners, sold out his interest for $140,000 to a newly formed corporation called the New Southern Inc. Stockholders were Jack McJunkins and Dane Harris, two of Owney's associates, and Agnes. On February 12, the newspaper reported that Agnes and Dane Harris had sold their interests in the Southern to Dino Soncini, George Pakis, Jack Pakis, and Gene Stonecipher and that it had closed. The article suggested that friction between local politicians had prompted one political leader to threaten to close the building as long as Agnes held an interest in it. What it failed to mention was that the four buyers were also close friends of Owney.

The man at the center of the trouble was Circuit Judge C. Floyd Huff, known locally as "Babe." Owney had poured money into his election campaign–$15,000 was donated in a single week on one occasion–to ensure a safe future for his business interests. Huff made demands which Owney resented and began to apply pressure on him. The Duke did not wish to fight him head-on. It was not his style. Instead, he publicly backed out of gambling in order to concentrate on Huff's political defeat.

"Huff is out and out crooked," Owney said at the time. "He used terrible tactics to gain control of gambling in Hot Springs, but he isn't going to control me. I feel like going out and shooting him, but he just isn't worth spending time in jail for."

Two days after selling her interests in the New Southern Inc., Agnes wrote an angry letter to the *Sentinel Record*, which featured it in its column, "The Reader Speaks":

"I think I am entitled to make a statement about parts of the story carried in the local papers regarding the sale of my forty percent stock in the New Southern Corporation. I sold my interest in Tropical Park race track in Florida some years ago because I preferred to invest my money in my home town. But I have now sold my stock in the New Southern Inc. because I do not care to own or conduct any business under the present political dictatorship. I do not like dictatorship in Russia, in Hot Springs, or elsewhere in America. Too much political interference in business is not conducive to the growth of a city or country. I was in business here under the political regimes, but nothing could compare to the present conditions.

"Personally, I do not think a city can build any growth of permanence on the quicksands of gambling. I do not approve of it in any form and was in perfect accord with Mr. Madden's part in closing the Southern Club casino. He would not accede to political demands. I understand there was a lot of laughing in some quarters after the transaction, but you know the old saying: 'He who laughs last, etc....'—Agnes Demby Madden."

It was Agnes at her finest—angry, protective, and with the sweetest hint of revenge. Airing his affairs in public was a recognizable touch of the Duke at work. He enjoyed drawing as much attention as possible to a particular scheme, while having little intention of going through with it. Owney had enough problems without the greedy harassment of Judge Babe Huff. A year or two earlier, in 1953, Hoover and the U.S. Bureau of Immigration had begun to reexamine his ten-year-old U.S. citizenship for flaws, with the prime intention of revoking it and deporting him. To ensure that every effort was made, the FBI director issued orders that Owney's file should be upgraded and given "Top Hoodlum Status"—the bureau's highest criminal category.

In the course of their inquiries, they swooped down on Mae West and another Hollywood star—probably George Raft—whose name has been mysteriously erased from the records. Neither told them anything. Later, Clark Gable was interrogated at his home about his friendship with Owney but also declined to cooperate with them.

For lack of evidence, Immigration finally dropped its case and turned its attention to Owney's brother, Marty. Marty, 63 at the time,

was running a racing stable in Charlottesville, Virginia, on money borrowed from his brother, and already had the weight of the Internal
Revenue Service and the FBI on him. The pressure was so intense that
he decided to take a vacation in Cuba until things had cooled down.
When he returned, the situation had worsened. Marty appealed to his
brother for help and Owney, through intermediaries, approached senators for help and also hired a New York law firm which specialized in
immigration matters. Since Marty had lived for most of his life in New
York City, Owney used his influence there to pull strings. Approaches
were made to Cardinal Spellman and, through a mutual friend, to his
old enemy, Governor Thomas H. Dewey.

The excuse for Marty's threatened deportation was a burglary conviction in 1911 and a felony in 1916. The story made front-page news—
but not all the papers were sympathetic with the authorities. "An elderly,
broken-down quiescent brother of Owney Madden, the old-time bootlegger and prizefight racketeer, is biding his time until we dump him,
friendless, forlorn, broke, and a stranger in his native Liverpool," wrote
Owney's old columnist pal Westbrook Pegler. As the date of his depar-
ture drew near, Marty and his case became a celebrated cause. "If they
force me to go back to England, I'll die within a year," he told reporter
James O'Connor. "I don't know a soul on the other side. I have no family or friends there.

"Forty years ago, I committed a couple of sins that I've already paid
for," Madden said, shaking his grey head, bitterness in his voice. "Isn't
that sufficient? Do they have to keep hounding me?"

It was, of course, Owney they were hounding, just as they had jailed
him for a murder of which he appears to have been innocent, returned
him to Sing Sing on the flimsiest of technicalities, exiled him against all
his constitutional rights, and tried unsuccessfully to have him deported.
The offenses of which he was guilty, they were incapable of proving. The
Duke, now in his early sixties and suffering from recurring bad health,
was to engage in more battles before his war was ended.

On September 10, 1953, the knock finally came on Marty's door. He was escorted by immigration officers and followed by a milling crowd of reporters, photographers, neighbors, and members of the public, down to the ferry to Ellis Island to await deportation. The grounds had been narrowed down to a vacation he took in Cuba in 1931, when he returned to New York and failed to declare that he had a criminal record. He had been on Ellis Island for less than an hour when the telephone rang in the immigration office, informing the duty officer that Marty could be released on $5,000 bail. As he stepped from the ferry back onto Manhattan, police had difficulty controlling the crowds surging to congratulate him.

"What was the trouble really about?" one reporter shouted. "Was it anything to do with Owney?"

"I don't want to say it," Marty called, "but I'm afraid it was."

The stay of execution was partly due to efforts by senators, including Senator John McClellan of Arkansas, to apply for a special private bill giving Marty citizenship. Owney conducted negotiations through a friend, Walter Ebel, from the local radio station, to whom all the correspondence was addressed. On July 10, 1954, Owney and Agnes wrote a private note to Senator McClellan: "Walter Ebel is attending your rally today, so we are taking this opportunity of asking him to carry our contribution to you for your campaign. We decided this was more prudent than going to any committee in Hot Springs, as it seems every two-bit politician and newspaper writer tries to make capital of everything connected with our name."

On July 15, 1955, the House Subcommittee on Immigration recommended that deportation proceedings against Martin A. Madden should be discontinued. Two years later, Marty, frail and in poor health since the case had been mounted against him, died. John McClellan and Owney were destined to meet again under different circumstances.

In 1954, FBI Special Agent Clay White was assigned to Hot Springs and worked from home on about twenty-five cases until the FBI rented office space in the spa's Federal Building. One of his cases was Owney

Madden, a retired racketeer from back east in whom Hoover appeared to have a lot of interest. Other agents worked out of the Federal Building—up to fifteen of them during the racing season—but White handled most of the surveillance on Owney. It was monotonous work, made more difficult in the heat of summer by Hoover's strict rules governing his agents. They were obliged to wear suits and ties at all times, have their hair trimmed to a regulation length, and never drive their undercover cars with the windows open. In the days when air conditioning was in its infancy and temperatures were in the high 90s, it was clammy, uncomfortable work. To make things worse, any man inclined to perspiring could find himself out of a job. At some stage in his career, every agent had to meet the director personally. Supervisors warned them to carry a handkerchief for the occasion. Hoover had been known to fire men who had moist palms.

"Owney Madden led a routine life," Clay White recalled years later when I visited him in Hot Springs. By then, he had retired from the FBI and was working in the Garland County Sheriff's Office. "Just about every day, he would go through the same pattern. He would get into his automobile and go down to the Southern Club, stay there a while, and drift back home after dark. For the first three or four years I was in Hot Springs, Owney Madden would not even speak to me. I would go into the Southern Club, maybe looking for someone, or just checking—activity was real extensive in Hot Springs at that time—and Owney Madden would ignore me. One day I had to do an interview for another office—I can't recall the name of the subject—but they wanted me to talk to Owney Madden about the individual.

"I called him up at home and told him who I was. Like I say, he had never even acknowledged my existence until that time, and I had never had any reason to talk to him or interview him.

"'How did you get my telephone number?' he asked.

"And I said, 'Well, you know, Owney, we have certain ways that I can get your number.'

"He thought about it for a moment and replied: 'Yeah, I guess that's right.'

"I told him I wanted to talk to him about a matter and he said: 'Well, I'll be in the Southern Club all afternoon. Come in there sometime this p.m. and we'll sit down and talk.'

"I felt that Owney was the type of individual that, if he said anything to you, you could take it as gospel. He would not lie to you. Now, he may not answer your question, but if he did, it was the truth."

White monitored Owney's movements, along with callers at the house, but found little to convince him that Owney was involved in organized crime. He said as much in his regular reports to Washington, but Hoover found it difficult to accept. White elaborated:

"The Bureau—and by that I mean supervisors at the seat of government working for the FBI—always felt that Owney Madden was still very active in organized crime, even after he came to Hot Springs. Now I am convinced, based on my investigations and what I knew about Owney Madden, that this was not true. I'm not saying he was completely free, but he lived a very different life to the one he led in New York City. There were some things that I'm sure he was involved in—things that we might not know about—but Owney Madden's activity in Hot Springs was not in the category of being involved in organized crime."

As an agent working almost alone on the case, in a town which had a tradition of not being entirely disposed to assisting federal officers, White was faced with a monumental task. Owney operated in a way which revealed nothing to a casual observer and little even to a trained agent. His everyday habits were deliberately commonplace, and he operated in a business which did not rely on striking daily deals and holding regular meetings. Like Washington, White could not be expected to have more than suspicions that something was happening beneath the surface. Owney had spent many years burying his affairs deep. He was every inch the perfect citizen and a sincere and generous contributor to local causes. Beyond that, he considered the rest of his affairs no one's business but his own and made sure they remained that way.

Hoover listed a series of headings under which he wanted detailed information. These included personal history, associates, criminal activities, legitimate enterprise, place of amusement or hangouts frequented, travel, personal habits and peculiarities, and general comments. He instructed his agents in Little Rock to immediately set up a network of informants among neighbors, acquaintances, and local merchants and gave strict deadlines for each report to be on his desk.

White met Owney, who was recovering from a bout of flu, at the Southern Club and quizzed him about his activities. White later reported: "The subject stated it was difficult for him to understand why the FBI would investigate individuals like himself when they were not violating any laws, and would not investigate individuals like Judge Huff. Madden maintained that he was aware of the fact that the FBI was investigating him at the present time."

White included a report of his surveillance:

"January 10th, 1958: Madden was observed at approximately 3 p.m. in the bar of the Southern Club, talking with the bar maid.

"January 21, 1958: Madden observed alone sitting at a table at the Southern Club Grill.

"January 22, 1958: Madden was observed at the Southern Club Grill talking to one of the waitresses."

For someone who had no financial interest in the Southern Club, Owney seemed to spend a great deal of his time there. Hoover read that he had no "places of amusement or hangouts," did not travel, and had no legitimate or illegitimate businesses. A neighbor, who had a clear view of the house, reported that "the Maddens have very little company and there is seldom an automobile parked outside their residence." Owney's physical description included the following three entries:

"Health: Poor

"Peculiarities: Nervous

"Appearance: Wears sports clothes and cap and scarf around neck."

Hoover, still undeterred, told agents in New York to track down Owney's first wife, Dorothy, and his daughter, Margaret—neither of whom he had seen in years—and interview them. Inquiries about them in New York, New Orleans, Pittsburgh, Chicago, and Saratoga Springs only drew blanks. Surveillance continued throughout 1958 and checks were made on every aspect of his life. The owner of the restaurant where he dined with Agnes on their wedding anniversary was interviewed and declared him "a gentleman." So did the mechanic who serviced his car and the residents who lived nearby. All remarked on how charming and thoughtful Owney was. The only time he ventured out all year was to watch a film of the Robinson-Basilio fight at a movie theater in nearby Little Rock.

Owney's health had deteriorated, and he remained at home for days, receiving regular visits from his doctor. His resilience, however, was remarkable and he was soon back at his table at the Southern Grill. After one bout of flu, which exacerbated his chest condition, Agnes confided to the wife of the police chief who lived next door that she did not think he would live long. But, Owney confounded them all and was soon going about his outwardly mundane routine.

For senior agents in the FBI's Washington office, Mondays and Wednesdays always made their stomachs churn with apprehension. Hoover held these twice-weekly meetings with them to discuss cases but often used them as a platform for his tantrums. There were times when the director was so volatile that it was impossible to predict what would please him. On one occasion, he fired an agent who wore a tie with bright colors, breaking the bureau's rule that tie and socks must match. Another agent was threatened with dismissal for reading *Playboy* magazine. The item which caused Hoover's face to cloud over this time was the report from Little Rock on Owney Madden. The report essentially was an admission by agents that they were unable to distinguish Madden from any other law-abiding citizen. And, despite his "Top Hoodlum" status, not a single photograph had been taken of him since his release from Sing Sing in the early 1930s. Hoover demanded that samples of Madden's signature and recent photographs of him should be sent immediately to Washington to update the files. The director also wanted a glimpse of the fox who had eluded him for so long.

17.

When the Bubble Burst

There was a sigh of satisfaction for Owney in 1958 when Judge Babe Huff was defeated in the local elections. Arkansas's governor, Orval Faubus, diplomatically left the question of gambling in the hands of Hot Springs officials, and business returned to normal. Little Rock's FBI office, unable to spend further man hours following Owney, decided to withdraw surveillance and rely solely on informants' reports.

By the following year, an experienced eye would have detected a slight change in Owney's routine. The Duke appeared to be spending more time than usual in discussions with his attorney, Q. Byrum Hurst. He also received visitors from New Orleans, where the syndicate operation was now directed by Carlos Marcello, a gangster of Tunisian origin who had risen to great heights in the southern mob hierarchy. One of Marcello's many ventures on behalf of Costello & Co. was a racing wire service, which took results from tracks all over the country and supplied them via telephone lines to bookies across the south. It fell into the kind of grey area that Frank loved. The service was arguably legal on a local level but still contravened the interstate gambling laws.

Clay White began to receive hints from informants that something was happening behind the scenes in Hot Springs. One version claimed that the syndicate's wire service was moving into Bubbles in a big way. Early one Sunday morning, when half of Hot Springs was asleep and the other half attending church, a pick-up truck pulled up at the Ritter Hotel on Exchange Street and a man in coveralls unloaded an assortment of ladders, tools, coils of wire, and a drill. The man, who worked during the week for the Southwestern Bell Telephone Company, went about his task with practiced ease. Within half an hour, two white ceramic insulators were bolted to the wall outside a suite of fifth-floor rooms. By the time he had finished for the day, telephone wires ran all over town like a web woven by an inebriated spider. The wires were tied to walls, then run through tree branches and twisted around nails here and there. The lines were hanging so low over Central Avenue that passing trucks threatened to drag them down.

Anyone who took the trouble to follow this crazy route, as Clay White did, would have been led to a network of bookie shops all over town. One final wire disappeared into the countryside, swinging from tree to tree across National Park land to a country club. Owney's black Chevrolet began to take a different route each day from his home on West Grand. Instead of spending afternoons in the Southern Club, he now disappeared into the Ritter Hotel and took the elevator to the fifth floor. The hotel, the FBI discovered, was owned by Q. Byrum Hurst.

White decided to meet Owney for a talk and later noted in his standard, leaden prose: "The subject Madden advised that he no longer frequented the Southern Club as he had in the past. He stated it had gotten to the point that he would not, due to the fact that certain individuals were always requesting that he lend them money. Madden stated, for example, on some occasions, he went to the club with $200 and when he departed in the evening he had loaned $190 of it to five or six different people. He indicated that he was now spending most of his afternoons at the Ritter Hotel and remaining in his residence at night and in the mornings."

As the number of people calling on Owney in cars bearing out-of-state license plates suddenly increased, the FBI went back to shadowing him. White tailed him most days in a Ford supplied by the

FBI—agents were not allowed to take their FBI cars home for fear of being accused of using them socially—and found Owney settled in his new routine.

White finally confronted Owney and asked him point blank if he was running a racing wire service. To his surprise, the Duke responded by inviting him in to show him around. White wandered through the three-room suite while Owney explained how the system worked. He received results via New Orleans and fed them out to eight local bookmakers. He had installed a tape recorder to log each transmission in case a bookie claimed that the wrong information had been given out. There were several men hard at work in the suite, including an ex-New Yorker named Jimmy Vitro, who appeared to be a jack-of-all-trades. Later, White checked with the Federal Communications Commission, which confirmed that someone from the Ritter had been in touch to ensure that they were not breaking any laws.

About this time, Owney ordered a new television set for his office from a local store and asked the dealer to install the aerial. "When he got up there, he found all these old wires running across the roof," one Hot Springs resident told me with a chuckle. "He didn't know they were important, so he ran them down and moved them out of the way. Next day, Mr. Madden came into his shop and introduced himself.

"'Do you know anything about wires on that roof?' Mr. Madden asked him. 'Why sure,' the store owner replied. 'They were just in the way so I took them down.'

"Then, Mr. Madden explained nice and quiet that those wires were real important. They were necessary for the race service, and without them the bookie shops couldn't get their results. The TV dealer was kind of surprised and shocked. After he put them right back again, he and Mr. Madden got along fine. I guess it must have been the beginning of a profitable friendship because Mr. Madden never forgot. Later, when he opened the Vapors Club, the TV store man, so I heard, was right there among the list of investors."

As soon as he received a report on Madden's wire service, Hoover fired off a message to Little Rock: "In view of Madden's important connections with the underworld on a national basis, and the fact that he currently controls the racing wire service, efforts should he made to step up your coverage of his activities to know the identity of persons with whom he is in contact."

The FBI office in New Orleans was put on alert to watch for any major crime figures who might be traveling to Hot Springs. Agents in the FBI's Little Rock office read the director's instructions with some dismay. They knew that squeezing blood from a stone was infinitely easier than finding out what Owney was up to.

Informants watching his house reported that the only callers were women visiting Agnes for regular meetings of her ladies' Republican Club. Owney maintained a routine which the FBI timed and found to vary only by a few minutes each day. His behavior betrayed little of the intense drama taking place. As occasionally happens in the twilight world of organized crime, Carlos Marcello had been experiencing problems with "young bloods" hungry to take over his New Orleans territory and otherwise burn a path through the south. The FBI had no inkling that the New Orleans underworld was in turmoil and on the verge of a bloody war.

Owney had already been apprised that the new elements intended to take over Hot Springs, and Marcello's hands were too full to help him.

When Owney's daily round became monotonous, the FBI scaled down its surveillance. The next time they checked on him, however, he had disappeared. White made inquiries and found that Owney was aboard an aircraft already heading back from Chicago to Hot Springs. He had just won the assurance of full protection for his enterprises from Tony Accardo, the supreme crime boss of the Windy City. Accardo ruled with such an iron hand that underworld violence had plummeted to almost zero since the Capone days, a feat due heavily to his fearsome reputation. Owney and Tony were old friends, and Accardo was prepared to lend as much muscle as necessary to help him out. The Duke, for his part, did not require practical help. He just wanted the reassurance that it was there if needed. The potential invasion of the young bloods from New Orleans was averted, and Hot Springs was never threatened again within Owney's lifetime. Such was his esteem among the Chicago mob that, a few months later, a delegation visited him in secret.

They checked into three picturesque cottages on the shores of Lake Hamilton, just outside Hot Springs, and the FBI unsuccessfully tried to monitor the conversations. To their embarrassment, the agents found that the press seemed to know more about the rendezvous than they did. One report showed that agents had sighted "two unidentified white males and three unidentified white women in a white Mercury convertible and a black Mercury two-door, both with Illinois license plates. Investigations failed to disclose if these individuals were visited by others at the Island Cottages, and there was no known meeting there." White, incidentally, was not on duty when the visit took place, and two other agents were assigned to this surveillance.

Their report to Washington was obliged to quote from a well-informed newspaper article which pointed out that the visitors, "Mr. Frank Thomas" and "Mr. J. Moran," were Dominic Hella and Joseph Di Varco. Staying nearby in another cottage was a Joseph J. Lucania. The agents' report went on: "The newspaper article related that the subjects under discussion were primarily organizational, to determine who was to take over if Joseph Anthony Accardo is forced to serve the six-year prison term for filing a false statement on his income tax returns, and the reopening of large-scale gambling inside Cook County, Illinois.

"It was further reflected in the article that one of the mobsters consulted was Owney Madden, former New York racketeer, who now presides over the Southern Club, one of the bigger gaming places in Hot Springs. It is stated that Madden, now nearly seventy, is still actively a part of the Crime Syndicate and serves as representative in Hot Springs. In any event, at least three times he was consulted by the visitors during afternoon confabs at the gaming club."

Hoover, it can be assumed, read the report with dismay. He disliked having his suspicions confirmed by newspaper reporters when his own highly trained staff was consistently unable to provide what he was looking for. Despite all indications to the contrary, it appeared that Owney was no more retired than in the old days when he ran New York. As a footnote to the incident, the Duke circled a paragraph from the news-in-brief column of his newspaper before snipping it out and putting it to one side. It reaffirmed something he had always suspected from personal experience: "John Byington, chairman of the Consumer Product Safety Commission, said in a radio interview at Washington that one-third of the federal government's employees were 'a disaster' and should be fired."

Hoover responded to the continued lack of success with Owney by sending another highly charged message to Little Rock. "It is imperative," he said, "that you develop and maintain a workable Criminal Intelligence Program. In connection with this you should give consideration to highly confidential techniques, including microphone surveillance. These latest developments must be exploited with the utmost enthusiasm and aggressiveness..."

Late in 1960, Owney was admitted to St. Joseph's Hospital. Hoover, unsure what course to take next, asked for every report that had been filed on Madden in the previous ten years. Owney's condition, an informant told White, was "very serious" and that "it is doubtful he will recover from his illness." Doctors at St. Joseph's diagnosed ulceration of his old gunshot wounds and observed that "he is encountering more difficulty than usual for a person with this type of illness." They felt reluctant to operate because of his age. Agnes and his friends sat at his bedside all week, talking to him and cajoling him along. A few weeks later he amazed everyone by making a complete recovery and was discharged from the hospital. Once home, Owney puttered about the garden and tended his pigeons but spent less time at the Ritter Hotel and the Southern Club.

It was a welcome opportunity to gather his thoughts. While he'd been in the hospital, a new sheriff and prosecuting attorney had been elected.

They took office on January 1, 1961, and lost no time letting it be known that they were unsympathetic to his activities. White called on the Duke to see how he was faring and reported: "Although his condition has improved considerably, his doctor does not consider him to be out of danger. He is planning to be very careful in the amount he exerts himself each day."

Owney's doctor was not alone in considering him not to be free from danger. In Washington, a brash young U.S. attorney general, considered by his subordinates to be ignorant and lacking finesse, was rapidly building his career in the well-worn tradition of racket investigation. Bobby Kennedy, backed by his brother, John, newly elected as president of the United States, had his sights firmly fixed on Hot Springs and was ready to squeeze the trigger.

On June 7, 1961, the *Arkansas Gazette* carried an Associated Press story from Washington which gave a hint of what was to come. Attorney General Robert F. Kennedy, it reported, was urging the Senate Judiciary Committee to act on half a dozen anti-crime proposals he had submitted. Among them was the urgent need for federal authorities to be given additional powers to deal with the underworld. To illustrate his case, he singled out "a race wire service in Hot Springs where several top racketeers could be prosecuted" if the new powers were granted. The *Gazette* further noted:

"The attorney general said the Justice Department had knowledge of a situation which developed last year when Louisiana racketeers traveled to Hot Springs in an attempt to move in on the race wire service there. 'The operator of the Hot Springs service traveled to Chicago to seek the help of the Chicago rackets overlord in fending off the New Orleans group,' Kennedy said."

A prosecution in Hot Springs, he concluded, "would be a distinct service to the nation."

Owney had lived through it all before several times over and now in his 70s was wearying of the war. The report made him particularly angry at Bobby Kennedy, "the young upstart." He considered Kennedy's actions to represent the timeless hypocrisy of politics.

"Jesus, Mary, and Joseph," he told his attorney. "I was in partnership with his father back in the bootlegging days. How can he do this?"

By his own measure, Owney felt that he had never had double standards and prided himself in the belief that he had prospered through straight dealing. Politicians—particularly ambitious ones—were a breed for whom he carried an enduring contempt.

J. Edgar Hoover was uncomfortable with the Kennedy administration. Lyndon B. Johnson was the only president he had followed obediently. Still, he appreciated Bobby Kennedy's stance on crime. To supply him with the fullest possible information, he ordered Little Rock to conduct further investigation into the wire service. At ground level, there was only one way it could be accomplished, and Agent White paid another call on Owney to ask for his help. The Duke obliged by taking him to one of the bookie shops supplied by the service, which by now had been registered as the Downtown Printing Company. Marcello, in New Orleans, called his end of the operation the Nola Printing Company. The two business names were to figure heavily in FBI wires across the country.

Owney explained the system in more detail to White, giving him the facts and figures he would need for his report. The phone bill to receive race results from New Orleans, for instance, cost $1,600 a month.

To reduce his overheads, Owney said he had approached bookies in Little Rock, who were receiving another wire service at $1,600 a month each. He proposed to cut their telephone bills in half by relaying the service he received from Nola to Little Rock. In order to do this, the telephone company would charge him an extra $170 a month. Thus, Little Rock would make more profit and Hot Springs's margin would increase. The idea crystallized the kind of venture which appealed to the Duke's business acumen.

Owney showed White around the Ritter Hotel suite a second time, pointing out details he had previously overlooked. There was a panel of switches—one corresponding to each Hot Springs bookie so that Owney could cut off the intercom in any betting shop he wished in case of a disagreement. In the corner of the office there was also a mimeograph machine which printed daily scratch sheets to bookmakers receiving the service.

White decided to visit all the bookies for his report, a tour that took him to the Blue Ribbon Club, the Cameo, Tim's Place, the formerly notorious White Front Club, the Pensioner's Club, the Citizen's, and the Bridge Street. All were crowded to the doors and doing heavy business. "The most elaborate and up to date," he reported to Washington, "was the Bridge Street Club with its entrance on Bridge Street, known as the "Shortest Street in the USA." The steps were covered with heavy carpeting and the club floor itself is likewise carpeted. The interior gave the appearance of an up-to-date stock market. There were four large boards on expensive, paneled walls listing race tracks in New York, Baltimore, Sportsman Park in Chicago, and Churchill Downs in Kentucky. An employee, whose first name was Herman, was the marker who kept guests and customers up-to-date with the progress of each race.

The room was equipped with expensive chairs and ashtrays. Also in the club were eight slot machines and a crap table which were receiving big play. Elsewhere in the room was an expensive stereo radio recording outfit and an extremely elaborate bar. The room had an acoustic ceiling, and there was heavy carpeting on the ceiling over the bar.

Hoover presumably found it interesting reading. Bobby Kennedy achieved the powers he was demanding, and a Senate investigation into gambling and organized crime was announced, chaired by Senator John McClellan of Arkansas. Richard Nixon called McClellan "the Dean of the Senate," and he was well-respected on Capitol Hill, despite his conservative misgivings about Kennedy's support of civil liberties. Bobby Kennedy was given full rein to express himself politically through the hearings, and he lost no time in drawing up a "hit list" of forty underworld figures. The president himself set the pace of things when he let it be known: "We have one rule around here. If they're crooks, we don't wound 'em, we kill 'em."

There was a certain enthusiasm about the whole business, which some commentators found curious. Lee Mortimer wrote in his "New York Confidential" column:

"I'M JUST WONDERING: (Or am I being naive?) Why Senator McClellan of Arkansas never mentions Hot Springs, with its open gambling, slot machines, and easy gals to entertain visiting Mafia and labor-union big shots from all over the country? They come to take the healing baths and reminisce with Owney 'The Killer' Madden, who is now Hot Springs's sage senior citizen and chief procurer. What goes on in Hot Springs makes Saratoga in the old days look like piker money. The Springs is where the Boys cut up the rackets and assign the boodle that McClellan is investigating... Why Senator Kennedy of Massachusetts never mentions conditions in Massachusetts? They are so favorable for mobsters and union boondogglers that Boston (and Worcester and Fall River) are the sites of clearing houses (behind a staid New England front) for the constant interchange of underworld information, orders, and loot. (I *am* being naive)."

As far as McClellan was concerned, he was not being at all naive. The senator had received several substantial campaign contributions from Owney and Agnes and was a friend of their attorney, state senator Q. Byrum Hurst. He shared little of Bobby Kennedy's enthusiasm for dumping the judicial equivalent of an atom bomb on his neighboring town of Hot Springs. The young attorney general went about his task with gusto, displaying a particular pride in his "Get Hoffa Squad"—a team of sixteen lawyers whose sole purpose was to convict Teamsters Union leader Jimmy Hoffa on as many counts as were humanly possible.

In his early career, Bobby Kennedy proved himself to be gracious neither in victory nor defeat. High on his "hit list" was Carlos Marcello,

Owney's New Orleans partner who, it was rumored, had handed a satchel containing $500,000 to Richard Nixon's campaign for the presidency in order to help keep Jack Kennedy out. Bobby finally evened the score, so to speak, when he discovered an old deportation order still out against Marcello which, for unknown reasons, had never been acted upon. Before he had time to call his lawyer, FBI agents rushed Marcello off in handcuffs to a government border patrol aircraft. The plane was already warmed up and, as soon as Marcello was aboard, it headed out of the country. He was dumped in Guatemala, a country which had once given him a certificate of citizenship in exchange for an undisclosed sum of money. Times had changed, however, and Marcello soon found himself back on a plane and headed for El Salvador. No one there seemed to know what to do with him, so he was thrown into jail.

A few days later, after considering the wisest course of action, officials drove him by jeep along bad roads, thirty miles into dense jungle. There, they threw him out, still wearing his hand-stitched suit and alligator shoes. Marcello, a small man of qualities which might be envied by the Green Berets, made it to civilization several pounds lighter and slipped back unnoticed into the United States.

In underworld terms, Robert Kennedy was perhaps the most intensely disliked of America's attorneys general. His brother, John, had the sympathy of the mob over his Cuban policy, and there are stories of their secret attempts to help the CIA overthrow Cuba's dictator, Fidel Castro. A return to the grand old days of wide-open gambling in Cuba was something the mob dearly wished to achieve. Bobby, however, before acquiring his reputation as a civil rights champion, was considered ruthless and ambitious. There are many transcripts of telephone taps in which gang bosses and union leaders expressed what they would like to do to him. They talked of plastic explosives, assassination with a high-powered rifle which could be blamed on southern segregationists, and knifing him. When Marcello finally made it through the back door of the United States and into New Orleans, he is said to have vowed to three associates: "Don't worry about that little Bobby sonofabitch. He's going to be taken care of."

Bobby, however, was successfully getting the political muscle he wanted from the Senate and, in August of 1961, a team of Washington "racket probers" descended on Hot Springs to gather evidence for the McClellan Committee. They made no secret of the fact that their main target was Owney's wire service.

"Hot Springs sources reported tonight that Owney Madden, former ganglord and big-time New York beer baron during the Prohibition era, who retired to the Arkansas resort city in 1935, was among three subpoenaed," the *Arkansas Democrat* reported. "Senator John McClellan (Dem. Ark.), chairman of the Senate investigating subcommittee, declined to give any details."

Soon after he was handed his subpoena by Jerome Alderman, counsel for the McClellan hearings who led the swoop on Hot Springs, Owney had a telephone call from a friend in Chicago who was also in trouble. Jimmy Hoffa, leader of the national Teamsters Union, had been charged with attempting to bribe the committee and needed a good lawyer. Not that Hoffa was ever short of good lawyers, but in the prevailing climate, he knew that Bobby Kennedy was making an all-out effort to put him in jail.

"Owney," he begged in a telephone call, "help me out. I've got to have an attorney I can really trust."

"There's a personal friend of mine sitting right here," said the Duke, handing the phone to Q. Byrum Hurst.

It was a selfless gesture. Hurst could not represent both men in Washington because it would not create a good impression to link them even in the slightest way. Owney would have to find another attorney to safeguard his own interest at the hearing. Q. Byrum Hurst agreed to represent Hoffa and introduced Owney to Charles Lincoln, a colleague from Little Rock, who would also represent Jimmy Vitro, the wire service manager.

In the meantime, there was some legal mopping-up to do. Senate investigators had not overlooked the fact that one of the wires from the Ritter Hotel crossed U.S. government property—Hot Springs National Park—which contravened federal law. Owney could be prosecuted, fined, and even jailed if the situation was not quickly rectified. Transmitting gambling information from one state to another across government land might be exactly the lever Bobby Kennedy was looking for to net both the Hot Springs and New Orleans operations. The information was handed to the U.S. attorney general at Fort Smith, Arkansas, who pursued it with interest.

Before he appeared before the subcommittee in Washington, Owney drew up plans to discontinue the wire service and attend to his legal affairs. Newspapers, hounding him for interviews, did not make the task easier.

"Are you engaged in any form of gambling?" a reporter for the *Memphis Commercial Appeal* asked him as he climbed into his car.

"No," Owney replied testily, "and you can tell that to the world, and you can be sure of it."

Owney called a meeting of all spa bookmakers and suggested that they close down on August 5, as he believed a new law was about to be passed making race-wire services illegal. Faced with the prospect of a jail sentence in the winter of his years, he also made arrangements for his casino interests to be bought out.

"How about the hearing in Washington, Owney?" Agent White asked, as they sat in the Southern Grill a few days later.

"Well, we don't actually know how to prepare for it," the Duke said, inhaling deeply on his cigarette. "All I can do is answer questions truthfully. But, I suppose I'll take the Fifth on one or two."

While Owney tidied up his affairs, his lawyers successfully put back the date of his appearance from August 8th to August 22nd. As the day approached, they managed to postpone it further to August 28th. The reason seemed puzzling, especially since there appeared little to be gained from attending on one day rather than another. I put the question to an old associate of Owney in Hot Springs. He took a long time to answer, but finally he said: "Well, Owney's line of thinking was that if he kept putting it back something might happen. Maybe Bobby Kennedy might fall dead or something. Then he wouldn't have to go at all."

A few days later, the district manager of Southwestern Bell had a visit from a McClellan Committee official who subpoenaed all his telephone records for Hot Springs. The U.S. attorney in Fort Smith had handed over the trespass case to the National Park Service with a recommendation to take action. The National Park, however, did not fully appreciate the urgency and shelved the file until someone got around to it.

On the eve of the Washington hearings, the *Arkansas Democrat* set the scene: "Owen Madden, formerly of New York City, told our reporter he would tell the committee nothing. Hot Springs witness James Vitro, reportedly an employee of Madden, also said he would not answer questions. The third witness is Julian Lytle of North Little Rock who, according to his attorney, would answer only to his name and address."

Owney took the night flight to Washington with Attorney Charles Lincoln and appeared next day in the Caucus Room of the old Senate Office building where Senator Joe McCarthy had conducted some of his celebrated hearings during the '50s with the House Committee on Un-American Activities. The Duke, no longer the wiry, tough-looking individual of his heyday, looked old and tight-lipped as he tried to shoulder his way through a wall of photographers. Inside, TV crews snapped on their blinding arc lights and thrust light meters in his face as he sat before the cameras and the panel. He had never before been exposed to such a glare of publicity, and it was clear from the outset that he disliked it.

Senator McClellan began by asking Jimmy Vitro, and then Owney, to identify themselves for the benefit of the committee. Both gave their names and addresses:

CHAIRMAN: Mr. Vitro, I do not believe you told me your occupation or your business.

MR. VITRO: I beg your pardon?

CHAIRMAN: I beg your pardon. I say I do not believe you told me your occupation or your business.

(The witness conferred with his counsel.)

CHAIRMAN: Can he not hear?

MR. LINCOLN: He is deaf in one ear.

CHAIRMAN: Use the other one.

MR. VITRO: I decline to answer the question on the grounds that my answer might incriminate me.

CHAIRMAN: Very well. Mr. Madden, did you give us your occupation?

MR. MADDEN: I am retired, senator.

CHAIRMAN: I beg your pardon?

MR. MADDEN: I am retired.

CHAIRMAN: You are retired.

MR. MADDEN: Yes, I am.

CHAIRMAN: Since when?

MR. MADDEN: A few years, quite a few years.

CHAIRMAN: You have been retired quite a few years from what?

(The witness conferred with his counsel.)

CHAIRMAN: You said you had been retired quite a few years.

MR. MADDEN: Yes.

CHAIRMAN: What did you retire from? What was your business or occupation?

(The witness conferred with his counsel.)

MR. MADDEN: I refuse to answer on the grounds of...

CHAIRMAN: I suggest you say "decline to answer."

MR. MADDEN: I respectfully decline to answer.

Owney, who had been prepared to see how events proceeded and possibly drift with the current, looked at the stone-faced members of the panel and the semi-circle of TV cameras, and decided to dig in his heels.

Jerome Alderman, the counsel who interrogated him in Hot Springs, took over the questioning:

MR. ALDERMAN: You were born in England, were you?

(The witness conferred with his counsel.)

MR. MADDEN: I object to that on account of pertinency.

CHAIRMAN: Were you born in England? There is no objection to that. We have had a lot of English people that are citizens. In fact a lot of our forefathers came from over there. I think they told me mine came from Ireland, and that is right close by.

(The witness conferred with his counsel.)

MR. ALDERMAN: What is your answer?

MR. MADDEN: What?

CHAIRMAN: Were you born in England? That is what he asked you.

MR. MADDEN: I object to the question on pertinency.

MR. ALDERMAN: I will withdraw the question. Are you naturalized? Are you a naturalized citizen of the United States?

MR. MADDEN: Yes.

MR. ALDERMAN: Do you have a place of business in Hot Springs called the Downtown Printing Company?

(The witness conferred with his counsel.)

CHAIRMAN: Is Mr. Madden hard of hearing too?

MR. LINCOLN: Yes, he is.

Alderman pushed hard with a series of detailed questions about the wire service and the Nola Printing Company in New Orleans. Owney took the Fifth Amendment to each in rapid succession. The Duke's appearance at the hearings caused such a flurry of excitement among TV crews vying for shots that he had difficulty hearing the questions clearly and blinked under the powerful lights.

"Does that light bother you?" Senator McClellan asked. The hearing continued:

MR. MADDEN: It bothers the hell out of me.

CHAIRMAN: I did not understand you.

MR. MADDEN: Yes, it bothers me. It bothers me a lot.

CHAIRMAN: All right, turn this light out. Turn the light out or turn it around so it will not be in his eyes. Is that better?

MR. MADDEN: That is fine.

Senator McClellan barely had time to ask another question before the TV men got in the way again. Finally, Owney's attorney, Charles Lincoln, had to intervene:

MR. LINCOLN: I am sorry, Senator, one of the TV men came up with a light meter, and he looked over at him and did not get your question.

CHAIRMAN: I do not care if you get pictures, but do not interfere. I have been very good to you boys and you have been very good to me. Let's not interfere with the witness while he is testifying. It is all right if you can take pictures. They have not objected to that.

Michael Connaughton, who worked for the Internal Revenue Service, testified that he had traced the racing wires from the Ritter Hotel in Hot Springs with a telephone company lineman. It proved to be a long and often hazardous job, taking them over rooftops, through a forest, and halfway up a mountain. "The total amount of wire strung was at least a mile in length and it was of the commercial type, often used to wire doorbells, and not too suitable for outside wiring," he testified. "The attachments were rather unorthodox, such as being hung on nails, wrapped around bricks, around other attachments, and laying on roofs."

When Owney's testimony—or what there was of it—ended, he wasted no time in catching a flight straight back to Arkansas. A reporter for the *Democrat*, who had been covering the hearings, was also on the flight. When Owney climbed aboard and walked down the aisle, he passed Senator McClellan, who was already in his seat, buckling his safety belt. The two men smiled, shook hands, and exchanged a few words together.

Years later, Q. Byrum Hurst would put it like this: "There were no hard feelings. It wasn't McClellan's fault—it was young Bobby Kennedy that had done it."

In Washington, J. Edgar Hoover studied reports on the hearings and was dissatisfied with the outcome. He ordered secret reports on the wire service to be passed on to National Park officials to encourage them to prosecute the Duke. But, the action was already too late. Superintendent Raymond Gregg of Hot Springs National Park had received a letter from Hurst, informing him that "five hundred feet of insulated communications wire was not, and was never, the property of Mr. Madden. My client specifically desires to inform you that the wire you complain of must have been installed many years ago for purposes unknown to Mr. Madden. It is a pleasure for this office to cooperate with the Interior Department and we do so in every way possible..."

Hoover demanded an explanation from his agents and was told that "prior to the arrival of National Park employees to remove the wire, it had been cut by unknown persons."

The wire service remained closed after the hearings and Owney retreated into a hermit-like existence. His health had deteriorated and, after sliding out of a chair at home, he took regular massages for his back. Behind the drawn blinds of the cool, white wooden house, he spent most of his time listening to the radio and reading newspapers while Agnes sewed. From the articles he circled and cut out, it seems that he may have been suffering from mild depression. Of the clippings he stored in an envelope, many were about health, medication, and statistics that related depression to suicide.

Hoover remained unconvinced that Owney was anything other than a dangerous criminal. He sent a coded radio message to his agents in Little Rock, ordering them to find out if Owney had any interest in the new Vapors Club, which had opened on the edge of town. When inquiries drew a blank, he reexamined the Duke's entire record and decided that it was now a matter of extreme urgency to obtain photographs of him. Hoover found it almost beyond belief that, in 1962, the only picture of the man he had designated a "Top National Hoodlum" had been taken thirty years previously.

Owney, by this time, was venturing out again. "He is continuing his normal routine of visiting the barber shop in the Arlington Hotel, where he obtains a shave at approximately twelve noon, takes a thermal bath at the Superior Bath House, and normally remains at the Southern Club the remainder of the afternoon," Agent White reported.

At the attorney general's office, Bobby Kennedy also was finding it difficult to accept that Owney's life had slipped so easily back to a normal routine. He asked the FBI to send the complete Madden dossier to his office for examination. Hoover, perhaps in fear of losing face with Kennedy, insisted that photographs of Owney should be taken immediately. No excuses would be accepted. "Little Rock is instructed to expand their efforts to determine Madden's current position in Hot Springs's gambling activity," Hoover noted further.

Kennedy, unable to assemble a case against his father's old business associate, decided to go for Q. Byrum Hurst instead. Hurst, who had successfully secured Jimmy Hoffa's freedom in Washington, found himself facing charges of tax evasion despite keeping meticulous financial records. It was a trying time, but Owney, having stepped in to help Hoffa, now went to the rescue of his old friend, Hurst. The Duke gave evidence in court that he had loaned money to Hurst, which cast a helpful light on the sums outstanding. The judge ordered Hurst's acquittal.

The next day, Hurst's lawyer, William Bowen, wrote a note to thank Owney for his help: "I am still enjoying the picture of you on the witness stand, answering so well the questions I asked you relative to your background and loans to Byrum. I particularly remember the outstanding manner with which you handled yourself when cross-examined by the government. Quite frankly, I had worried about your testimony and was most pleased and gratified by the manner in which you handled yourself."

On December 13, 1963, Agent White sent a note to Hoover that read: "Photographs of Madden were secured by use of a hidden camera. However, other individuals blocked portions of Madden and the photos are not suitable for hoodlum album purposes. The FBI laboratory is being requested by separate communication to furnish necessary equipment to obtain photographs from a distance of 100 yards." The photos, White promised, would be obtained as soon as possible.

While waiting, Hoover ordered senior agents in Las Vegas, Beverly Hills, Fort Lauderdale, New Orleans, New Jersey, Oklahoma City, and St. Louis to find out anything they could about Owney. None of them were able to make a positive report.

At the age of 72, the exiled Duke continued to take his thermal baths and linger reflectively at the Southern Club. By March 10, 1964, agents from the Little Rock office of the FBI were still trying to photograph him but had no success. "Several photographs of Owen Vincent Madden have been obtained by the use of concealed cameras, but the results are not of sufficient quality," read one report. "Efforts are still being made to obtain photos of subject." On May 12, 1964, the FBI finally managed to get its man in the viewfinder. It was a day to remember—the first photograph the bureau had ever managed to take of him in his long and varied career. With the exception of his prison shots from decades earlier, it was the only official photograph of him in existence.

Robert Kennedy, frustrated by a similar lack of success, announced that he "could not believe" that there was no connection between organized crime and the illegal gambling in Hot Springs. The spa city continued to do a roaring business, with major stars appearing at the Southern Club, the Belvedere, and the Vapors. Singer Tony Bennett tried out a new number on an engagement at the Vapors called "I Left My Heart In San Francisco." "I didn't think it would go down well," he said later, "but Hot Springs seemed to like it."

Reporters from the *New York Times* and the *Daily News* descended on Hot Springs in response to Kennedy's statement to find out what was really going on. Journalists arrived in a town awash with gamblers, filling every hotel room and playing every game of chance invented. The *News*, in a two-part series, concluded that Bubbles was "the biggest, non-floating dice game in the land—only 64 miles from Camden, home of Senator John McClellan." The *Times* interviewed Prosecutor David Whittington, who told them: "If I try to change things, I'll be voted out of office and the public will elect any bum who will give them what they want." To which Police Chief John Erney, Owney's next-door neighbor, added: "The citizens of Hot Springs want an open town. We've had people run who want to close up, and they get beat."

As articles portraying Hot Springs as a renegade town defying the law appeared across the country, authorities in Washington were both outraged and embarrassed. William Hundley, chief of the Justice Department's organized crime section, condemned Hot Springs as the biggest illegal gambling operation in America and announced a major investigation. Bobby Kennedy, it seemed, was determined not to be defeated by Owney in the eyes of the public. The pressure proved too much for Arkansas governor Orval Faubus and, with great reluctance, he stepped in and ordered the closure of Bubbles' teeming gaming houses. Police Chief Erney made the rounds personally to tell everyone that Saturday, March 28 was their last night in business. "I don't anticipate any trouble," he said.

Governor Faubus's order was quickly followed by a resolution in the Arkansas House of Representatives that banned illegal gambling. Everyone in Hot Springs knew that the bubble had finally burst.

On Saturday evening, TV cameras from CBS and NBC pulled into town to record the wake, along with journalists from every major newspaper in the country. One wire service reporter grabbed a telephone and dictated: "This is 'last fling night' in the most luxurious gambling houses east of Las Vegas." On the stroke of midnight, Dane Harris, Owney's partner in the Vapors Club, had the last word. "All this," he said, sweeping his hand desolately across the tables covered in dustcloths, "has been a way of life here so long, it's more like a grocery store."

Less than a year later, on February 17, 1965, Agnes called the family doctor to the house. He examined Owney, weak from a chest complaint, and confined him to a wheelchair. The following day, a Thursday, was the last time he ventured out from the white house on West Grand. By April 22, four days after Easter, he was admitted, pale and breathing with difficulty, to St. Joseph's Hospital. The doctor who treated him was Henry Chenault, his brother-in-law, the husband of Agnes's sister, Kat, whom she had visited in Panama. At ten minutes past midnight on April 24, 1965, the Duke of the West Side finally outwitted them all. The exile in his chosen country slipped painlessly into sleep and died peacefully.

In the Federal Building, Agent White rolled a sheet of paper into his typewriter and filed his report: "Owen Vincent Madden died as a result of chronic emphysema. *Sentinel-Record* newspaper is receiving extensive number of telephone calls from eastern newspapers regarding his death and requesting background and photos."

Newspapers in England, where Owney had entered the world seventy-three years earlier, recalled "a blazing underworld career spanning two decades of bootlegging and racketeering. In later years he was a generous contributor to charities, particularly those benefitting young people. He rigorously avoided publicity."

At the time Owney died, everyone in Hot Springs had been anticipating bad weather. Tornadic activity and heavy rains were in the forecast. Tornadoes and high waves had pounded the Mississippi River flood zone, flattening houses in a 300-mile trail up through the South. Hot Springs was taut with apprehension. Early on the day Owney was buried, the twisters blew themselves out and the rain fell all morning. Water ran down the spouts of little wooden houses facing Greenwood Cemetery and trickled among the wildflowers peeping through the spring grass at the roadside. Everyone took shelter and waited for the rain to subside. They took turns comforting the widow and nursing their own private memories of Owney. When the downpour stopped, they emerged from beneath the steaming oak trees. Family and close friends stood shoulder to shoulder with anonymous men in overcoats who had flown in from Chicago, L.A., New York, and New Orleans to pay their last respects. Also present were city hall officials, members of the Arkansas Bar Association, business owners, and representatives of the city and state police.

"The service lasted approximately one hour," the *Hot Springs Sentinel-Record* reported, "the afternoon sun casting long shadows across a gentle eastern slope in Greenwood Cemetery, where Madden's casket was placed in its vault and lowered into the grave."

Among the 250 onlookers was Owney's attorney and friend of thirty years, Q. Byrum Hurst, who addressed the crowd. His eulogy might have been written in Hollywood, but they knew what he was talking about: "Page after page of sensationalism has been written about him," Hurst told them, "but when Owney Madden got off that train in Hot Springs, he became a truly different man and a real citizen.

"He was mild of manner and small of stature. I couldn't name all the people he helped. Every down-and-outer learned that a helping hand for those really in need could be found in Owen Madden, often called 'The Duke' by those who knew and loved him. He shunned publicity. He never wanted to take credit for the good he was doing."

Hurst had canceled a business meeting in Los Angeles the day before and arrived back in Hot Springs only an hour before the funeral. He recalled that Owney had ordered a local restaurant to serve a meal to anyone who was hungry and could not afford it and send him the bill.

"If Owen made a dollar, it was rapidly given to someone else who needed it more. We know not or care not what happened before he came to live with us in Hot Springs. We don't care what they say in New York, Chicago, or Washington. We simply know he was a kind, good man."

Among those listening, heads bowed, were the honorary pallbearers—tough men with faces like granite—who knew Owney well. They included Ray DeCarlo from New Jersey, Joe Jacobson and Oscar Gutter from Chicago, Joe St. John out of St. Louis, Joe Poretto, who worked with "Carlos the Bad" in New Orleans, Owney's next door neighbor,

Police Chief John Erney, Mayor Dan Wolf, former prosecutor Walter Herbert, and detectives Ernest Dodd and Jack Harvey.

"It has been said there is much good in the worst of us, and so much bad in the best of us," Hurst told the gathering, "that it doesn't behoove any of us to criticize the rest of us." Heads nodded.

With more irony than syrup, he added: "There is no ball park named after Owen Madden, no silver cup bearing his name. But it is written on the hearts of all the people he helped—with money, by deed, and by words of encouragement in their dark hours."

Owney, as those gathered around the graveside knew, had given generously to churches, the Navy League, the Boys Club, the YMCA, the United Fund, and the Salvation Army. He had equipped local schools with sports equipment, fitted out the Hot Springs baseball team, and donated the money for a public park. His wish for anonymity suited many of the recipients. Because of his notoriety, some of them preferred not to publicly acknowledge his kindness to them.

When the service was over and the mourners began to make their way back to the white house on West Grand Avenue, a spokesman for the Gross Funeral Home looked relieved. Agnes had worried them by requesting an open funeral instead of a private service. "We knew that there would be a lot of friends," he said. "We just had to take a chance that we would not be overrun with curiosity seekers."

The next day, the New York newspapers published Owney's obituary, along with the picture he hated most. It was a decades-old photo, showing him with a sullen look. A reporter had once sent him a hundred copies of the photograph with a note advising him to hand them to his friends. "Tell them that's the picture we'll be using when you're dead," he said.

A few days after the funeral, Agnes offered to install, at a cost of $10,000, a stained glass window in memory of her mother in a new church under construction. The congregation turned her money down on the grounds that it was "tainted." Mae West sent a sympathy card bearing the picture of a naked Greek god and a message that said Owney was the sweetest guy she had ever known. George Raft felt unable to pay his last respects. Agnes was hurt and puzzled until some friends wrote and asked her not to hold it against him. "Ever since his mother died, he has shunned and avoided anything which reminded him of mortality," they explained. "George, in his own way, is probably trying to outrun death himself." Raft and the co-star he once said stole everything but the cameras died within two days of each other in November of 1980.

Agnes, alone with the memories of a secret and turbulent life, seldom ventured out of the house they once shared together. When I visited with her in the mid-80s, she was in failing health and walked with difficulty from room to room. She was surrounded by memories, like someone with the belief that the present can never outweigh the fullness of the past. By his own standards of loyalty, charity, and straight-dealing, Owney Madden was a good man—even a great one—they said in Hot Springs. He also made a lot of money from the proceeds of his crimes— many millions is a conservative estimate. Many of them were crimes which no longer remained crimes as the attitude of America changed.

And those who once sought to bring him to justice were not entirely unstained by the system in which they were raised. History, with a little help from Hollywood, has taught us to differentiate between the good guys and the bad. Owney was somewhere in that no-man's land which the law has no capacity to acknowledge. He was loved by his friends and hated by his enemies—all for reasons which bear no relation to issues of right and wrong.

Perhaps the most honest way to measure a man is by human values through the eyes of his friends. In the words of an old pal, boxer-turned-gangster Micky Cohen: "Owney was really a guy to respect and admire— quite a guy, a man of his word all the way through. His faithfulness to his own kind is the strongest thing a man can have. If Owney felt you were the right person, there wasn't nothing that he wouldn't do for you."

When I reached the end of my journey to write the life of Owen Vincent Madden, Michael Cherkasky, chief of Manhattan's Rackets

Bureau, was preparing a case against members of a West Side gang whose activities, one investigator claimed, "are bigger than Murder Inc." The Westies, as they are known, were described as the most violent gang to emerge from New York in living memory. "These are people," Cherkasky told me, "who would cut off a guy's head and take it to a bar to show his friends how bad they were." Newspapers followed the story avidly. "The predominantly Irish gang evolved out of a bootlegging operation begun in the 1920s by Owney Madden, owner of the celebrated Cotton Club," one paper wrote. "The Westies have become renowned in criminal circles for their enthusiasm for violence."

What would the quiet, old sage of Hot Springs make of New York life today, I wondered. Would he have welcomed an opportunity to be close to the madness again? I imagined the shy smile breaking over that lean, pale face.

"Not for all the tea in China," I guess he would have replied.

Acknowledgments

The full story of Owney Madden will never be known. He was shy, private, clever, and cunning when asked about his full and secretive life. Owney never gave interviews and declined to discuss his affairs, even with friends he had known for years. Everyone has their own story to tell about the pale, thin Englishman who became a cornerstone of American organized crime. Those who knew him recall him with loyalty and affection. He was a gentle man, at ease with his friends, who ranged from world champion fighters to movie stars to leading members of the National Crime Syndicate. Most of all, he was happiest at home, flying his pigeons.

Great question marks hang over periods when no one knew where he was or what he was doing. Because of the solitary nature of the man, this book is not complete. No book on Owney Madden ever could be. Inaccuracies are hopefully few. Mysteries and incongruities are inevitable. As a story, however, it deserves telling, and without the help, kindness, and hospitality of the following during my visit to Hot Springs in the mid-1980s, it would not have been possible:

In Hot Springs, Arkansas: Mrs. Agnes Madden and Roger Rucker for kindly making available Owney Madden's personal papers and family photographs; Inez Cline and Bobbie and Sonny McLane of the Garland County Historical Society; Q. Byrum Hurst; Hot Springs historian Mark Palmer; former FBI agent and Garland County Sheriff Clay White; Maxine Jones; Melinda Gassaway, executive editor of the *Hot Springs Sentinel-Record*, and Alroy Puckett, Garland County Probation Office.

In New York: Ken Fink and Rebecca Peterson of CBS News; Kenneth Cobb of the New York Municipal Archive; the staff of the City Clerk's Office; the New York Bar Association; the *New York Times* Library; Jimmy Murphy and Michael Cherkasky, Manhattan Rackets

Bureau; Michael Daly, *New York* magazine; Jimmy McManus, District Leader, Hell's Kitchen; and Ray Arcel, retired boxing trainer.

In Washington: the Library of Congress staff; the National Archives Trust Fund Board; and the Federal Bureau of Investigation.

Elsewhere in the U.S.A.: Benjamin and Candy Shalleck of Palm Beach, Florida; historian Stephen Fox of Cambridge, Mass., and Kevin Thomas of the *Los Angeles Times*.

In England: Tommy Prior for access to his comprehensive library of gangland literature; Andrew Rosthom; Jack "Kid" Berg; Liverpool City Libraries; Leeds City Libraries; and Paul Hick, House of Campbell.

Sylvana Nown for collating the research material and patience beyond the call of duty. Grateful thanks to David Holmes of Ward Lock Publishing for his encouragement and the offer I couldn't refuse.

The author would also like to thank the following publishers for permission to quote from the following books: Dell (New York), *The Last Testament of Lucky Luciano* by Martin A. Gosch Sr. and Richard Hammer; Dial Press (New York) for *Gang Rule in New York* by Craig Thompson and Allen Raymond; Facts on File (New York) for *The Encyclopedia of American Crime* by Carl Safiki; Hodder & Stoughton (London) for *Frank Costello– Prime Minister of the Underworld* by George Wolf; Lyle Stuart (Secaucus, New Jersey) for *Gangster Number Two–Longy Zwillman* by Mark A. Stuart; Prentice Hall (Englewood Cliffs, New Jersey) for *How Dry We Were– Prohibition Revisited* by Henry Lee; Raines & Raines (New York) for *Lanky* by Hank Messick; Robson (London) for *The Cotton Club* by Jim Haskins; Rose Publishing (Little Rock, Arkansas) for *A Man For Arkansas* by Jim Lester; and W. H. Allen (London) for *George Raft* by Lewis Yablonsky.

While every effort has been made to trace publishers of works quoted, the author apologizes for any omissions.

Bibliography

Asbury. Herbert: *The Gangs of New York* (Garden City Publishing, New York, 1927).

Black, Mary: *Old New York in Early Photographs* (Dover, New York, 1976); *New York Then and Now* (Dover, New York, 1976).

Block, Alan: *East Side, West Side* (University College Cardiff Press, Cardiff, Wales, 1980).

Bonanno, Joseph: *A Man of Honor* (Simon & Schuster, New York, 1983).

Brown, Dee: *The American Spa* (Rose Publishing, Little Rock, 1982).

Cashin, Fergus: *Mae West* (Star, London, 1982).

Cashman, Sean Dennis: *Prohibition–How the Land Lies* (Free Press, New York, 1981).

Churchill, Allen: *The Year the World Went Mad* (Thomas Crowell, New York, 1960).

Cohen, Micky: *In My Own Words* (Prentice Hall, Englewood Cliffs, NJ, 1975).

Cohn, Art: *The Joker Is Wild–The Story of Joe E. Lewis* (Random House, New York, 1955).

Eells, George and Musgrove, Stanley: *Mae West* (Morrow & Co., Scranton, PA, 1982).

Fried, Albert: *The Rise and Fall of the Jewish Gangster in America* (Holt, Rinehart & Winston, New York, 1980).

Garrett, Richard: *The Search for Prosperity–Emigration from Britain 1815–1930* (Wayland, London, 1973).

Gosch, Martin A. and Hammer, Richard: *The Last Testament of Lucky Luciano* (Dell, New York, 1974).

Granlund, Nils T.: *Blondes, Brunettes and Bullets* (David McKay, New York, 1957).

Haskins, Jim: *The Cotton Club* (Robson Books, Ltd., London, 1985).

Jones, Maxine: *Maxine–Call Me Madam* (Pioneer Press, Little Rock, 1983).

Kennedy, Ludovic: *The Airman and the Carpenter* (HarperCollins, UK, 1985).

Lawes, Lewis E.: *20,000 Years in Sing Sing* (Ray Long and Richard R. Smith, New York, 1933).

Lee, Henry: *How Dry We Were–Prohibition Revisited* (Prentice Hall, Englewood Cliffs, NJ, 1963).

Lester, Jim: *A Man for Arkansas* (Rose Publishing, Little Rock, 1976).

Lynch, Denis Tilden: *Criminals and Politicians* (MacMillan, New York, 1932).

McCabe, James D., Jr.: *New York by Gaslight* (Arlington House, New York, 1984).

Maurois, Andre: *A History of the USA* (Weidenfeld and Nicholson, London, 1962).

Messick, Hank: *Lansky* (Berkley, New York, 1971); *The Private Lives of Public Enemies* (Dell, New York, 1974); *The Silent Syndicate* (MacMillan, New York, 1967).

Nash, Jay Robert: *Citizen Hoover* (Nelson Hall, Chicago, 1972).

O'Connor, Richard: *Hell's Kitchen* (Redman, New York, 1958).

Pasley, Fred D: *Muscling In* (Faber & Faber, London, 1932).

Peterson, Virgil W.: *The Mob–200 Years of Organized Crime in New York* (Green Hill, Ottawa, Illinois, 1983).

Reeve, Arthur B.: *The Golden Age of Crime* (Mohawk Press, New York, 1931).

Salerno, Ralph and Tompkins, John S: *The Crime Confederation* (Doubleday, New York, 1969).

Sann, Paul: *Kill the Dutchman* (Arlington House, New York, 1971).

Sculley, Dr. Francis J.: *Hot Springs, Arkansas* (Pioneer Press, Little Rock, 1966).

Sifakis, Carl: *The Encyclopedia of American Crime* (Facts on File, New York, 1982).

Stuart, Mark A.: *Gangster No. 2–Longy Zwillman, the Man Who Invented Organized Crime* (Lyle Stuart, Secaucus, NJ, 1985).

Thompson, Craig and Raymond, Allen: *Gang Rule in New York* (Dial Press, New York, 1940).

Walker, Stanley: *The Night Club Era* (Blue Ribbon, New York, 1933).

Whithead, Don: *The FBI Story* (Random House, New York, 1956).

Wolf, George: *Frank Costello–Prime Minister of the Underworld* (Hodder and Stoughton, London, 1974).

Yablonsky, Lewis: *George Raft* (McGraw-Hill, New York, 1982).

Index

About the Author

Graham Edmund Nown was born on November 3, 1944, in Rainhill, a small village in the northwest of England, where Robert Stephenson's *Rocket*, an early steam engine, set off on its famous trial run in 1829. An award-winning journalist, Nown was widely published as a non-fiction author in the U.K. where he wrote two best-sellers.

Nown wrote on a diverse range of subjects including biographies of Mrs. Beeton, the famous Victorian cook, and Sherlock Holmes. He was commissioned to write TV tie-in books and co-wrote a number of successful books with British celebrities.

His interest in Prohibition came through researching Owney Madden's story and led to invitations to write distillery histories for Laphroaig, The Edradour, and Ballantines. He contributed to newspapers and magazines and made regular radio broadcasts in the United States on the subject of single-malt scotch whiskies.

Nown lived with his wife, Sylvana, and daughter, Rose, in a Victorian coach house alongside the sand dunes on the northwest coast of England. Tramping over the dunes with his faithful dogs each day refreshed and inspired him. He died suddenly on Sunday, September 7, 1997, at home. Sylvana Nown noted that he is "dearly loved, greatly missed, and in our hearts forever."

Printed in the USA
CPSIA information can be obtained
at www.ICGtesting.com
CBHW030902090424
6616CB00001B/3

9 781935 106517